Nietzsche's Economy

Also by Peter R. Sedgwick

CULTURAL THEORY: The Key Concepts (*co-author with Andrew Edgar*)

CULTURAL THEORY: The Key Thinkers (*co-author with Andrew Edgar*)

DESCARTES TO DERRIDA: An Introduction to European Philosophy

NIETZSCHE: A Critical Reader

Nietzsche's Economy

Modernity, Normativity and Futurity

Peter R. Sedgwick

palgrave
macmillan

First published 2007 by
PALGRAVE MACMILLAN
Houndmills, Basingstoke, Hampshire RG21 6XS and
175 Fifth Avenue, New York, N.Y. 10010
Companies and representatives throughout the world

PALGRAVE MACMILLAN is the global academic imprint of the Palgrave Macmillan division of St. Martin's Press, LLC and of Palgrave Macmillan Ltd. Macmillan® is a registered trademark in the United States, United Kingdom and other countries. Palgrave is a registered trademark in the European Union and other countries.

ISBN-13: 978–1–4039–9066–2 hardback
ISBN-10: 1–4039–9066–2 hardback

This book is printed on paper suitable for recycling and made from fully managed and sustained forest sources. Logging, pulping and manufacturing processes are expected to conform to the environmental regulations of the country of origin.

A catalogue record for this book is available from the British Library.

Library of Congress Cataloging-in-Publication Data
Sedgwick, Peter R.
Nietzsche's economy: modernity, normativity, and futurity / Peter R. Sedgwick.
p. cm.
Includes bibliographical references and index.
ISBN-13: 978–1–4039–9066–2 (cloth)
ISBN-10: 1–4039–9066–2 (cloth)
1. Nietzsche, Friedrich Wilhelm, 1844–1900. 2. Economics—Philosophy.
3. Civilization, Modern. I. Title.
B3318.E36S43 2007
193—dc22 2006052507

10 9 8 7 6 5 4 3 2 1
16 15 14 13 12 11 10 09 08 07

Printed and bound in Great Britain by
Antony Rowe Ltd, Chippenham and Eastbourne

I Dafydd ac er cof am fy nhad
For Dafydd and in memory of my father

Contents

Preface

It hardly needs to be stated by anyone with a more than passing acquaintance with Nietzsche's books that they have always invited a plethora of conflicting interpretations. The contrasts are highlighted by Jacques Derrida's comment on readings that find justification in Nietzsche for a left- or right-leaning politics[1] and by the fact that he has even been considered to be an a-political or anti-political thinker.[2] Disagreements on what Nietzsche means are often stark. Such things are symptomatic. They attest powerfully to the seductive nature of Nietzsche's writings and their ability to draw us into a relationship with them whereby we become tempted to find something of ourselves mirrored therein. This happens to a degree that it would be hard to conceive of in relation to thinkers like Kant or Frege. Doubtless, much of the appeal that provokes this temptation is to do with Nietzsche's self-consciously personal tone. This tone echoes through his provocative, occasionally outlandish, sometimes funny assaults on what are still cherished beliefs, or the fact that he speaks in a literary voice that places personality before feigned objectivity even as he plays the game of philosophy. Nietzsche's self-consciousness strikes a nerve. However we may differ from him, he is, like us, irredeemably modern.[3] In the words of Ronald Hayman, Nietzsche's 'various voices speak compellingly to a sensibility for which paradox is the only truth, plurality the only consistency, fragmentation the only integrity'.[4] As befits someone who has on many an occasion been rendered a mirror, Nietzsche does not merely look but above all sounds like an uncanny pre-echo of our own self-consciously modern anxieties.[5] No surprise, then, that Nietzsche has been seen both as a fighter against modern times and as typifying them.[6]

Modernity has always been a problematic concept. Nevertheless, it would be hard to understand Nietzsche outside the context of modernity. His obvious fondness for the phrase 'we modern men'[7] pays sufficient testimony to the self-conscious nature of his entanglement with modernity. Even in the midst of his untimely struggle with his own era, Nietzsche is an avowedly modern thinker in terms of his concerns and sensibilities. The restlessness of his thought is an acknowledgement of the restlessness of his times. We moderns are changeable spirits, insecure, uncertain and all too aware of our own contingency. Consider a comment Nietzsche makes in Section 111 of *Human, All Too Human.* Here he argues that where for our primitive ancestors it was the case that they experienced themselves as regular and calculable beings and the natural world about them as irregular and incalculable, precisely the opposite holds for us. Nature has become 'the great means of composure for the modern soul'. Nature conceived under the duress imposed upon it by modern science now looks law-like to us (whether or not this appearance is something of an illusion is irrelevant in this respect). However, the need to see nature as something that inspires tranquillity testifies to the inner turmoil of the modern soul. It tells us that the modern psyche understands itself in terms of its own increasing irregularity and lack of composure.

The modern soul, whether it likes it or not, is part of the contemporary industrial subjugation of nature. This is why things can get uncomfortable for self-reflection. Every encounter with nature that aims at further subjugation through technology has the side effect of making our subjectivity itself seem simultaneously amenable to and horrified by the prospect of that subjugation. The more regularised we become by our wish to dominate nature the less easily we seem to be able to cope with the idea.[8] It is easier to contemplate a nature that is pliant and indifferent to human desires. Thus conceived, its ability to remind us of the consequences of our limitless desire for appropriation is negated. We need not, for that moment, consider precisely what we do and that it is we who do it. Modern subjectivity must, however, always return to itself. What compels it to gaze outwards, the desire to escape from the manifold nature of its self-awareness, is also at the same time what obliges it to return to restless self-reflection. As David Harvey has noted, the tension between the two elements within Baudelaire's famous 'dual formation'[9] of modernity captures the sense in which our self-understanding oscillates uncomfortably between extremes. At one moment, one kind of aesthetic practice dominates; at the next, an inverted image stands alongside or advances to subvert its now reflected counterpart. This sense of instability, of not knowing how things stand and of not being at home in the world that one inhabits, lurks behind every gesture of modernist practice. To put it another way, 'modern' denotes the state of being aware that one's identity is bound to time and place and the *simultaneous* sense that the meaning of such concepts is open to constant revision in the light of speeding change. This change is integral to the dynamic of modern society, for it is the change driven by industry and technology. The world of modernity is also the world of economics in its most assertive of historical forms.

Even more than in Nietzsche's times, our own feelings in the West concerning the unstoppable social transformations that occur at the hands of technological development reinforce the sense of bewildering diversity. This ensures we remain true moderns endowed with the sensibility that makes us receptive to Nietzsche in a manner that has kinship with the attitudes and concerns of his earliest readers.[10]

In this book, I offer an interpretation of Nietzsche's work that situates it in relation to the notions of modernity and the sphere of economic and industrial culture just briefly considered. I see him, in other words, as a thinker who is inescapably bound up with his times, and this above all in relation to his treatment of the economically inspired notions of exchange, credit, debit, sacrifice, labour, possession, expenditure, surplus, measuring, weighing, evaluating and the like. Nietzsche's work, I argue, is permeated by a concern with economics to the extent that it is constitutive of his thought. In connection with this, Daniel W. Conway has written revealingly of Nietzsche's analysis of modernity as an 'economy of decadence' and Derek Hillard equally so of the role of the exchange principle in *On the Genealogy of Morality*.[11] Graham Parkes has also made an important contribution to our understanding of the role of economic language in Nietzsche's psychology.[12] Jürgen G. Backhaus and Wolfgang Drechsler have also edited a volume that examines the relevance of Nietzsche's thought to contemporary economic theory.[13] My own aims, however, are rather different. It is possible to construct a narrative account of Nietzsche's entanglement with the world of economy extending from his early to his late writings. Starting with the *Untimely Meditations*, one can see at work a critical interest and engagement on Nietzsche's part with the realm of commercial culture. This is continued into the so-called 'middle period' works (*Human, All Too Human, Daybreak, The Gay Science*) which engage in sustained criticisms of the domination of modern culture by mercantilism and consider the consequences of this for our self-understanding. These works also speculate on the implications of modern industrial economy for the spheres of language, politics and education. Their central criticism of modernity is that it is dominated by the belief that efficiency of consumption is a virtue. At the same time, even these works deploy a conception of economy that runs deeper than this critical aspect. Economic notions are envisaged as being at work in all areas of human endeavour. The domain of human prehistory likewise receives an economic characterisation. Nietzsche constructs an account of modern society as an amalgam of contemporary practices residing upon ancient economically derived foundations. The concept of exchange, it turns out, has primeval roots. We are in our essence measurers, weighers and estimators whose identity emerged out of our ancestors' adoption of the practices associated with such concepts. Our self-transcending ability, celebrated most of all by the figure of the overman, is an endowment of this ancient inheritance. The primeval roots of economy are explored most tellingly in the accounts of the morality of custom offered in *Daybreak* and *On the Genealogy of Morality*. These, in turn, are increasingly harmonised with the notion of a 'great economy' of the affects governing human preservation (first outlined in *The Gay Science*). This great economy comes to attain an ever more prominent status in Nietzsche's later writings. As this aspect of economy is emphasised, so the more socially aware side of Nietzsche's thinking dwindles. Mechanised exploitation ceases to be horrifying to him. The self becomes ever more akin to material fit for moulding at the hands of industrial processes. He uses the notion of the great economy to justify his contention that societies are necessarily hierarchical and his view that exploitation is a condition of life. Likewise, he begins to consider the nature of culture in terms permeated by the economic language of household budgets, credit, debit, expenditure, surplus and squandering – terms that his earliest writings recoil at. Industrial notions of mechanised conformity also begin to fascinate Nietzsche in new ways in the later writings (and in the notebook entries of the late 1880s). This gives rise to his conception of the 'culture-complex': a sphere in which the total administration of environmental and human resources could be put to use with the aim of attaining a cultural Renaissance. At the same time, economic notions can be seen at work in Nietzsche's analysis of the self in *Thus Spoke Zarathustra* and in relation to his conception of human enhancement, epitomised by his conception of philosophers of the future (*Beyond Good and Evil*).[14]

One could pinpoint possible influences with regard to the economic aspect of Nietzsche's thought I have just mentioned. The writings of Emerson are one possible source.[15] His interest in the writings of the English political economist Walter Bagehot might be cited as an obvious case. Nietzsche was certainly well acquainted with Bagehot's *Physics and Politics, or Thoughts on the Principles of 'Natural Selection' and 'Inheritance' to Political Society* (1872).[16] From this it might be easy to regard Bagehot's analysis of economic principles and his related discussion of primitive social conditions as resonating with the mature Nietzsche's interest in 'prehistory' and his characterisation of it as a world dominated by the exchange principle and the relationship between creditor and debtor.[17] As the title makes clear, Bagehot's book also conjoins economics with the thought of Darwin, of whom Nietzsche was obviously very well aware. The discourse of political economy thereby cross-fertilises with that concerning the primitive conditions of human social evolution.[18] Likewise, and in connection with this, one might also cite Darwin as an obvious influence. Nietzsche is often cited as a critic of Darwinian thought, especially of social Darwinism.[19] Whatever may be the case with regard Nietzsche's apparent or genuine rejection of Darwinism, *The Origin of Species* has its own specific investment in economic theory that could be cited as being relevant. In this regard, it is well known that Darwin's central contention that life is governed by a 'struggle for existence' reflects the influence of economist Thomas Malthus's *Essay on the Principle of Population* (1797), a work that Darwin read in 1838.[20] More germane to our consideration of Nietzsche, however, is Darwin's repetitive stressing of the notion that an 'economy of nature'[21] governs the operation of the mechanism of natural selection.[22] One might be tempted to consider Nietzsche's own deployment of the notion of a 'great economy' of human preservation in the light of this. It is not my intention, however, to cite such influences as being in some sense decisive when it comes to the role of economy in Nietzsche's thinking. My preference, as should now be clear enough, is to take Nietzsche as voicing something about the cultural–industrial forces at work in his own times and paying testimony to them (sometimes critically, sometimes less so) in the domain of thought. In this way, Nietzsche is situated in the midst of the very marketplace from which some critics have sought to fence him off. It is in turn to be hoped that this preliminary act of situating him thus will provide some small basis for further investigation of his thought especially in its political and social registers.

1

Economy and Society in Nietzsche's 'Middle Period' Works: *Human, All Too Human, Assorted Opinions and Maxims, The Wanderer and His Shadow, Daybreak*

The great problems are to be encountered in the street.

(*Daybreak*, 127)

1. *The realms of politics and economics are spheres of concern from the time of Nietzsche's early writings. Above all, texts like the* Untimely Meditations *demonstrate a deep concern with the relationship between mercantilism and culture. The latter is, through education, rendered an instrument for the furthering of mercantile interests and the profit motive. The third* Meditation *opposes both philosophy and the realm of nature to this. The economy of nature sows the philosophical seed at random – it is wasteful, extravagant and self-destructive. It operates at a loss. Nature and modernity are thus opposed. Scholarship is not immune to being co-opted into the social process. The increased mediocrity of the first is matched by increased profit of the second. Economic power, in other words, permeates modern society. It does so, Nietzsche notes, even to the extent of infiltrating his own language. The essay 'On Truth and Lie' can be cited as an early example of this kind of infiltration. In it, metaphysical 'truths' are envisaged as the conceptual perversions of unconscious economic behaviour.*

As early as his *Untimely Meditations*, Nietzsche shows concern with the everyday world of politics and economics. Although disparaging any possibility of political solutions to philosophical problems (*Untimely Meditations*, III, 4), the *Meditations* remain at the same time texts that self-consciously place themselves in the context of social, political and economic forces. They are, in short, deeply sensitive to the fact of their own place within cultural modernity. The world of which Nietzsche writes in these relatively early works is one in which change is rampant.

Hitherto cherished beliefs are being overturned. Change manifests itself in the accelerating decline of organised religion, the increased sense of political hostility between European nations, the burgeoning of scientific research 'in a spirit of the blindest *laissez faire*' and the fact that the 'educated classes' are now held in thrall to 'a hugely contemptible money economy [*Geldwirthschaft*]' (ibid.). Barbarism looms on the horizon as culture is overrun or perverted by financial interests. Those who command the new economic wealth that characterises modern times, Nietzsche argues, would like culture to support and thereby legitimate them. They invest accordingly. They also expect a return on their investment. Take the example of education. The new forces that command society require education to be

> the means of which, through demand and its satisfaction, one becomes time-bound through and through but at the same time best acquires all the ways and means of making money as easily as possible. The goal would then be to create as many current human beings as possible, in the sense in which one speaks of coin as being current [. . .] Thus the sole intention behind our modern educational institutions should be to assist everyone to become current to the extent that lies in his nature [. . . and thereby prepare him . . .] for the accumulation of the greatest possible amount of happiness and profit.
>
> (*Untimely Meditations*, III, 6)

Society, in other words, is being inexorably subjected to the demands of mercantilism. The process of the mercantile absorption of culture reveals itself in the modern desire to assert a necessary connection between property ownership and intelligence, wealth and culture. Even more, Nietzsche argues, the specifically *moral* nature of this connection is taken to be unquestionable. The investment in education stipulates a return in terms of the educated person's suitability for the world of work. At the same time it limits *how much* culture a person ought to be allowed to absorb. Culture is in this way rendered a tool of mercantile interests. Modern economic society dictates that a person should have as much culture as accords with the interests of the general earning of money and world trafficking for economic gain that is now the norm.

The third *Meditation* ('Schopenhauer as educator') paints a picture of its contemporary world as a realm in which the demands of capital are beginning to swamp the development of culture. The word 'culture' for

Nietzsche here means the development of something that exceeds the merely everyday concerns of daily life, the cultural expression that finds its paradigm in the tragedies and epic poetry of the Ancient Greeks. In contrast, modern society is driven by the demand that its members manage their affairs well – by which is meant profitably. A good person, one might say, is by contemporary norms a good housekeeper. For Nietzsche, the contemporary assertion of a necessary link between financial wealth and culture means that culture is on the retreat, that culture is coming to be defined by terms that are extraneous to it. It ought to be the other way around, of course – and, at one level, it forever remains the case that it is. Thus, when in the third *Meditation* Nietzsche looks to something with which to oppose mercantile dominance, he selects the combination of philosophy and nature. No less than anything else, nature makes the philosopher. It then fires its creation into the midst of an unsuspecting humanity: 'it takes no aim but hopes the arrow will stick somewhere [. . .] Nature is just as extravagant in the domain of culture as it is in that of planting and sowing.' In the world of plant reproduction, nature takes no care to ensure that its products are sown wisely. All too often, seed falls on barren ground and is stunted or simply fails to develop at all. Nature is a spendthrift. The world of nature is one of profligacy, of the waste and squandering of precious, finite resources. Nature, in short, does not operate in order to make a profit. Unlike the dominant tendency of modern society, nature does not assess all things in terms of the returns on its investments. Likewise, the philosopher, the person of culture, can be born in good conditions or bad. There is no telling where or when such a being will be thrown up. Nietzsche can then drive his point home. Philosophy and culture are subject to the vicissitudes of nature. Nature does not manage its economic affairs intelligently; its outgoings are routinely much larger than the returns they might yield, and therefore, however much wealth there may be at nature's disposal, it will, at some point down the line, run itself right into the ground and ruin itself. Nature and modernity thus stand opposed with regard to their dominant tendencies within Nietzsche's text. Modernity, for the Nietzsche of the *Untimely Meditations*, is characterised by the obsessive concern with efficiency and accumulation. It is a sphere that is driven above all by the need to oil the gears of the great earning – and 'power-machine' (ibid., IV, 6).

Of course, modernity is also for Nietzsche the age of burgeoning science. In this regard, it is an era in which the powerful religious illusions that dominated past societies no longer appear to hold sway. But science is no less susceptible to being hooked into the social process.

It does not have the power to save culture through learning, for science, no less than education, can be rendered subordinate to the demands of a world dominated by production, exchange and the requirement for labour. Thus,

> the present age is [. . .] supposed to be an age, not of whole, mature and harmonious personalities, but of labour of the greatest possible common utility. That means [. . .] that men have to be adjusted to the purposes of the age so as to be ready for employment as soon as possible: they must labour in the factories of the general good before they are mature, indeed so that they shall not become mature [. . .] Believe me: if men are to labour and be useful in the factory of science before they are mature, science will soon be ruined just as effectively as the slaves thus employed too early. I regret the need to make use of the jargon of the slave-owner and employer of labour to describe things which in themselves ought to be thought of as free of utility and raised above the necessities of life; but the words 'factory', 'labour market', 'supply', 'making profitable', and whatever auxiliary verbs egoism now employs, come unbidden to our lips when one wishes to describe the most recent generation of men of learning. Sterling mediocrity grows ever more mediocre, science ever more profitable in the economic sense [*ökonomischen Sinne*].
>
> (Ibid., II, 7)

The modern world is the world of the factory, of labour and exploitation. This is the case no less for the realm of knowledge than it is for the apparently differentiated world of work. The world is economic through and through. The more the demands of economy grow, the more its influence deepens. The greater the pressure of the 'money-business [*Geldwirthschaft*]' (ibid., III, 4), the more the world of intellect, too, becomes a matter of 'dream- and thought-business [*Traum- und Denkwirthschaft*]' (ibid., 8). At the same time, Nietzsche is aware of the degree to which these detestable but dominant norms infiltrate his own language. He, too, acknowledges that he *must* speak in terms of the economy of business and ownership even as he criticises it. This acknowledgement betrays an awareness characteristic of Nietzsche's mature works no less than the earlier writings under consideration here. Nietzsche may seek consistently to be 'untimely' in his philosophy, but he remains at the same time self-consciously sensitive to the dilemma of being enmeshed within the context from which his thought erupts. However much he speaks against contemporary life, his language must be that of his times no less than that of the passer-by in the street. In this sense, he must speak against himself.

The essay *On Truth and Lies in a Nonmoral Sense* (written in 1873 – the time of the first of the *Untimely Meditations*) provides a prime example of this kind of self-conscious undermining of the norms that Nietzsche must nevertheless use in order to make sense at all.[1] Having posed the question 'What then is truth?', he offers an answer that has become justifiably famous. Truth, he says, is

> A movable host of metaphors, metonymies, and anthropomorphisms: in short, a sum of human relations which have been rhetorically and poetically intensified, transferred, and embellished, and which, after long usage, seem to people to be fixed, canonical, and binding. Truths are illusions which we have forgotten are illusions; they are metaphors that have become worn out and have been drained of sensuous force, coins which have lost their embossing and are now considered as metal and no longer as coins.[2]

In order to stake a truth claim such as this, Nietzsche at least provisionally presupposes the validity of the conventions of truth he is seeking to place in doubt. He also here posits a *mechanism of forgetting* in which the original meanings of terms have been lost to us through *use*. What is stated here is that the illusion of the 'fixed' status of the so-called 'metaphysical truths' comes from the fact that the memory of their initial practical use in human conduct has been erased. The paradigm case of such use Nietzsche turns to is that of the symbolic exchange of money. In other words, the mechanism whereby the original value of certain concepts is first forgotten and then reinterpreted into something fixed and abstract is itself clarified in terms of an economic metaphor. Thus, what was once understood and used as mere coinage, as a representation without significance beyond its practical use, has as a consequence of that use become misinterpreted and taken to stand for something greater. The once sensuous power of the imagery of thought has been sucked out of it and replaced by abstraction. Through his use of the coin metaphor, Nietzsche provides us with a startling image. The metaphor envisages a world of exchange, a past world in which humanity goes about its business unthinkingly using symbols to stand for things. The world people unconsciously inhabit is a world of exchange-value. The world of exchange is thereby naturalised here: it is simply what was once the case, it signifies a form of behaviour that is taken as a given. What is 'unnatural', in contrast, is to take the concept of exchange to stand for something timeless and abstract. The text thereby implies that there is nothing more natural than the use of money. It is part of the peculiar power of Nietzsche's argument to seek to show how once concrete practical behaviour can, through its very pursuit, give rise to increasingly abstract and empty behaviour. What we call 'truth' is the forgetting of convention, the devaluation of the practical currency of everyday exchange behaviour into an illusory projection that now promises to point beyond this everyday world.

2. *The texts of* Human, All Too Human *and* Daybreak *demonstrate deep involvement with economic issues.* Human, All Too Human *opposes metaphysical to historical philosophy and the spirit of scholarship. The threat to metaphysics, which holds truth to be timeless and eternal, is reflected not merely in the academic arena but in the modern social milieu. Modern society is characterised by restless change. This takes several forms: increasing state power, revolutionary agitation, popular power, the rise of the public sphere as one of open debate. For Nietzsche, the public realm is held in thrall to the power of money. Modern culture is the culture of financial power, pure and simple. Nietzsche's conception of historical philosophy can be situated within this diagnosis of his own times. It establishes the time-bound nature of thought. The person who is a critic of their own times is condemned to them in terms of the dictation of tastes, values and desires. This self-awareness is the hallmark of modern consciousness: we are inexorably trapped within our own times as historically constituted beings and actually aware of this. The spirit of a person's times constitutes their identity to the extent that even their taking a critical stance towards their own age evidences that age's contradictions. The modern critic thus stands as a figure who must speak against his or her own times from within them, devoid of recourse to eternal moral truths capable of transcending them and thereby lending their words unique authority. This self-awareness is the essence of historical philosophy, which spurns the aspiration to a God's-eye view on the world. The critic, as the bad conscience of their age, stands communing with their own thoughts, a solitary in a crowded marketplace.*

As we have seen, the youthful Nietzsche is critical of the mercantilism that he perceives as becoming increasingly dominant within contemporary culture. Nevertheless, he has no immunity from the language and conceptual apparatus of economy that he himself identifies as permeating the contemporary social order. To speak against this order means at the same time to speak within it, using the conventions that one inherits from it. But Nietzsche's critical entanglement with economy does not receive its defining characterisation with the *Untimely Meditations* or the essay 'On Truth and Lie'. Consideration of these works can at best form a prelude to a larger examination of the role of economics within aspects of Nietzsche's thought. In the works that follow the *Meditations,* the text of *Human, All Too Human* (1878), and the two works that Nietzsche subsequently decided would make up its second volume, *Assorted Opinions and Maxims* (1879) and *The Wander and His Shadow* (1880), his concern with economy becomes increasingly apparent. These works, along with *Daybreak* (1881), show a side to Nietzsche that has, I think, been underplayed by many commentators. In them he reveals himself to be a philosopher occupied by political and economic concerns. In what follows, I shall seek to show the manner in which the spheres of economics and politics are confronted and analysed in these works. This does not involve merely examining Nietzsche's overt references to these things. As we will see, the notion of economy as it occupies Nietzsche in these texts runs far deeper than his mere invocation of this one word.[3]

Human, All Too Human opens with a bold, general observation that takes us to the heart of a philosophical problem: 'Almost all the problems of philosophy once again pose the same form of question as they did two thousand years ago: how can something originate in its opposite, for example rationality in irrationality, [. . .] logic in unlogic, [. . .] truth in error?' (*Human, All Too Human,* 1). Nietzsche poses what looks like a simple question about the *origins* of concepts. His next move is to invoke two approaches to answering this question. The first approach is that of 'metaphysical philosophy'. Metaphysical philosophy extols a traditional understanding of how we answer such questions. Metaphysical philosophy, Nietzsche argues, takes the view that such oppositions are fixed. Thus, reason, in this view, cannot be derived from unreason, logic cannot have its origins in illogic, and error cannot be the source of truth. Metaphysical philosophy holds this position because it attributes a 'miraculous source' underlying experience 'in the very kernel and being of the "thing in itself" ' from which reason, truth and logic spring. Metaphysical philosophy, in other words, exhibits an urge that runs counter to experience: it invokes a realm that is supposedly beyond experience in order to justify its claims. This turning away from experience is one of the things that allows Nietzsche to characterise metaphysical philosophy as *metaphysical.* But metaphysical philosophy is metaphysical in another way, too. When practitioners of metaphysics invoke a realm that lies beyond the confines of experience they are at the same time claiming to have possession of a supra-historical standpoint on reality. The metaphysician claims that he or she has access to a perspective that is outside history. Metaphysics, according to Nietzsche, thinks it has a monopoly when it comes to the ownership of a standard of measurement that will allow us to determine what 'reality' is. This standard, because it is such a standard, never changes. That is why, according to Nietzsche, metaphysics takes the meaning of the word 'true' to mean that which does not change.

Metaphysical philosophy, for Nietzsche, is opposed by 'historical philosophy'. Where metaphysics wants to locate eternal truths, historical philosophy starts by identifying knowledge as being the product of finite beings situated in a physical context. The historical philosopher envisages knowledge as a matter of development. This development is essentially linked to the material conditions of the form of life (namely, us) that developed knowledge. One unshakeable consequence of this is that although our knowledge has arisen under material and historical conditions, the very conditions of its development meant that our thought itself was constituted in terms of habits and rules from which we cannot now escape. In simpler terms, all thought involves presuppositions that cannot be shaken off even by the most devout scepticism. We live in a world where all thought is facilitated by unquestionable assumptions. These assumptions, Nietzsche argues, originate in the remote prehistoric past of humanity (ibid., 2). Ignore this, and you fail to address the fact that our present cognitive habits are rooted in a past that, at least in part, determines them. Metaphysicians uncritically adopt the assumption that the conditions that govern human life today are timeless structures that consequently allow us to have knowledge of 'reality': 'They involuntarily think of "man" as an *aeterna veritas* [. . .] as a sure measure of things [. . .] Everything that the philosopher has declared about man is, however, at bottom no more than a testimony as to the man of a *very limited* period of time. Lack of historical sense is the family failing of all philosophers [. . .]'. What is needed in place of metaphysics is 'a *chemistry* of the moral, religious and aesthetic conceptions and sensations, likewise of all the agitations we experience within ourselves in cultural and social intercourse, and indeed even when we are alone [. . .]' (ibid., 1). Against metaphysics, Nietzsche thus opposes the spirit of science.[4] What is needed is not metaphysical speculation but a systematic and rigorous analysis of the moral, religious and aesthetic domains.

Human, All Too Human may be permeated by the spirit of scholarship, but it is at the same time, like the *Untimely Meditations* before it and the works that immediately follow it, dominated by a concern with culture and modernity. If contemporary metaphysics suffers from an inherent instability and the imminent threat of collapse, it is in this regard no different from the social realm in which it finds itself situated. Nietzsche sees in modern society something that is permanently on the move. It is characterised most essentially by change. The change that marks cultural modernity takes several forms. Most obvious, even to a casual reader of Nietzsche's texts from the late 1870s and early 1880s, is that they paint a world in which the state looms large. Modern society is a place where, Nietzsche says (with no little irony), 'one has learned to believe in the necessity of the state' (ibid., 101). Nietzsche also perceives this to be a world in which socialists agitate for a revolutionary overturning of political order and the destruction of individuality (ibid., 463, 473). It is a society that is increasingly dominated by public opinion. Political debate is rampant. However, in his view, such debate is neither genuine nor free, for it is determined by powerful financial interests. Hence, Nietzsche's texts from this period seek, amongst other things, to expose the rise of a mass culture in which 'anyone possessing money and influence can transform any opinion into a public opinion' (ibid., 447). As the public realm expands, so the inner realm of the individual contracts in its potential: 'Public opinions – private indolence' (ibid., 482).

One may speak against one's times, and thereby be 'untimely', but this does not mean that one has an identity that is thinkable independently of the spirit of one's times. We are historical beings, and this condition is as inescapable as metaphysics is illusory. This is the chief lesson of historical philosophy. We cannot will our way out of the present. Indeed, the urge to do so would amount to wanting to will oneself out of existence altogether. The historical mode of thought which forms the basis for anti-metaphysical, historical philosophy thereby serves to situate modern consciousness in temporal confines of which it is all too well aware. Its sense of temporality defines its self-awareness. We are prisoners of our own historically constituted essence. For Nietzsche, this historical condition at the same time determines even the manner in which both our senses perceive and our understanding comprehends our environment:

> *In prison.* – My eyes, however strong or weak they may be, can see only a certain distance, and it is within the space encompassed by this distance that I live and move, the line of this horizon constitutes my immediate fate, in great things and small, from which I cannot

> escape. Around every being there is described a similar concentric circle, which has a mid-point and is peculiar to him. Our ears enclose us within a comparable circle, and so does our sense of touch. Now, it is by these horizons, within which each of us encloses his senses as if behind prison walls, that we *measure* the world, we say that this is near and that far, this is big and that small, this is hard and that soft: this measuring we call sensation – and it is all of it an error! According to the average quantity of experiences and excitations possible to us at any particular point of time one measures one's life as being short or long, poor or rich, full or empty: and according to the average human life one measures that of all other creatures – all of it an error! [. . .] The habits of our senses have woven into us lies and deception of sensation: these again are the basis of all our judgements and 'knowledge' – there is absolutely no escape, no backway or bypath into the *real world*!
>
> (*Daybreak*, 117)

Nietzsche is no straightforward empiricist after the manner of Locke or Hume. As with a thinker like Hume, for Nietzsche, we are beings whose perceptions, feelings and passions define us. Yet, at the same time, our senses are confined within the boundaries of a horizon of possibility beyond which we can neither understand nor perceive anything at all. The realm of the senses (feeling, in its most general sense) is in fact structured in its possibilities according to the logic of measurement. The senses are not passive receptors of information (sensory stimulation) since the realm of sensation is measured, delineated and thereby determined in advance of any sensation. To put it another way, for Nietzsche our world is always already interpreted *before* we even get to the point of grasping it as something to be perceived. In order to be perceived by us it must be measured, and measurement is a notion that has an intimate connection with economy. As will become clear, the notion of measurement also has a central role in Nietzsche's account of our nature. We are first and foremost *measurers* of our environment. That we come to self-understanding through procedures of measurement (the notion of equivalence, for instance, which, the mature Nietzsche will argue, underlies the development of justice) is an insight that will take on an increasing importance in Nietzsche's thought, finding its most telling expression in *On the Genealogy of Morality*.

Nietzsche remains fascinated by the contemporary developments he charts and sees them in himself no less than in the world around him. In this, he too remains stubbornly and self-consciously modern, a representative of the spirit of his own age. One may rage against one's time, but one also cleaves to it in spite of everything. Thus, in *Assorted Opinions and Maxims* Nietzsche argues that a foolish attitude to the past is evidenced by the desire to have lived at some other time than one's own. Historical philosophising tells us that we must become ever more aware of being locked in the finitude of our own age, that there is nowhere else to go. This is the case in an even more devastating sense than the mere prohibition on time travel imposes upon us. All genuine study of the past leads to one firm conclusion: 'Anything rather than back to that!' (*Assorted Opinions and Maxims*, 382). If a person was transported back to another age, he or she would find the 'spirit of that age' to be unbearably oppressive, bearing down 'with the weight of a hundred atmospheres'. One's own time may be a prison, but any other time would be experienced as poison. Modernity would not be immune to the same judgement being made of it by those looking back from the standpoint of some future time. No period would be an exception to the rule that every person from every age would find every other *unendurable*. Yet every person finds that their own era is something that can be borne, and the reason for this lies in the fact that the spirit of a person's age 'does not only lie *upon* him but is also *within* him. The spirit of the age offers resistance to itself, bears up against itself.' It is not possible to stand 'outside' one's own time. But it is possible to stand against one's time *from within it*.[5] One can become the mouthpiece of the contradictions and tensions of one's age – or in moral language, the *conscience* of one's time. One can stand within the marketplace, the realm of everyday life and concerns, but not play the game of the market. One can seek to grasp mass society's rules, ruses, power plays and the like, but simultaneously resist adhering to the purposes usually advocated as being intrinsic to the social game. It may be possible to bend the rules, to challenge them where needed, even if it is ultimately impossible to escape to a pure realm that lies beyond all rules, marketplaces and politics. This, Nietzsche reminds us, is the wisdom of Epictetus, a man who learned to be content with communing quietly with himself. Such 'wisdom is the whispering of the solitary to himself in the crowded marketplace' (ibid., 386). It is the wisdom of a person who speaks but is condemned to being misunderstood by his or her contemporaries.

3. *Nietzsche's 'middle period' works offer a consistently critical commentary on the mercantile culture of their times. By way of example, like the third* Meditation, *so* Human, All Too Human *focuses upon contemporary education as a means of exploring the interrelationship between the*

> *cultural, economic and political spheres. Nietzsche's frequently cited contempt for the realms of economy, society, politics and mass culture might be cited in favour of considering this a marginal concern. However, even as he denigrates contemporary political and commercial culture, Nietzsche cannot help but do so in economic terms* (Daybreak, *179*). *This is because modernity is the age of economic management par excellence, from which on his own admission Nietzsche cannot escape. His reflections on modernity often arise in surprising contexts. Contemporary dietary habits, for example, betray the modern worship of money and the power of capital. The worship of false wealth is in turn contrasted with the pursuit of spiritual wealth, but the one is thereby expressed in the language of possession characteristic of the other.*

In actual fact, Nietzsche does not exactly whisper to himself. Rather, he states publicly (i.e. in print), frequently and in the most unambiguous terms where he thinks the importance of commerce lies. In the works that span the period from *Human, All Too Human* to *Daybreak*, he consistently offers his readers a commentary on the social–commercial culture of his times. As is often the case with Nietzsche, nothing cuts in one direction only. He is happy to offer the following kind of analysis of the social and political forces that operate within modern society, dominated as it is by the state (*Assorted Opinions and Maxims*, 320). Envisage, Nietzsche tells us, the following situation. The ideal tool of state power (from the state's point of view, at least) would be found in the combination of the army with the education system. The army exploits upper-class ambition and also the strength of the lower classes – both classes being composed of moderately or poorly gifted individuals. The education system in its turn allows the state to appropriate those from a background of poverty endowed with natural *talent*, 'especially the intellectually ambitious semi-poor of the middle classes'. Education is falling increasingly within the domain of the state. Home education is discouraged, as is private education. Teaching posts are created which promote the increased control of the state by making the posts themselves able to offer 'only *meagre* nourishment' to their occupants. Teachers driven by relative poverty become obsessed by advancement and in this way more open to state control. A body of teachers thus 'physically and spiritually curbed' brings about the education of the populace to a level of culture that satisfies the aims of the state, but crucially does not exceed those aims. '[A]bove all, the immature and ambitious spirits of all classes are almost imperceptibly imbued with the idea that only a life course recognized and authorized by the state can bring immediate *social* distinction.' Bestowal of qualifications, in other words, is linked to social status and acceptability. Qualifications become essential for getting work, recognition and the like. The young are thereby trapped within a 'net of expectations'. If, in turn, national service becomes an obligation and then a custom, the state can then 'venture the masterstroke of weaving *together* school *and* army'. The army would become the path of advancement for the intellectually gifted, who accept its culture unquestioningly.

> Nothing is then lacking but opportunities for great wars: and this will be taken care of, as a professional matter and thus in all *innocence*, by the diplomats, together with the newspapers and stock exchanges: for the 'nation', as a nation of soldiers, always has a good conscience when it comes to wars, there is no need to worry about that.
>
> (Ibid., 320)

Nietzsche here demonstrates the socially aware dimension of his thinking, articulating the complex possibilities of relationships between the spheres of politics, education, culture, state and economy. The social realm is grasped as an interrelated whole. Society is a network of elements, susceptible to being organised and harmonised according to the dominant interests of state and commerce.

The above commentary Nietzsche offers picks up on the importance of political and economic forces for the development of culture. Nevertheless, given the expression here of a deep suspicion of state and commercial interests, it should perhaps come as no surprise that Nietzsche can elsewhere state the following:

> Political and economic affairs [*wirthschaftlichen Verhältnisse*] are not worthy of being the enforced concern of society's most gifted spirits: such a wasteful use of the spirit is at bottom worse than having none at all. They remain domains for lesser heads [. . .] better to let the machinery fall to pieces again! But as things now stand, with everybody believing he is obliged to *know* what is taking place here every day and neglecting his own work in order to be continually participating in it, the whole arrangement has become a great and ludicrous piece of insanity. The price being paid for 'universal security' is much too high: and the maddest thing is that what is being effected is the very opposite of universal security, a fact our lovely century is undertaking to demonstrate: as if demonstration were needed! To make society safe against thieves and fireproof and endlessly amenable to

> every form of trade and traffic, and to transform the state into a kind of providence in both the good and the bad sense [. . .] Our age may talk about economy [*Ökonomie*] but it is in fact a squanderer: it squanders the most precious thing there is, the spirit.
>
> (*Daybreak*, 179)

Clearly, political and commercial pursuits are regarded here as being of the second rank compared with the higher interests of intellectual life. But Nietzsche's point is more complex. For one thing, he is using the very domains he denigrates to *define* modernity. Modernity is here encapsulated as the age in which politics, trade and economics are abiding concerns, even to the extent that intellectuality itself cannot avoid being invaded and colonised by them. This, at the same time, exhibits the grossest waste of intellectual resources. What Nietzsche attacks about modern life, in other words, is the paradox of an age that is obsessed with economics but lacks genuine (intellectual and cultural) economic sense. What he criticises is not merely the spirit of modern life (its tastes, its interests, etc.) but above all its wastefulness. Modernity is a spendthrift: through it people are sucked into triviality. In this way, people of talent have their abilities and potential squandered. Likewise, the increasing obsession with everyday economic and political life is also a waste in the sense that it turns people away from the domains of interest and activity appropriate to them. The idea that there ought to be public debate about political and economic policies is anathema to Nietzsche. Yet, at the same time, he himself cannot help but enter into and adopt the terms of this debate even as he denigrates it. For one thing, Nietzsche cannot resist attacking contemporary political discourse for its insufficiencies in *economic* terms. Thus, he accuses modern life of exhibiting the tendency to bad management of resources. Nor is it obvious that he really wants to avoid talking in such terms. What Nietzsche is criticising here is neither consideration of economics nor politics as such, but something more general: the contemporary manifestation of the public sphere and the way in which it subordinates intellectual pursuits to specific discursive constraints. This is a political issue, for when economics and political and party political squabbles dominate the realm of social intercourse what are, for Nietzsche, the more important concerns of culture are denuded of significance and come to seem irrelevant or even meaningless. Suffice to say that from early on his preference is for politics on a different scale from that exemplified by the public sphere. What Nietzsche prefers is a 'grand politics' that stands apart from a Germany dominated by 'the political and nationalist lunacy' (ibid., 189, 190).

However much it is to be detested, modernity is inexorably *the* age of the priority of production, money, exchange and economic management. If one wishes to talk about values, and Nietzsche almost always wishes to do so above anything else, one cannot avoid thinking about that which exemplifies the values of one's times. Indeed, as we have already seen and if we are to take him at his word (*Assorted Opinions and Maxims*, 382), Nietzsche would hardly be able to bear being anywhere else anyway. Sometimes, surprising areas of consideration can take us abruptly into reflection upon this inescapable aspect of modernity. Take modern food and the habits of modern eating. Both, for Nietzsche, are appalling. Even eminent scholars, he tells us, 'load their table in the same way as the banker loads his': with too much and too many different things. That, today, people are inclined to eat thus does not, however, mean that they are gourmonds. So why do their meals take this form? What is the point of eating in this overtly excessive manner? Such meals are

> *representatives*! Representatives of what, in the name of all the saints? Of rank? – No, of *money*: we no longer possess rank! We are 'individual'! But money is power, fame, dignity, precedence, influence; the amount of money a man has determines his moral prejudices! No one wants to hide it under a bushel, but no one wants to lay it on the table either; consequently money needs a representative which *can* be laid on the table: and hence the meals they eat!
>
> (*Daybreak*, 203)

Modernity is thereby epitomised as a world dominated by the possession of capital, a domination that brings with it the need to demonstrate one's social status as a possessor of goods. In short, modern society is in thrall to the naked celebration and worship of money: 'what one formerly did "for the sake of God" one now does for the sake of money [. . .]' (ibid., 204). The danger is that a society permeated by this tendency can come to celebrate itself in such a way that it loses good sense, good manners and becomes facile, boastful and lacking in dignity. The need to display wealth evidences the need to *show* that one is an 'important' (i.e. rich) person. Such wealth is false wealth, for Nietzsche. True (intellectual/spiritual) wealth, in his view, takes a rather different form: to recall a point already made, it is like the wisdom possessed by Epictetus (ibid., 546). Nietzsche's praise of Epictetus indicates that he does not consider the concept of property possession to be a necessarily bad thing. It is the *kind* of possessions that we pursue which matter, for what we pursue has a habit of defining who we are. But more of this in due course.

4. *Nietzsche comments continually on the cultural implications of the materialism of modern society. Thus, he, for example, considers commercial forces giving rise to the dominance of a single language in order to facilitate the pursuit of trade. Language is thereby seen as being subject to the domain of larger cultural forces (production and exchange) and the practices constitutive of them. By the same token, the power of modern capital threatens to overturn the political unit of the nation state. Modern economy thereby brings a mix of good (the possibility of a unified Europe, technological advance, scholarly rigour) and bad (greed, superficiality, mediocrity, politicisation of class divisions). Above all, modernity is the age of the machine and the depersonalising consequences it gives rise to. In consequence of mechanisation, the age of capital is the age of 'impersonal slavery' and social conformity. Contemplation (the philosophical life) is thereby threatened and the meaning of labour denuded by industrialised compulsion. The demands placed on labour intrude into the realm of thought, endangering it with the possibility of becoming as superficial and detached as the casual railway passenger's knowledge of the landscape he or she skims across between point of departure and destination. The 'free spirit' stands in opposition to this: an outsider trapped within the social body.*

Nietzsche may detest the excess and wastefulness of modern life with its domination by economics and management culture, but this does not stop him from continually extrapolating the cultural implications of this fact. His repugnance at the sight of the modern money-world cannot stop him from being fascinated by it. He cannot, in other words, remain silent about economics and its influence upon society and individuality for very long. This influence is pervasive. For instance, the power of the forces unleashed by capital can permeate the sphere of language. A person may learn many languages, but the effects of such acquisition are potentially harmful. Great facility in language 'stands in the way of the acquisition of thorough knowledge' (*Human, All Too Human*, 267). A person's wide linguistic knowledge can lead to others drawing the false inference that the person is knowledgeable in a more general way. But knowledge of a wide variety of linguistic elements is not the same as concrete knowledge arrived at through reflection and analysis. The illusion is created of a depth of understanding in the richly endowed polyglot that may not in reality be there. Genuinely deep understanding may even be prevented by the very ability that others take to be a sure sign of considerable intelligence. Languages, however, do not stand in the world like unchanging monuments immune to the power of social pressures. Rather, the presence of many languages in the world is likely to change due to the power of commercial forces. The requirements of trade and industry will cause a narrowing of the wide linguistic diversity that is current. Commercial trafficking between people 'is bound to grow ever more cosmopolitan and efficient [. . .]'. A nineteenth-century London merchant is required to have the command of several languages in order to do business, but this 'necessary *evil*', says Nietzsche, will sooner or later be overcome. The *need to trade* will ensure that 'at some distant future there will be a new language for all – first as a commercial language, then as the language of intellectual intercourse in general – just as surely as there will one day be air travel'. Nietzsche here asserts the primacy of economics in the constitution of linguistic conditions. In its turn, the economic traffic in goods will, via language, influence the trafficking in ideas. He makes this prediction on the basis of economic activity. Culture and commerce are inseparable, for commercial conditions constitute the ground and driving force for the development of the intellectual sphere. Equally striking is the harmony implied to exist between technological-commercial development (the creation of the technical know-how required for air travel is envisaged as being inevitable) and linguistic change. Language answers to the demands of trade no less than technology answers to them.

The influence of trade and industry goes deeper even than this. Trade transgresses national boundaries. The mixing of languages and their possible sedimentation into a unified single language to satisfy commercial demands is merely one aspect of the general restless mixing of cultures evident in the contemporary world. To be modern is to live in this continual state of cultural unrest (ibid., 285). Fervent economic and business activity typifies modernity and finds its expression at every other level of life. 'Trade and industry, the post and the book-trade [. . .] rapid changing of home and scene, the nomadic life now lived by all who do not own land' are what Nietzsche sees when he looks about him (ibid., 475). This situation will in its turn have an historical consequence of tremendous proportions, for it will initiate the 'abolition of nations' in Europe. One should, Nietzsche tells us, follow this trend set by economics and become 'a *good European* and [. . .] work for the amalgamation of nations' (ibid.). This is something positive and to be wished for. However, as he gazes upon the landscape of modernity, Nietzsche's judgement oscillates. His is an attitude of ambivalence, pure and simple. Modernity is envisaged above all in terms of its restless potential, and this potential conjures visions both positive and disastrous in equal measure. A world dominated by economic production can offer the possibility of political change for the better (a unified Europe, for example), it can lead to technological advance and can transform language in a manner that may lead to greater intellectual rigour. But it can also foster material greed and in doing so create superficiality and mediocrity. Likewise, a world dominated by production is also a world of class divisions, of transformed relations between individuals, of political movements like that of socialism and a realm that threatens individuality.[6] It is all these things because the age of production is at the same time the age of the division of labour according to the dictates of the machine.

Modernity is always a matter of social relationships determined in terms of the terrain of impersonal relationships with technology. It is the age of the machine: '*Premises of the machine age.* – The press, the machine, the railway, the telegraph are premises whose thousand-year conclusion no one has yet dared to draw' (*The Wanderer and His Shadow*, 278). Nietzsche's dares, if sometimes only tentatively. Machines are impersonal. A machine 'deprives the piece of work of its pride, of the individual *goodness* and *faultiness* that adheres to all work not done by a machine [. . .]' (ibid., 288). In the past, Nietzsche notes, goods were purchased from artisans. Purchasing was a sign of conferment and distinction on both maker and buyer. In this way, objects became signs of 'mutual esteem and personal solidarity'. The world that preceded mechanical production was a social formation in which relations were cemented through personalised modes of exchange and individualised labour. In modernity, the realm of mass production, the machine causes the sense of personality to evaporate: 'we now seem to live in the midst of nothing but an anonymous and impersonal slavery' (ibid.). The machine thereby creates social conformity with telling political consequences.[7] It teaches the 'mutual co-operation of hordes of men in operations where each man has to do only one thing' and in so doing proffers the 'model for the party apparatus and the conduct of warfare' (*The Wanderer and His Shadow*, 218). In an impersonal context of alienated labour, genuine contemplative activity is rendered problematic. The decline in the contemplative life due to the machine-driven age of mass production has occurred in tandem with the corruption of labour itself. Nietzsche describes a world patterned by forces of mass production that have not merely transformed but corrupted both contemplation and labour. This is a society in which 'work and industry – formerly adherents of the great goddess health – sometimes seem to rage like an epidemic. [... The...] time for thinking and quietness in thinking are lacking, one no longer ponders deviant views: one contents oneself with hating them. With the tremendous acceleration of life mind and eye have become accustomed to seeing or judging partially or inaccurately, and everyone is like the traveller who gets to know a land and its people from a railway [...]' (*Human, All Too Human*, 282).[8] Industrialisation intrudes upon the world of contemplation. The enforcement of the demands of labour constrains the pursuit of knowledge by imposing conditions on the management of time. Work, once a sign of good living, now becomes a raging illness that delimits the possibility of thoughtful reflection. The more that time management at the hands of organised labour becomes a defining characteristic of the everyday, the greater the degree of shallowness that infects life. Nietzsche's invocation of a paradigmatic image of industrialisation here to communicate the decline of contemplation is significant. The landscape he depicts is one scarred by railway tracks. The ease of access to different and increasingly distant places that this affords belies the lack of concrete knowledge that the modern traveller thereby gleans. The traveller does no more than simply pass through. He or she skates across the surface of a world that, because of this very mode of interaction's effect on the life of the mind, must become increasingly superficial. The life of the modern traveller is, in this sense, not lived through and as an experiencing of concrete conditions. Nowadays, Nietzsche in effect says, a person does not really encounter anything much at all beyond their own lazy self-image – which is not the same as critical self-reflection. The traveller and voyager of modern life has become a passenger, a distant and unconnected onlooker upon a landscape that remains forever (and reassuringly) held at an arm's length from genuine contact and understanding. To be like this passenger on a train, we might say, is to be like a visitor to a foreign country who arrives and proceeds to learn the language spoken there with the sole aid of a dictionary, talking as little as possible to any actual people. The visitor returns home with the illusion that he or she has attained something like a proper understanding of the language and culture of the country visited. But what they really have is an at best formalised grasp of the relations between words formed on the basis of projections of what they already know. This is not equivalent to a genuine understanding of the nuances of meaning that are to be encountered in different social contexts within any culture, since such meanings remain stubbornly context specific. One truly learns only by making mistakes, by being confused and subsequently corrected by observing the behaviour and listening to the speech of others.[9] In short, keeping the world at a distance is a sure means of misunderstanding it. In doing so, one likewise misunderstands oneself because one is content to believe that one already knows oneself and the nature of things sufficiently well to discharge oneself of the responsibility for further reflection on the sometimes disturbing demands presented by different views. An industrious and industrial world, in short, is at the same time an intellectually lazy one.

Because society becomes ever less inclined to contemplation, the 'free spirit' – a phrase that for Nietzsche signifies all that is praiseworthy in a person able to engage in critical reflection upon their own times and values – is regarded by it as a disreputable figure. Such an attitude is taken 'especially by scholars, who miss in his [the free spirit's] art of reflecting on things their own thoroughness and antlike industry' (ibid.). The scholars' 'ant-diligence' bespeaks the fact that even they, for Nietzsche, have become subject to the modern tendency to depersonalised labour – as does their sense of 'shame' when confronted with idleness and the pursuit of leisure (*Human, All Too Human*, 284). The free spirit, in contrast, stands as a symbol of resistance to this tendency and 'has the quite different and higher task of commanding [. . .] the whole militia of scientific and learned men and showing them the paths to and goals of culture' (ibid., 282). What the free spirit thereby resists is the tendency of society to transform the individual into something akin to the production machine, a mere piece of equipment and adjunct to the social demand for ever-increasing productivity.

5. *Industrial forces reify subjectivity. The worker's relation to the social order is reduced to being one determined by the exchange of labour for money. Subjectivity is thereby rendered an object of exchange value. Modernity's pursuit of great wealth through this social arrangement is regarded by Nietzsche as folly and is spurned in favour of a philosophy that extols the virtues of moderate poverty. Capitalism and socialism are rejected in equal measure. Instead of revolution, Nietzsche advocates the mass desertion of Europe by the working classes in favour of the colonisation of other lands. This reveals Nietzsche's reluctance to consider the relationship between capital, mass production, mechanisation, and colonisation. His dislike of socialism, in other words, resides in an unwillingness to question the concepts of property and ownership. Socialism, however, is best resisted*

> *by the abandonment of the unrestrained pursuit of wealth. Socialism and unrestrained capital accumulation thus stand equally as modern manifestations of the same destructive, philistine false consciousness – the greed of the hypocritical property owner would make them a revolutionary socialist if they did not have possessions. Possession is, or ought to be, a privilege, according to Nietzsche. It is best reserved for the most spiritual types of person. The unimaginative pursue wealth without thought, and their attainment of power distorts the meaning of culture. Culture becomes equivalent to the possession of material goods. Such possession is always distorted, not least because of the principle of exchange. Through this principle exploitation is encouraged and this leads to alienation.*

Society is dominated by impersonal and depersonalising mechanistic forces that transform individuals into equipment. One symptom of this is to be found in the fact that it has become populated by 'factory slaves' (*Daybreak*, 206). More pay, Nietzsche notes, would not serve to liberate these slaves from the misery of their condition, for this condition and the suffering that defines it is fundamentally linked to the depersonalisation they have undergone. Their servitude is 'impersonal enslavement', pure and simple. The belief that such impersonal servitude could be regarded as something virtuous and worthy of reward (e.g. in the shape of increased pay) is disgusting to Nietzsche. Thus, he is appalled at the very idea of allowing a price to be set on oneself in this way and allowing one's personhood to be given an exchange value. To value oneself in this manner is repellent, for through it one accedes to being denuded of one's personality and rendered a mere bolt suitable for incorporation into the machinery of modern industrial existence. 'Are you accomplices in the current folly of the nations – the folly of wanting above all to produce as much as possible and to become as rich as possible?', Nietzsche asks. What one needs, rather, is to set up a contra account that demonstrates how much by way of inner worth is abandoned when one seeks such goals:

> But where is your inner value if you no longer know what it is to breathe freely? if you no longer possess the slightest power over yourselves? if you all too often grow weary of yourselves like a drink that has been left too long standing? if you pay heed to the newspapers and look askance at your wealthy neighbour, made covetous by the rapid rise and fall of power, money and opinions? if you no

> longer believe in a philosophy that wears rags, in the free-heartedness of him without needs?
>
> (Ibid.)

The current foolishness of nations desires productivity above all things. This creates a culture obsessed with material need. In turn, the greater the domination of the desire for purely material satisfaction the less the degree of freedom possible. There is more to value than money, wealth and power, Nietzsche argues. There is 'inner value', as opposed to 'outer' material wealth. The philosophy that wears rags stands as a symbol for the rejection of this materialism, for it embraces a spirituality that spurns the capitalist accumulation of wealth even as it balks at the *bestia triumphans* espoused by socialist visionaries.

Nietzsche may object to capitalist exploitation, but he does not espouse revolution. What Nietzsche then suggests the working classes of Europe do is, however, rather surprising. He urges them to renounce the identity imposed upon them by embarking on a path of active protest that involves escaping from the geographical confines of industrialised Europe:

> This would be the right attitude of mind: the workers of Europe ought henceforth to declare themselves *as a class* a human impossibility [. . .]. [T]hey ought to inaugurate within the European beehive an age of great swarming-out such as has never been seen before, and through this act of free emigration in the grand manner to protest against the machine, against capital, and against the choice now threatening them to be *compelled* to become either the slave of the state or the slave of a party of disruption [i.e. socialism] [. . .] Only in distant lands and in the undertakings of swarming trains of colonists will it really become clear how much reason and fairness, how much healthy mistrust, Europe has embodied in her sons.
>
> (Ibid.)

Notable here is the manner in which the machine-like tendencies of industrialised culture are conjoined with financial power. In this way, an explicit connection is made between depersonalisation through automation and capital. Nietzsche does not advocate political revolution in the face of this threat, after the manner of socialist thought. Rather, he espouses a form of action that, while standing as a declaration of war upon the excesses of the contemporary capitalist industrial order, at the same time reflects his own entanglement with this social order.

His answer to class exploitation here is permeated with the spirit of colonialism through and through. As much as a *quarter* of the population of Europe, Nietzsche suggests, should express their dissatisfaction at the class situation by simply going elsewhere, by becoming colonisers of other lands and cultures. Nietzsche does not entertain the possibility that emigration and colonisation is itself only thinkable because the inexorable expansion of industrial markets has already exerted its influence. What, for example, is the relationship between industrial scale commerce and contemporary colonisation? He does not pause to wonder whether large-scale industry and its systems of transport and distribution of goods would be needed to make possible the kind of mass exodus he advocates, nor that the colonisers might impose the very thing they flee from on the colonised. What is not challenged, in other words, is the view that property possession and its unequal distribution, which are what lie at the heart of modern commercialism no less than they grounded medieval social life, are inevitable conditions of human existence.

It is in terms of this last point that Nietzsche most opposes the socialist revolutionary thinking of his times. Contemporary radicalism may hold property possession to be unjust, but the solutions usually proffered as a remedy to this source of injustice (forced equal distribution of goods or the abolition of property and the creation of communal ownership) are equally problematic (*The Wanderer and His Shadow*, 285). The first option has, Nietzsche argues, been tried on a limited scale, with much social conflict and misery resulting. One problem is that digging over boundary stones means digging over morality, too. The distribution of goods in any society, in other words, is intimately linked to its moral norms and the continued acceptance of their validity: a change in the one initiates a crisis in the other. In any case, 'for how long would this equality, unhealthy and poisoned at the roots as it is, endure! Within a few generations inheritance would have here divided one allotment among five people, there given one person five allotments [. . .]'. Socialist collective ownership, on the other hand, would 'destroy the land. For upon that which he possesses only in passing man bestows no care or self-sacrifice, he merely exploits it like a robber or dissolute squanderer.' Possession, it follows, implies care, frugality and cultivation. It is, in this sense, something to be cherished. Against Plato's view that the evils of self-interest and egoism shrivel when property is abolished, Nietzsche argues that with this 'the four cardinal virtues' would also disappear. Property possession, although problematic when it becomes excessive, nevertheless indicates something about the strengths of the human soul.

The only genuine means of resisting socialism that the wealthy liberal has is recourse to the strategy of living with modesty and sufficiency (*Assorted Opinions and Maxims*, 304). In other words, the rich person should abandon the pursuit of wealth for its own sake and live within sensible means. Unsurprisingly, the bourgeoisie would hardly be well disposed to considering this course of action, says Nietzsche. The reason for this is simple enough: hypocrisy. The wealthy bourgeois liberal is, when it comes down to it, not so very different from the socialist he or she despises. Addressing the liberal, Nietzsche says, it is your own heart's deepest convictions 'that you find so fearful and threatening in the socialists, though in yourselves you consider them inevitable, as though they were something quite different' (ibid.). Fundamentally, socialist and liberal are not that dissimilar. They are each of them a different refraction of the same social and cultural milieu. Had the wealthy bourgeois not the need to consider his own fortune and the care for its preservation, his fundamental convictions would make him a socialist, too: 'possession of property is the only thing that distinguishes you from them'. Neither socialist revolutionary nor exponent of industrial-scale liberal capitalism, Nietzsche seeks an alternative way. The desire for property should be cultivated, but only to the extent of allowing 'the accumulation of *moderate* wealth through work'. What should be prevented is the

> sudden or unearned acquisition of riches; we must remove from the hands of private individuals and companies all those branches of trade and transportation favourable to the accumulation of *great* wealth, thus especially the trade in money – and regard those who possess too much as being as great a danger to society as those who possess nothing.
>
> (*The Wanderer and His Shadow*, 285)[10]

This last point might be expressed in slightly different but telling terms. Possession is a privilege that ought to be the sole right of those with an intellectual and spiritual dimension to their personality: 'Only he who has *spirit* [*Geist*] ought to have possessions: otherwise possessions are a *public danger*' (*Assorted Opinions and Maxims*, 310). Nietzsche gives a straightforward enough reason for endorsing this view. If this intellectual and imaginative aspect is lacking in a person who possesses even only moderate wealth, their financial success coupled with their spiritual barrenness will lead them to pursue yet more wealth. If successful, they will become capitalist accumulators who glory in 'riches which are in fact the glittering product of spiritual dependence and poverty'. Such individuals are cast as deceivers and self-deceivers: 'They only *appear* quite different from what their wretched origin would lead one to expect because they are able to mask themselves with art and culture: for they are, of course, able to *purchase* masks.' Again, the key danger here is linked to the combined ills of economic power, cultural superficiality and the stirring of socialist sentiment. The poor feel resentment when presented with the contrast between their own poverty and the luxury of the ostentatious capitalist. They, in turn, aspire to material wealth, and with this aspiration a 'social revolution' has the way paved for it. Thus, modern society creates the illusion that material success is akin to spiritual and intellectual refinement. This illusion creates social turmoil by fostering unsatisfied and insatiable desires. The labourer is condemned to exchange their time for money under the illusion that in doing so they are pursuing a moral good when they are answering to the call of such desires. But modern society is a place where work cannot be fairly evaluated due to the dominance of supply and demand in estimating financial value. Hence, work cannot be fairly rewarded. To arrive at a just evaluation of someone's labour 'we would have to place the entire person on the scales, and that is impossible. Here the rule must be "judge not!" [. . .] no personality can be held accountable for what it produces, that is to say its work: so no *merit* can be derived from it [. . .]' (*The Wanderer and His Shadow*, 286). Likewise, the value of any object if it is determined according to the rule of supply and demand is distorted to such a degree that basic conditions of honesty and justice are ignored:

> An exchange [*Tausche*] is honest and just only when each of those participating demands as much as his own object seems worth to him, including the effort it cost to acquire it, its rarity, the time expended, etc., together with its sentimental value. As soon as he sets the price *with reference to the need of the other* he is a subtler brigand and extortioner. – If money is the exchange object [*Tauschobjekt*] it must be considered that a shilling in the hand of a rich heir, a day-labourer, a shop-keeper, a student are quite different things: according to whether he did almost nothing or a great deal to get it, each ought to receive little or a great deal in exchange for it: in reality it is, of course, the other way round. In the great world of money the

> shilling of the laziest man is more lucrative than that of the poor and industrious.
>
> (Ibid., 25)

Supply and demand, in other words, is unfair in so far as it allows for a distorted price put upon objects of exchange. Differences between classes become especially polarised when it is money that is exchanged, for the notion that a coin has a fixed value denoted by the figure embossed upon it, which in turn determines what can be purchased with it, is also inherently unfair. The exchange value of money is equally determined by class divisions, which dictate conditions that penalise the poorer and reward the richer because the amount of labour expended by each in order to get money is not reflected in its purchasing power. A person who works hard for, say, a Swiss Franc *ought* to receive more for it than a person who simply happens to be in possession of a fortune through the mechanism of inheritance. The money-world is hence inherently a world of exploitation. The labourer works from utility, and by obliging him or her to live thus society gambles with dangerous forces: 'The *exploitation* of the worker was [. . .] a piece of stupidity, an exhausting of the soil at the expense of the future, an imperilling of society.'

6. *Modernity is the age of money worship. This is its greatest illusion. Illusions, however, are powerful motivators. In this case, – they drive the modern industrial economy. The resulting industrial enslavement is universal – the wealthy as much as the poor are bound in servitude to the demands of capital. The evaluative habits of the trader mentality come to dominate. European culture recedes, colonised by the consumerism it created. In this way, not only the individual but culture itself is reified, rendered an object subject to exchange principles. Modernity is, in blunter terms, the age of the cultural philistine. The youthful Nietzsche thereby stands as an involved critic of the capitalism and consumerism of his times.*

Everyone in modern society, from the wealthy and uncultured to the poor and equally uncultured, comes to believe that what really matters in life can always be satisfied with money. This is the fundamental illusion that drives the money economy. But such a belief can only ever be at best partially true, for 'while it is to *some* extent a matter of money, it is *much more a matter of spirit*' (ibid., 25). Possessions may be to a limited but essential degree a prerequisite of the freedom needed for independence of thought. Nevertheless, when the priorities are wrong material wealth itself comes to be the master. The apparent independence and ease promised by money creates its own servitude: 'the possessor becomes a slave [. . .] obligated to a society, nailed into a place and incorporated into a state' (*Assorted Opinions and Maxims*, 317). With this the sense for values gets distorted. Modern society is a society of obsessive traders, and it is this that uncovers the heart of the modern soul. Modern European humanity is characterised most essentially by commerce, just as the high estimation of personal contest in Ancient Greece or the love of war and justice in Ancient Rome typified these cultures. As with Greece and Rome, what characterises European modernity in this way represents an expression of the colonisation of its values by the culture of traders:

> The man engaged in commerce understands how to appraise everything without having made it, and to appraise *according to the needs of the consumer*, not according to his own needs; 'who and how many will consume this?' is his question of questions. This type of appraisal he then applies instinctively and all the time: he applies it to everything, and thus also to the productions of the arts and sciences, of thinkers, scholars, artists, statesmen, peoples and parties, of the entire age: in regard to everything that is made he enquires after supply and demand in *order to determine the value of a thing in his own eyes*. This becomes the character of an entire culture, thought through in the minutest and subtlest detail and imprinted in every will and every faculty: it is this of which men of the coming century will be proud: if the prophets of the commercial class are right to give it into your possession! But I have little faith in these prophets.
>
> (*Daybreak*, 175)

The trader is a being separated from what is produced and is, as such, unproductive, relying upon the activity of others in order to exist. The key point that is developed from this, however, concerns not so much the implied sterility of commercial humanity as the manner in which values are estimated by the trader mentality. The point that really matters for Nietzsche is the considerable power of that mentality to invade the social realm generally. Values, from the trader perspective, are not a matter of personal need but determined by the wants and requirements of other people. In turn, since this behaviour yields a profit, the guiding instinct of the trader is to apply this evaluation universally. Everything thereby becomes subject to the judgement that it is valuable or worthless according to its utility or indispensability for consumption. Consumption, which springs from industrial European culture, ends up by colonising it. The 'consumer' becomes the archetypal human being: a reified entity that is merely the object of the trader's calculations concerning potential for profit and loss. Subjectivity is in this manner rendered an empty projection of commercial considerations. The subject becomes the consumer whose essential freedom is the choice of mode of consumption. The formalised individual/consumer, in its turn, serves as a means of bringing to abeyance the spheres of art, science, thought, nationhood and culture. Ultimately, culture becomes commerce through and through. Of course, for Nietzsche such a culture is like the death of culture. Culture becomes impossible in a world where everything has a price put upon it according to the needs of others, where exchange value is the only form of value. Modernity is the era of the philistine.

From the above discussion it is clear that Nietzsche, in the works spanning the period 1878–1881, sketches a picture of modernity in which its character as an unstable period of change is inseparable from its domination by concepts of capital, exchange, accumulation, economy and trade. He is a socially oriented thinker who sees in the social milieu in which he dwells an inescapable invitation to philosophical thought. To think about language, knowledge and truth, ethics, philosophical contemplation or individuality means to do so in the context of a society that has become inescapably patterned by exchange culture, mechanisation and class divisions. Nietzsche may want to situate himself as a critic of these dominant characteristics, which decisively define his times, but he does so only in virtue of them. An additional issue immediately arises from this observation. It can be framed in a simple enough question: to what extent does the world of economics and exchange not merely arouse in Nietzsche a critical response, but also infiltrate and occupy his thought in such a way as to constitute something essential about it? This is a question that I begin to broach in the next chapter.

2
Humankind, the Measurer of All Things: Modernity and Primitive Economy in *Human, All Too Human*, *Daybreak* and *The Gay Science*

1. *The impermanence and fluidity that characterises modern society permeates individual self-consciousness. Modern mercantile society is dominated by our tendency to role-play due to the pressures of commercial and social forces. We moderns are actors. As such, we have ceased to be the material upon which a society in the old sense can be built. Another way of putting this matter is in terms of exchange and sacrifice: we are no longer able to sacrifice the present in exchange for the future aspirations. Moderns find it hard to conceive in such terms since they live in a social world in which the transitory is emphasised at the expense of permanence.*

As the texts spanning the period from the *Untimely Meditations* to *Daybreak* display, the power of commerce in culture, the entwined spheres of exchange, production, consumption and labour, encircle Nietzsche's hand as surely as it encircles the pen that writes. Even as he stands against it as its critic and looks beyond it, Nietzsche's is a voice of its time. Modernity is Nietzsche's chief concern because he himself is indubitably and self-consciously modern. Modernity means restless change, the unsettling of established social orders and convictions, the overturning of cherished values. It is a 'time of transition' (*The Gay Science*, 356) of which the famous announcement of the 'death of God' (*The Gay Science*, 125) is only the most dramatic of symptoms.[1] The consequences of such a transitional and 'jittery age'[2] are complex. The advent of a sense of modernity does not merely signal a historical transformation in ways of living and their accompanying beliefs that leaves issues of selfhood untouched. What marks out modernity is specifically the fact that this historical transformation brings with it the inner experience and articulation of a refashioning of the self (of self-understanding – in short, self-consciousness) at the hands of external social forces. It is this refashioning that provokes the raising of issues concerning human nature and its domains. One could encapsulate an important aspect of Nietzsche's concern here in two simple questions: 'What is nature?' and 'What is culture?' What, in other words, is 'natural' about humanity and what is socially constituted when it comes to our dominant characteristics, passions and propensities? As we will see, Nietzsche's concern with these questions will take us on a path that leads back from the modern self to primitive humanity via a consideration of the ancient practices of sacrifice and exchange. Nietzsche's reflection on these invokes prehistory and the power of custom in such a way that the relationship between past and present, between the primeval and the modern, is shown to be far closer than it might at first appear to be. This, in turn, allows for a situating of modernity in the context of the primeval conditions that constitute its possibility. These conditions are practices: those of custom and tradition. Custom, tradition and sacrifice together intimate the economic constitution of human identity, which comes to light in the guise of the human ability to calculate, itself the precondition of all civilisation.

For Nietzsche, an enforced rumination on personal identity follows inevitably from modern life. A Europe in radical transition is somewhere where accepted social roles and identities are rendered doubtful. So, Nietzsche notes, he finds himself in a world where many people have vocations and are obliged to do so. But in the atmosphere of restless social change and concomitant variety there is no necessity for a person to pursue one particular vocation rather than another. People slip (or are pushed by accidents and need) into careers and hence social roles. Even from the standpoint of their own experience, the impersonal forces that push them hither and thither are not hard to delineate. Approaching the later years of their life, however, people 'become the victims of their own "good performance" [. . .]' (ibid., 356): the role becomes the person, and the person becomes increasingly disinclined to acknowledge this fact. In other words, the vocational individual that Nietzsche describes here as being typically representative of modern European society is a player, an actor par excellence. The problem is that people in modern life are actors to the extent that their self-understanding is unconsciously moulded and distorted by the act itself. This is evidenced by bad faith. Such individuals, Nietzsche tells us, progressively fail to accept the degree of chance that led to them leading the life they ended up leading. This kind of person comes to ignore the impersonal indeterminacy that was really involved in their taking up the particular 'vocation' that they later came to regard as a matter of personal destiny. That they condemn themselves to bad faith is understandable. In a world dominated by the labour market the sense of individual identity is generated ever more by one's being passed through the sieve of selection and service. For reasons of self-respect, one denies to oneself that what happened was not really very much to do with one's own propensities and choices at all. The modern self is in danger of becoming an actor through and through in so far as one is now what one does in this most public but narrow of senses. The individual has become the role he or she plays and nothing more: 'Considered more deeply, the role has actually *become* character; and art, nature.' What may be perceived as being 'natural' for a person is in reality socially constructed. To put it another way, for us moderns, the fact of being socially constructed is rapidly becoming our 'natural' condition in so far as we are role players before all else. That we may come to understand our lives as flowing inevitably from some mythical 'inner nature' evidences the self-delusion characteristic of all bad faith. Unable to believe in a rigid 'order of things' that determines and thereby sanctions our fate we try to claw it out of ourselves and resort to fantasy as a means of doing so.

In the not so very distant past, Nietzsche says, things were different. A contrasting *lack* of the faithlessness that presages bad faith was the norm. People tended to accept the notion of being personally destined for a particular form of work unquestioningly because it was sanctioned by a sense of the order of things (God, church and state colluded). Illusions firmly and honestly cleaved to give a sense of personal destiny. Social hierarchies constructed along the lines of the medieval period, for example, had the virtue of durability because of this faith – and one should never forget that 'duration is a first-rate value on earth'. Authentically democratic ages, in contrast, are marked by the loss of the belief in a predestined role for the individual. An impertinent faith rises up which is the opposite of this one: that one can be what one wishes and take on any role one wills. Nietzsche now flips the reader's expectations on their head: although typically modern, there is at the same time nothing especially new in this faith. This was the belief dominant in the ancient Athenians of the 'Periclean age'. It is also

> the faith of the Americans today [and one] that is more and more becoming the European faith as well: The individual becomes convinced that he can do just about everything and *can manage almost any role*, and everybody experiments with himself, improvises, makes

> new experiments, enjoys his experiments; and all nature ceases and becomes art.
>
> (Ibid.)

Culture and nature thus collide in the modern self. In the case of the Ancient Greeks, this '*role faith*' drove them to such a degree that they finally became actors and nothing more. It was in this guise, Nietzsche claims, that the Greeks overcame the rest of the world: the Romans were enchanted and 'vanquished' not by Greek culture but by Greek artifice. The illusory possibilities proffered by role-play are seductive.

Modern Europe's mirroring of Periclean Athens in fact follows the cultural lead of the United States. Nietzsche is not too keen on this prospect: 'what I fear, what is so palpable that today one could grasp it with one's hands, if one felt like grasping it, is that we modern men are even now pretty far along the same road; and whenever a human being begins to discover how he is playing a role and how he *can* be an actor, he *becomes* an actor'. We are coming to live in a world dominated by phoney people. This fact makes modernity interesting because it is an age in which 'the "actors", all kind of actors, become the masters', and who knows what might happen if an actor or some other kind of role player should become a monarch or a president. But, interest value aside, this burgeoning of thespian humanity has its debit side: with the growth of the actor comes the decline of grand 'master builders'. A society of actors is one in which everyone fashions their identity according to dominant trends and is as changeable as those trends; it is a place where there is no perceived need to construct from the base up something unique and lasting. The actor may be an artist, but such solely mimetic art is impotent when it comes to the abilities needed to construct durable cultural forms:

> The strength to build becomes paralyzed; the courage to make plans that encompass the distant future is discouraged; those with a genius for organization become scarce: who would still dare to undertake projects that would require thousands of years for their completion? For what is dying out is the fundamental faith that would enable us to calculate, to promise, to anticipate the future in plans of such scope, and to sacrifice the future to them – namely, the faith that man has value and meaning only insofar as he is *a stone in a great edifice*; and to that end he must be *solid* first of all, a "stone" – and above all not an actor!
>
> (Ibid.)

Culture is conjoined here with dwelling. Dwelling means to live with a sense of one's place within a grand order of things. The grounding belief in one's own futurity that allows for great plans to be made, for great social experiments to be undertaken, requires that the individual first and foremost think of himself or herself as part of this larger order. Dwelling, in other words, is never simply a matter of 'personal choice' when it comes to the range of meaningful modes of living that are available. The belief system exemplified by the master-builder mentality shapes the self in a manner that is contrasted with the identity of the modern actor. Exemplifying fluidity, the modern actor-self adopts and adapts their identity with the requirements of role-play in mind. The contrasting belief that the individual is part of a ground plan and that his or her life gains significance through being situated within this plan implies a sense of selfhood as distant as possible from the realms of mode and modernity that conjoin contemporary Europe and Periclean Greece. Whereas the actor-self is constantly in danger of being as transitory and superficial as the social world from which it springs, the self that is endowed with sense through the belief that it is situated within a coherent totality that encompasses it is made of stronger stuff. It has to be. Like the bricks of a grand edifice, a self that is formed according to the demands of such ambitious beliefs is at the same time hardened by the discipline that accompanies those beliefs. The implication of the discussion is simple enough: modernity lacks staying power since it lacks the cultural capital that its Periclean predecessor could trade on. This lack of durability is modernity's most appalling characteristic. The contemporary social world of fluidity and change is dynamic but, paradoxically, at the same time one of paralysis. It is akin to a structure built on a beach with dry sand grains: their very fluidity and dynamism in relation to one another means that one can make little out of them and certainly nothing that cannot be blown away by the slightest breeze – you need to add water. In modernity, genuine construction is impossible. Quite simply, there will be no future issuing forth from it. We moderns cannot make societies, at least not as they have hitherto been understood: 'What will not be built any more henceforth, and *cannot* be built any more is – a society in the old sense of that word; to build that, everything is lacking, above all the material. *All of us are no longer material for a society*; this is a truth for which the time has come' (ibid.).[3]

The transition from the durable and fashion-resistant social order to the impermanent and modish is articulated by Nietzsche in terms of a diminution of the ability to reckon in terms of the extreme long-term future. The individual no longer feels part of a grand plan and hence lacks the courage needed for self-sacrifice. To put the matter slightly differently, what modernity lacks is the faith needed to undertake a specific kind of exchange: the sacrificing of the comforts of the present for the aspirations of the future, and the giving over of the future to large-scale plans and projects. Ceaseless change at the same time denotes the ceaseless present; the modern world is a world of immediately felt and acted-upon desires dominated by its own overwhelming sense of the power of the transitory. This does not mean that we moderns cannot think of possible futures. There is no greater limit to our imaginings than there ever was. But our envisaging of any possible future is undertaken without the necessary surety. We are hence incapable of really acting with a view to attaining one or another future. Modernity is too indulgent, too full of self-doubt for this. Another way of putting this would be to say that we have become liberals. Liberal pluralism means a multiplicity of directions cutting across the social milieu, many isolated individual goals mediated by social convention and commercial capital, but no large-scale cultural venture participated in by agents subscribing (albeit unwittingly) to the beliefs and practices necessary to bring it about. Modern Europe, as Nietzsche surveys it, is dominated by the economic power of commercial capital. For him, this hegemony of commercial economy is antithetical to the sacrificial economy of exchange that is necessary for the endowment and building of cultures and societies.

2. *Although critical of commercial society, Nietzsche does not oppose 'pure' culture to corrupt economics. Rather, his analysis of modernity concentrates upon articulating the notions of economy and exchange at a level deeper than that evidenced by their modern mercantile manifestation. His use of these notions may be initially approached by consideration of one of his discussions of scholars. An emotionally distorted specimen of humanity, the scholar has exchanged their spiritual well-being for expertise and is a living example of sacrifice to their discipline. Although repulsive the scholar has integrity when compared with what modern life would like to replace him or her with: the 'man of letters'. The scholar's self-sacrifice in the pursuit of knowledge articulates a specific economy underlying the scholar's development. This economy resists market forces: the genuine scholar refuses to sell their knowledge for profit. The 'man of letters', in contrast, sells culture with precisely this in mind. For the latter, culture is a mere commodity, something akin to a series of bite-size chunks of 'knowledge' to be consumed in the most efficient manner possible. Both are governed by the notion of exchange. What*

> *differentiates them from one another can be grasped in terms of their respective goals. The economy of expertise is opposed to the commercially inspired economics of culture consumption.*

What should immediately be clear is that Nietzsche is not presenting us with a simplistic choice that opposes commercial economy to pure 'culture'. Rather, the manner in which Nietzsche offers his analysis suggests that the stakes in his cultural discourse are understandable *only* in the context of a generally applicable concept of economy. What we are presented with are two manifestations of a deeper logic of economy and exchange which will become increasingly apparent as one examines Nietzsche's ideas about the nature of both modern and primitive social relations. This point may be initially clarified by turning to a section of *The Gay Science* that discusses scholars and which deals with modes of subjectivity and exchange.

Scholars are, Nietzsche tells us, pretty repulsive specimens of humanity who are likely to be emotionally stunted or distorted. The reason for this is that the scholar is susceptible to being deformed by his or her very expertise. The pursuit of specialist knowledge changes one into a kind of being that one would not naturally have become. A scholarly book always mirrors a 'crooked soul'. This is inevitable. There is no means of escaping from having to meet the cost of pursuing a scholarly life. Mastery is always paid for one way or another. In the scholar's case, narrowness in emotional and intellectual matters ensues. However, Nietzsche continues, these conditions of payment do not concern merely one kind of person's existence. Such payment constitutes an essential characteristic of life in general: 'On this earth one pays dearly for every kind of *mastery*, and perhaps one pays too dearly for everything' (*The Gay Science*, 366). In the case of the scholar, the cost of being a specialist means that 'one pays by also being the victim of this speciality'. The specialist is himself the sacrifice made at the altar of his speciality. This portrayal of the scholar may not be very pleasant, especially for anyone contemplating a life of scholarship (or worse, for someone who has already embarked upon it). Nevertheless, as is often the case with Nietzsche, things are not as they initially seem to be. Although not exactly picturesque, ugly scholars look much better when set aside their modern usurpers. The modern tendency is to want things to be different from the costly state of affairs that bespeaks the scholarly expert. Better, perhaps, to replace the mangled specialist, a person at home in his subject but hardly anywhere else, with the multidisciplinary generalist?

But, Nietzsche asks, what does that produce? His answer: a kind of person even more repellent:

> [I]nstead of the craftsman and master, [we get] the 'man of letters', the dexterous, 'polydexterous' man of letters who, to be sure, lacks the hunched back [. . .] the man of letters who really *is* nothing but 'represents' almost anything, playing and 'substituting' for the expert, and taking it upon himself in all modesty to get paid, honored, and celebrated in place of the expert. No, my scholarly friends, I bless you even for your hunched backs. And for despising, as I do, the 'men of letters' and culture parasites. And for not knowing how to make a business of the spirit. And for having opinions that cannot be translated into financial values. And for not representing anything that you are not.
>
> (Ibid.)

The exchanges involved in becoming a scholar are different from the exchanges that the 'man of letters' participates in and welcomes. The scholar, in spite of his or her limitations,[4] stands apart from the realm of commerce. The scholar lacks the knowledge needed to press their expertise into the language of cash value just as much as he or she spurns the temptation to prostitute expertise in that way. An economy governs the scholar's life no less than that of the 'man of letters'. Scholarly existence is governed by the logic of costs and benefits, of sacrifice and ensuing mastery. The difference lies in the terms and goals of the exchange. The scholar's dedication is to their domain of expertise. In this regard, the scholar is no actor, is not superficial, and pursues something capable of transcending his or her own material self-interest. The 'man of letters', in contrast, is a mere shop assistant of the spirit and cultural baggage handler. His expertise resides precisely in knowing how to profit from 'culture'. In the 'man of letters' culture becomes financial profit, pure and simple, a mere object of trade, a resource to be exploited for personal gain, but one whose exploitation precludes anything like the kind of deep knowledge characteristic of the expert.

The question that is posed to separate the scholars from the literati finds its answer in matters of competing economies of life. Nietzsche criticises commerce when commerce invades the culture of expertise and scholarship, but he does not seek to enter a domain free of economy. The life of the scholar is governed by exchange no less certainly than the life of the 'man of letters'. What is contrasted here is a matter of knowledge of values. What the commercial realm does is seek to adapt thought to its own instrumentalist dictum that what is valuable can be readily consumed, that a thing's ease of consumption is a condition of its being deemed valuable. But such ease is illusory: ease of consumption should not be confused with the apparent ease that accompanies the spectacle of mastery. That one thinks one has 'understood' or 'appreciated' something when it has first been repackaged in readily digestible form and transported to one's doorstep by a professional conduit of culture is an illusion. The 'Best of . . .' anthology is more likely to sidestep the difficult and really interesting aspects of something or someone than address them. The point of the easily accessible collection is to sell copy, not to educate and challenge. The disgrace of the 'man of letters' is that he willingly participates in propagating the illusion that acting out something is the same as mastering it. Of course, he does this not least because he has an interest in doing so, his own purported mastery being no less illusory than that promised by the stripped down, cleansed and superficial material he pedals.

3. *The ease of consumption demanded by modern sensibilities brings with it a distinctively modern experience of time. Time has come to be regarded as a commodity that needs to be economised. Europe has begun to imitate the American social model in this regard. This has resulted in ever less time for reflection and an increasingly superficial attitude to life. In turn, such individuality as has hitherto been possible is receding. Modern industriousness, ironically, bespeaks spiritual laziness. The superficiality of the actor is confirmed as the paradigm of individuality in modern society in all social strata, but this is an 'individuality' stripped of all genuine content.*

The ease of consumption demanded by commercialism is reflected by modernity's understanding of time. For something to be easily consumed means at the same time that it must be amenable to rapid consumption. Modernity is synonymous with the neurosis of time management techniques. This transformation of our understanding of time is international: modern commerce is a global phenomenon. Again, Nietzsche cites a point of contact where Europe meets with an increasingly powerful America, the former absorbing the influence of the latter (*The Gay Science*, 329). For him, 'the breathless haste' with which Americans work, something which is 'the distinctive vice of the new world', is beginning to spread across 'old Europe' in a manner that can be likened to a 'contagion'. One distinctive consequence of this is the development of a rather strange dim-wittedness. The reason is not hard to see. In a world dominated by market economics and the obsessive economising of time one eats one's lunch while reading about the latest trading news on the stock market in the *Börsenblatt*. All is work. There is no time given to reflection. 'Virtue has come to consist in doing something in less time than someone else' (ibid.). The destruction of good taste and culture is the aim of such virtue. A life of restless activity such as may be led by bureaucratic and business classes, although frenetic enough on the surface, ultimately lacks genuine individuality (*Human, All Too Human*, 283). When it comes to the cultivation of their personality (their individuality) the restlessly active individual is an idler: 'The active roll as the stone rolls [. . .]' (*The Gay Science*, 329). In this way, individuality becomes impoverished:

> 'Rather do anything than nothing': this principle, too, is merely a string to throttle all culture and good taste. Just as all forms are visibly perishing by the haste of the workers, the feeling for form itself, the ear and the eye for the melody of movements are also perishing. The proof of this may be found in the universal demand for *gross obviousness* in all those situations in which human beings wish to be honest with one another for once [. . .] One no longer has any time or energy for ceremonies, for being obliging in an indirect way, for *esprit* in conversation, and for any *otium* at all.
>
> (Ibid.)

The economising of time finds expression in the crude and blatantly obvious plainness of modern manners. This, in turn, exemplifies the deficiency of contemporary commercial culture. Modern industriousness is spiritual and intellectual idleness. The modern conception of honesty with others demands a mode of communication devoid of the trappings of courtesy, which is a prerequisite of culture, due to the same demand for efficiency that justifies the 'man of letters'. In all things, time is at a premium and must be used up sparingly. The modern playfulness of the actor-self thereby conceals a boring seriousness in all things. Lack of imagination permeates from the lowest to the highest strata of the social order. The industrialist, for all his or her wealth, is a bore and boorish with it. Little wonder then that Nietzsche can sum up by saying that the so-called 'industrial culture' is in general to be taken as 'the most vulgar form of existence' there has yet been (*The Gay Science*, 40).

4. *Modern economic life rests upon a deeper economy. This is intimated by the example of contemporary attitudes to sacrifice. Take the example of*

the youth that works in the service of society until in a state of physical ruin. Behind the camouflage of moral praise for this person's self-sacrifice lurks social utility. The modern virtues of industriousness and obedience are really tools that encourage individuals to act in accordance with the broader interest of economic expediency. The instrumentalism of modern culture resorts to a sacrificial logic to justify itself. Sacrifice is amongst the most ancient of concepts and yet is present in the modern milieu. Modern society, in other words, retains elements of primitivism. Sacrifice presupposes the concept of exchange. Likewise, sacrifice needs to be articulated in the context of Nietzsche's analysis of the notions of custom, tradition and morality. Understanding these involves accounting for the basic conditions present in all social orders.

However, full of contempt, Nietzsche's swinging criticism of contemporary culture frequently reveals his heightened awareness of the economic workings of social life in things great and small. One can turn, in this connection, to his comments on the socio-economic aspect of sacrifice in contemporary culture in *The Gay Science*. These show Nietzsche not simply as social critic but also as an employer of the very normative structure he has identified as typically modern. There is a good reason for this. While exemplifying modernity, this structure has a logic that runs far deeper than the contemporary world of industrial production; for the notion of sacrifice, which denotes one of the most ancient of human practices, is entwined with the equally primeval notion of exchange.

From the apparently civilised perspective of modern life one might be tempted to think of sacrifice as something at once primitive and ritualistic. In so far as we are modern, this thought might run, we have at least overcome the primitive superstition that sacrifice and sacrificial practice exemplifies. We have seen that Nietzsche himself notes modernity's lack of sacrificial energy, its contentment with seeking material comfort rather than spiritual goals with their concomitant hardships. Society's preference for ease of consumption and its weak stomach at the sight of the scholarly grotesque serve to confirm this as a general tendency. But modern society is in its way no less a sphere of sacrificial violence than the most autochthonous human social arrangements. Industrial society is a place in which it makes sense to praise the hard worker, even though not only the power of their vision but the 'naturalness and freshness' of their mental well-being is irreparably damaged by their diligence (ibid., 21). For the modern spectator of this miserable state of affairs, the feeling of sorrow aroused at the sight of the youth who has been drained by the industrial system even to the dregs of their being, is not rendered meaningful through an appreciation of this person's individual tragedy. Rather, sorrow is provoked by the feeling that 'a devoted *instrument*, ruthless against itself – a so-called "good man" – has been lost to society by his death'. The diligent youth is a sacrificial animal who has been trained to wield the knife against himself and to find a sense of purpose and meaning in so doing. The individual is sacrificed to the social body and what is essential is that the assessment of this act is strictly impersonal. What is lost is not a person but a means to a social end, a tool. Thus, in modern society, the notion of sacrifice is granted warrant by the act of the neighbour witnessing the death of the instrument. This, says Nietzsche, has a great social advantage: the fact 'that a sacrifice has been made and that the attitude of the sacrificial animal has once again been confirmed for all to see' is affirmed most powerfully by all concerned. The praise of the modern virtues (industry, obedience, selflessness, etc.) is really an affirmation of their instrumental worth as social preservatives.

The incarnation of this instrumentalism may be quintessentially modern in so far as the sacrificial act and its witnesses are all actors on the stage of modern commercial life, but within it at the same time there lurks something primitive and violent. The person who labours without abating in pursuit of the illusory comforts and honours promised as rewards for hard work is praised because *their sacrifice* has social utility:

> The neighbor praises selflessness *because it brings him advantages*. If the neighbor himself were 'selfless' in his thinking, he would repudiate this diminution of strength, this mutilation for *his* benefit [. . .] This indicates the fundamental contradiction in the morality that is very prestigious nowadays: the *motives* of this morality stand opposed to its *principle* [. . .] and thus one preaches in the same breath, a 'Thou shalt' and 'Thou shalt not'.
>
> (Ibid.)

The demand that individuals be socially expedient and acquiesce to offering themselves up as sacrifices is dressed up as virtue but really conforms to the social requirement that the talented person is justified through their being useful. In short, the economic needs of the social body take precedence over personal needs; the communal asserts its priority over the individual. Others are happy to stand by and laud the person of talent for offering themselves up in this way for selfish reasons. The neighbour's praise of 'virtue' rests upon economically mediated relations of self-interest that point to a principle as ancient as the social realm itself. The neighbour quite literally profits from the other's self-destructive labour and therefore rejoices in the sacrifice made. In a manner reminiscent of Adam Smith,[5] Nietzsche thereby envisages an invisible hand of normative social force directing and regulating the behaviour of the individual. The goals the individual is taught to aspire to are, as in Smith's theory, ultimately unsatisfying and empty, but the personal wealth accumulated by individual industry ultimately profits the social body. Modern society, it follows, can be no less a sacrificial structure than the most primitive of social orders. Society makes its demands and it does so on the basis of considerations that, at bottom, come down to matters of economic expediency. The fate of the individual within this context is not an overriding concern.

Consider the modern celebration and conjoining of the virtues of hard work and success. Virtue and personal advantage are often held to be kin for very practical social reasons. 'Blindly raging industriousness' which is 'the typical virtue of an instrument' is today advertised as the means to riches and reputation. This may actually be the case, says Nietzsche, for hard work can bring material rewards. The problem is that even if a person may end up being rich they at the same time pay dearly for it in other ways. Hardened by incessant labour, the diligent worker becomes unable to enjoy the wealth such labour may produce. Their life of hard work has at the same time denuded 'the organs of their subtlety, which alone would make possible the enjoyment of wealth and honors [. . .]' (ibid.). In short, unrelenting hard work makes a person crude and insensitive. The successful entrepreneur may have wealth in abundance, but the very pursuit of this wealth has denuded them. The entrepreneur knows about market values and about how to generate profit, but they cease to know what to do with their profits. Success may be displayed, of course. But the grand display of success does not mean that wealth is being truly enjoyed, that its potential is being fulfilled. Our age may indeed be the most industrious age there has ever been, and this in the most literal of senses. However, it is an age that no longer knows what to do with the fruits of its industry, apart from how to use it to make 'still more money and still more industriousness'. The organisation of modern industrial economy is for Nietzsche such that a crude materialism and instrumentalism lurks at its heart. This calculating aspect of our modern nature, however, betrays something else. Modern industrial culture may be the most repulsive form of existence yet imagined, but for Nietzsche its roots go far deeper than the surface patina of modern life would initially suggest. Societies are economically organised structures not merely because of the need to satisfy modern industrial requirements. The modern requirements of industrial living have themselves sprung from something that constitutes an essential and ancient characteristic of human existence and which endures within us today no less than it did in our distant ancestors. The sacrificial element present in modern society just noted betrays this fact. This most ancient of practices endures in modern garb.

A sacrifice is something given in *exchange* for something else. In the case just considered, Nietzsche explores the manner in which individual interests are forfeited for those of the community. Sacrifice, however, can only be properly grasped when thought in terms of the past. Primarily, as we will now see, Nietzsche's understanding of sacrifice needs to be considered in connection with his treatment of the related notions of custom, tradition and morality. Taken together, these notions (or more precisely, the practices they denote) stand at the heart of all human society and, consequently, constitute the origins of individual identity. Their consideration will also lead down a path that takes us directly to the economic origins of human nature.

5. *Modernity, characterised by the dominance of 'vulgar' commercial culture, is also marked by a diminution of the power of custom. Another way of putting this is to say that modernity is the age of moral decline in so far as morality is for Nietzsche no more than the traditional observance of customs. Humans are in this regard essentially creatures of convention: if tradition is lacking, then morality is lacking also. For Nietzsche, the basic conventions governing thought and action can be traced back to the prehistoric observance of customs. The task of historical philosophy is to unearth these primitive conditions and show the manner in which they are articulated in modern times. Nietzsche's basic contention is that modern culture is imbued with a prehistoric heritage that stems from the feeling of respect and awe in the face of the authority of custom. The earliest form of this Nietzsche calls the 'morality of custom'. There are two kinds. Both involve the observance of conventions and both involve the making of sacrifices. Morality emerges as the making of sacrifices to customs – the greater the sacrifice the more 'moral' the person making it. Primitive society developed on the basis of an exchange principle governing human behaviour exemplified by the notion of sacrifice. The observance of custom, it follows, is the prerequisite of all human culture.*

We have already seen that from the *Untimely Meditations* onwards modernity is characterised by ceaseless change and the rise of industrial production. As Nietzsche notes in *Daybreak*, such conditions can be articulated especially clearly when described in terms of a specific social transformation: the tremendous decline in 'the power of custom' (*Daybreak*, 9). Modern life is life where custom and tradition are in retreat. The appearance of ceaseless change as a now prominent characteristic of society is one significant symptom of this. Another way of formulating this claim, and considerably more shocking if one holds certain fond preconceptions about the superiority of moral considerations over all others, is to hold that we live in an age of moral decline. This is shocking because to argue that the diminution of the power of custom and tradition is equivalent to the loss of morality is to argue that morality, custom and tradition are really one and the same thing. There is, in other words, nothing special designated by the word 'morality' that distinguishes it from the other habits that we all of us know go to make up the fabric of our daily lives. Having noted the immorality of modernity Nietzsche can then furnish us with the following definition of morality itself:

> [M]orality is nothing other (therefore *no more*!) than obedience to customs, of whatever kind they may be; customs, however, are the *traditional* way of behaving and evaluating. In things in which no tradition commands there is no morality; and the less life is determined by tradition, the smaller the circle of morality. The free human being is immoral because in all things he is *determined* to depend upon himself and not upon a tradition: in all the original conditions of mankind, 'evil' signifies the same as 'individual', 'free', 'capricious', 'unusual', 'unforseen', 'incalculable'.
>
> (Ibid.)

Morals are merely stipulated ways of doing things within a cultural milieu. The particular ensemble of practices within any social order combined with the arrangement of those practices in relation to one another is what determines the identity of the moral tradition. It follows that in so far as we are moral beings we are creatures of convention. This does not mean that obedience to convention is merely a necessary condition of moral discourse, thought and action but that such obedience is just what these things come down to, and nothing more. Nietzsche's conception of the nature of ethics takes its place here as part of his more general philosophical concern with the question of what it means to be human. To recall the point made in the previous chapter on the distinction Nietzsche draws between metaphysical and historical philosophy (*Human, All Too Human*, 2), the nature of contemporary humanity is something that can only be addressed by way of reflection on the prehistoric conditions that gave rise to it. This distinction plays on the insight that it is possible to trace the basic conceptual apparatus of our thought back to assumptions that originate in the remotest prehistoric eras. This prehistory remains present in hidden and sometimes surprising ways. That is why it is no good looking at the thin slice of time occupied by modern humanity, as metaphysicians do,[6] and thinking that the skimpy piece of icing thereby skimmed off the top of the temporal cake is sufficient for drawing ambitious conclusions about human nature, morality, reality and the like. The bigger temporal slice that is obtained by cutting deeper into the past combines an awareness of human history with prehistory and with this comes the understanding that contemporary life has been determined unconsciously by elements that both precede it and abide within it. Historical philosophy begins with the contention that we have become who we are and that our very becoming such as we are has left its stamp upon us. The contention in *Daybreak* that morality is nothing more than the *observance* of customs is another exercise in the domain of historical philosophy, for it likewise comes down to staking the claim that we are the living legacy of the assumptions made by our prehistoric forbears. Being a 'modern', it follows, does not denote something that is independent of prehistory. Rather, modernity is strictly unthinkable without consideration of this prehistory. The 'immorality' of today that Nietzsche jokingly alludes to at the commencement of Section 9 of *Daybreak* is defined by way of its contrast with the 'morality' (strict obedience to norms) of yesterday and the day before. It is only possible to appreciate what is specifically modern about us when the question of what in us cleaves to the prehistoric past and how it does so has been asked and answered.

The term 'prehistory' denotes 'the tremendous eras of "morality of custom" which precede "world history" '. These are 'the *actual and decisive eras of history which determined the character of mankind* [. . .]' (*Daybreak*, 18). The essential aspects of human nature, therefore, are fixed firmly in place long before people are tempted to dwell upon their own metaphysical, psychological or material constitution. The prehistoric world Nietzsche envisages is a mirror image of our own. It is alien in that customary valuations of today are reversed, uncanny in its being an inverted reflection of the present. In the distant epoch of human prehistory, Nietzsche tells us, atrocity, pretence, revenge and denial of reason counted amongst the virtues. In contrast, well-being, thirst for knowledge, peace and pity were regarded as dangerous, while being pitied for something and engaging in labour were seen as disgraceful. It was a world, in other words, where what we today consider to be good was considered bad, and vice versa. Prehistory is the epoch in which the sphere of human existence as a domain of meaningfulness was determined as such. What sense we can endow life with today is owed to this primeval epoch. Prehistory also denotes the time when the concept of the fixed and unchanging was itself first celebrated as pertaining to the highest value. Change, in contrast, was taken to be something immoral (i.e. uncustomary) and as such was regarded as being 'pregnant with disaster' (ibid.).

It is clear from even these two sections of *Daybreak* that the term 'prehistory' is rich in meaning for Nietzsche. 'Prehistory' denotes the manner in which an unknowing prehistoric humanity established the conditions of its future possible development through the laying down of its own defining characteristics. Pointing towards us, although without any predetermined necessity, prehistory is the epoch in which the conditions under which we too draw up our decisive conclusions about the world were fabricated. The fact that our prehistoric forbears were creatures of custom determines decisively what kinds of beings we are today. In other words, 'prehistory' is a concept that has shock value as far as our self-understanding goes, for 'we moderns' are not as far removed from our supposedly dim and distant ancestors as we might sometimes like to believe. Picture the world of prehistory, says Nietzsche: 'Do you think all this has altered and that mankind must therefore have changed its character?' If you do then you should consider if you do not need to become better acquainted with yourselves (ibid.). Becoming has determined human identity and it is because of this that people are better understood as the articulation of a long-term and complex development. Contemporary industrial society, in other words, is a complex articulation of prehistoric principles. Thus, modernity is unrelentingly modern but at the same time permeated by primeval elements. Indeed, the self-conscious revealing of these elements might be said to be one of modernity's essential characteristics, for self-consciousness is a necessary prerequisite of the lack of faith that Nietzsche uses to define modern existence. We have seen that for Nietzsche modernity is an era where the power of custom has been denuded. In this regard modernity exhibits tendencies that run counter to the principle of social cohesion and, indeed, to the very conditions that make societies possible at all.

All social orders have their origins in prehistory and the ability the human species developed in that era to formulate and observe customs: 'Originally [. . .] everything was custom' [. . .] (*Daybreak*, 9). Custom, in other words, is the *enabling condition* of all human life since we are essentially social beings. In so far as human society even began to exist it did so because customs were observed and arranged in the form of traditions. Tradition fixes custom (the web of practices) together in relation to one another, it is the glue of all primitive social cohesion. In their most ancient manifestation these conditions constituted what Nietzsche terms 'the morality of custom'. There are, according to Nietzsche, two kinds of morality of custom. There is the kind that requires the most frequent performance of the customary observances. Frequency of observance indicates a mode of consciousness that is dominated by the letter of customary law and which regards all situations, however trivial, as potentially subject to that law. Then there is the kind that insists on the most demanding performance of the requirements of custom; this requires the law be performed in even the most arduous cases. What is essential about the two forms of morality of custom is that both involve *sacrifice*: 'The most moral man is he who *sacrifices* the most to custom: what, however, are the greatest sacrifices?' (ibid.). Whatever is stipulated by a morality to be of the greatest importance always requires abstinence. What is sacrificed (i.e. whether we are talking about the observance that requires frequent obedience or that which requires the greatest obedience when observance is the most arduous) in turn characterises and distinguishes one culture from another. Cultures are differentiated in so far as they are the outcomes of different normative demands. These demands, in their own turn, are determined by environmental and historical conditions.[7] Whichever form of observance is involved, *all culture* is customary and all culture is rooted in sacrifice to the demands of custom. There is no such thing as a civilisation that has not sprung from this primeval combination of customs and sacrifices. That is why Nietzsche talks of 'the mighty proposition with which civilisation begins: any custom is better than no custom' (*Daybreak*, 16). The continuity of customary observances is what we call 'tradition'. Consequently, Nietzsche is telling us, where there is no tradition founded upon custom and sacrifice there can be no culture. If modern society is a domain in which sacrifice is practised and celebrated that is because even in its fluidity and the accompanying diminution of the power of custom modern social order still hangs by the thread of primitive ancestral rites.

6. *In so far as all social orders are rooted in custom and the respect for authority they are also structures permeated by power. Morality is an expression of power, the moral act its fulfilment. The moral individual is a creature of conformity, lacking in genuine individuality. Morality, it follows, springs from the peculiar human sensitivity to the power of custom. We obey customs and are thus rule-followers. Norms and power are intrinsically connected. The moralism exemplified by Socrates and Plato arose in opposition to the power of the morality of custom. Against the sacrificial demands of tradition they espoused the view that acting morally is also acting in one's self-interest. The difference between the morality of custom and Socratic moralism hence lies in the emphasis on the individual. Where tradition sees the individual as a sacrificial object, fit for satisfying the necessities of communal life, the moralist sees the individual as an autonomous being, a goal in his or her own right. For this reason, people of all kinds who have stressed individual independence have been deemed 'evil'. The power inherent in social orders is hence essentially normative, for it is opposed to the centrifugal forces that individualism invokes.*

Raising the question of morality in terms of its origins in custom, sacrifice and tradition does not mean only raising universal questions about history, tribal descent and cultural identity. *Power*, too, enters the frame, and must do so as soon as the word 'tradition' is uttered and acknowledged. All societies are domains of power relations. Power is a primeval social characteristic. This is because as soon as anyone answers to the demands of custom they are situated as a subordinate within a relationship of authority. Answering to traditional authority is not a matter of personal utility. One does not obey the demands of tradition because these demands happen to suit one's tastes or interests. If personal interest always tallied with social convention the demands that tradition makes would not be necessary. Tradition makes its demands as something one stands before in a state of awe. Faced with these demands the primitive human being is prepared to sacrifice all self-interest. This is because tradition is a 'higher authority one obeys, not because it commands what is *useful* to us, but because it *commands*' (ibid., 9). Tradition is the articulation of imperatives. The reason one obeys these imperatives is that one feels in some way bound to do so simply in virtue of their being the commands that they are. This last point concerns their origins. It is their supposed *source* that legitimates the commands of tradition. The traditional imperatives that framed the prehistoric social world were obeyed, Nietzsche argues, because of the ancient power of superstition. The authority of tradition therefore denotes a kind of 'fear in the face of...'. What one stands in the face of here, the referent around which the web of practices making up a tradition is organised, must remain unspecified, an unknown 'X'. In order to inspire the awe necessary to command obedience the source of authority must remain as indefinable as it is thought to be supremely powerful. The supremely powerful is hence at the same time the inscrutable and unknowable, pointing towards that which escapes the formal conceptual abilities of the believer and follower of tradition yet simultaneously legitimating them so long as they remain faithful to tradition.

The observer of customs is moral because inspired by a state of superstitious fear they recognise this authority by acting according to the requirements that tradition lays down as appropriate for them. Thus understood, the moral person simply performs an action and is moral in virtue of this performance rather than any inner state of consciousness: he or she does something inspired by feelings that are barely different from those that prompt flight in the face of an onslaught by a dangerous animal. Contradicting beliefs we might be tempted to entertain about the nature of freedom and ethics which take ethical action to be based in reflective consciousness and individual responsibility, Nietzsche insists that being moral cannot be taken to denote anything more than the traditional observance of dominant norms. The moral person is not, in other words, by any means a *free being*. Consequently, the moral person is not acting in any manner that can be deemed 'individual', either. If, as Nietzsche contends, morality comes down to the observance of norms, then such observance of necessity contradicts the possibility of any individual action. 'Being moral' can signify nothing more here than following a convention due to the compulsion of fearing something dreadful will happen to oneself and one's fellows if one does not (ibid.). The moral agent is no more an individual in virtue of being moral than the person who follows the convention of knocking on another's door before entering their room is endowed with individuality as a consequence of following that convention. Such knocking cannot be taken as 'individual' or as implying freedom of agency. Knocking on someone's door in a manner that might be deemed 'individual' is a possible but not a conventional act. As soon as a person knocks on a door 'individually' (i.e. 'oddly') the knocking no longer signifies an observance of the custom of politeness but means something else –

possibly leaving the room's occupant disinclined to invite the person on the other side of the door in. In any case, to act conventionally as the tribal ancestor does when answering to the demands of tradition is to act in the context of perceived authority, and hence of power.

Rigidly governed by convention, the world of prehistory is envisaged by Nietzsche to be a place of lurking terror where authority rests on blind fear. Equally, from the outset the social world of human society whenever or wherever it may be is always already *a structure of command.* Power and society are inseparable. This structure of command consists of practices that can in individual instances be observed or ignored but which are adhered to as a rule. The dominance of the rule in turn tells one that, as a member of a community, one rebels against custom at one's peril.[8] Such rebellion risks the wrath of your fellows, for by it one immediately stands apart from the community of which one is a member.

It is important to note here that any custom, on Nietzsche's account, is basically practical in origin. A custom has a specifically collective utility. What customs stand for is the pooled experience and judgement of ancient communities concerning what is beneficial and harmful *to them.* But what allows Nietzsche to characterise all human societies as being from the outset not merely ways of living enshrined within networks of custom but because of this also structures of power is the *observance of tradition itself.* The fact that every era of human life is shot through with traditions implies that, right from the point at which they could first be described as truly human, people have always been endowed with that instinct or feeling for custom and the customary which gives rise to traditions. It is this *feeling* that is subsequently called morality (*Daybreak,* 19). The sensibility which disposes us to be persuaded to do something because it is the custom (i.e. the disposition to adhere to norms) is independent from the judgements that become regimented into various customs and whose different arrangements in the form of traditions make up one social world or another. For Nietzsche, then, the common and hence universal propensity we have (what it is that endows us with our specifically *human* nature) is that we are rule followers. What rules we happen to follow is a contingent matter. Equally, it is because we are rule followers and thus adherents to conventions that we are by our very nature subjected to power. Following any rule means observing some convention or other; and doing this involves the acknowledgement of some kind of authority that has power over one. 'Morality' is a word that stands for the propensity we have to understand the world in terms of this feeling for power. Morals, in so far as they are acted out, are modes of disclosure in which cultural identities are asserted. Our sensibility in this regard is nothing less than an ability to comprehend or 'feel out' things and situations in terms of power relations. It is this feeling that constitutes the basis of our social nature. Things either feel appropriate or inappropriate, that is the basis of their legitimacy. Power is normative. This, as we will see, comes down to a matter of estimation, of measurement. Estimation, in turn, expresses an economic propensity.

Of course, the dominance of the morality of custom and all this entails is not the only feature of society. But it is the basic constituent and any other features will be in some manner or other related to it. Nietzsche can, for instance, contrast the morality of custom with the moralism inspired by Socrates and Plato (ibid., 9). In contrast to the morality of custom's stress upon obedience to conventions in the face of an authority that dwarfs self-interest, thinkers who follow Socrates and Plato argue for a morality in which mastery of the passions is justified precisely because it is in the individual's self-interest. When it comes to the broader question as to how societies and cultures function, however, this kind of thinking about morals is the exception not the rule. If it does not look this way to us, says Nietzsche, this is because we live in a culture that has been fashioned in close proximity to Platonism. The truth is that platonic moral thinking represents a radical attempt at breaking away from the power of morality of custom. All who follow Plato in this regard 'take a new path under the highest disapprobation of all advocates of morality of custom – they cut themselves off from the community, as immoral men, and are in the profoundest sense evil' (ibid.). A paradigmatic example of the morality of custom is a virtuous Ancient Roman citizen of 'sterling qualities'. He would have regarded any Christian he came across as something disgusting and evil because of the latter's abiding concern with individual salvation. The individualistic self-interest epitomised by Platonic moral thought therefore runs counter to the key premise of the morality of custom, which is a *collective morality*. Moral collectivism, which lies at the origins of human development, is where sacrifice finds its source. From the standpoint of an adherent to the morality of custom, the individual must always be sacrificed to the demands of the higher authority of tradition. This is the most ancient of imperatives. Individuality, in the sense in which we moderns value it, is a very recent invention. The individual is, if you like, merely the icing on the top of the temporal cake that historical philosophy seeks to cut deeply into. That is why morality still retains the power to provoke strong feelings in us just as much as in our ancestors.

7. *Modernity is a blend of the opposed tendencies exemplified by the morality of custom and Socratic moralism, one prehistoric and the other ancient in origin. Both tendencies are rooted in the conditions of sacrificial exchange that make up the primitive economy of human relations. Modern humanity has thus been created out of the combination of the primitive sacrificial economy and the internally generated forces that rose in struggle against it. Human rationality is a good example of this: it was achieved at great expense through struggle against the normative conditions in which it first began to appear. Human identity is something that has been paid for by such struggles with the primeval conditions of human sociality. Thus, modern humanity no less than primitive humanity is, for Nietzsche, governed by primeval notions and practices. Another way of putting this is to say that we no less than our forbears are prone to being gripped by the emotional pull of primeval ideas: the notion of sacrifice has tremendous emotive force today, just as it always did.*

Although from the standpoint of our ancestors we might be deemed horrifyingly immoral in our lack of respect for custom, we moderns also remain dominated by conventions. As Nietzsche notes in Section 21 of *Daybreak*, we no less than our ancestors remain prone to responding to the feelings engendered by the sacrificial propensity. The power of tradition may have been challenged by industrialisation and the burgeoning power of mercantilism, but today as much as in ancient times the rule applies which states that for the cause of morality people will still make 'every kind of sacrifice, self-overcoming and martyrdom' (*Daybreak*, 183). The weakening of morality that the decline of tradition bespeaks is not equivalent to its destruction. Modern society is a complex blend of ancient normative reflexes and contemporary industrial requirements. This is why there is not such a great distance separating the ancient blood lust that found exaltation contemplating human sacrifice and the self-interested 'neighbour' of industrial society contemplating another's sacrifice to the common social interest. Only the latter's detached and self-consciously concealed approval, their hypocritically moralistic exaltation at the spectacle, sets them apart as a specifically *modern* spectator.

We have seen that for Nietzsche the social world out of which the human character was fashioned was one in which custom and tradition dominated. This domination was rooted in an exchange structure: tradition demanded respect for authority in exchange for taming the invisible forces that were envisaged by superstitious fear to threaten human communities. The prehistoric human thus celebrated the virtues of sacrifice because of its propitiatory effect. For Nietzsche, it is the case that today we are still governed by the powerful sensibility that this feeling bespeaks. At the same time, we are also the outcome of fearsome struggles fought valiantly against it – which is why Nietzsche's attitudes towards Socrates and Plato or towards rationality are more complicated than one of the parody and dismissal they can all too easily be taken to be[9]:

> Every smallest step in the field of free thought, of a life shaped personally, has always had to be fought for with spiritual and bodily tortures: not only the step forward, no! the step itself, movement, change of any kind has needed its innumerable martyrs through all the long path-seeking and foundation-laying millennia [. . .] Nothing has been purchased more dearly [*Nichts ist theurer erkauft*] than that little bit of human reason and feeling of freedom which now constitutes our pride.
>
> (Ibid., 18)

The logic of sacrifice thereby exerts itself in domains that extend beyond the social conventions that lead the modern neighbour to applaud the youth's self-sacrifice to industry. Our sense of individuality, the extent to which a personal existence of reflection and decision is at all possible for anyone today, is also linked to ancient struggle and sacrifice on another level. Nothing was won at greater cost than our morsel of rationality and our sense of autonomy. Our pride rests upon this. This pride, in turn, is what prevents us from seeing that the prehistoric world abides in us even in the midst of the factory, the academy, the literary society, or the stock exchange. We are, it follows, beings that have been paid for in various ways by our forbears through their travails. Another way of putting this would be to say that prehistory has for Nietzsche set up the terms according to which human history has developed. Significantly, this is a history composed of various, sometimes profound and sometimes trivial, *exchanges*. The logic of sacrifice that governed the development of tradition and the institution of human society also governs the unfolding of historical consciousness. Modernity, which is after all the age of industrial rationality, of a manipulative reason capable of excavating and fashioning the natural resources of the world, is unthinkable without this logic of sacrificial exchange. The question of modernity is therefore at one and the same time a question of the new and the prehistoric in combination. Modern consciousness and the society dominated by material exchange that it reflects are the outcome of an exchange structure according to the demands of which some things have had to be sacrificed in payment for others. That is why our identity has been purchased by our forbears: they gave and sacrificed themselves in exchange for the cultivation of our rational abilities (albeit without knowing what they were doing). In modern humanity, the feeling of freedom exemplifies this sacrificial logic. With this feeling one assumes one's thoughts to be autonomous, to be governed by the spontaneity of an inner spark of awareness that dwells in the eternal newness of the living present. As the power of tradition recedes this feeling comes ever more to the fore. Individual self-consciousness might, in this sense, be described as always already potentially modern in terms of the conditions upon which its self-understanding is articulated. But it is both an articulation of and remains gripped by the sacrificial idea; and in so far as it remains gripped by this idea modern consciousness does not represent a radical break with its pre-modern ancestral conditions of possibility. That is why, when asked if 'we' have changed that much from the humans of millennia long since past, Nietzsche's short answer is, 'No!'

8. *Nietzsche elucidates the logic of sacrifice, the most primitive form of exchange; but he also employs it. He does so both as a means of decoding contemporary social practices and of articulating the value of attitudes he himself applauds. Hence, genuine science, like scholarly sacrifice already considered (Section 2, in this chapter), is founded on a sacrificial logic. Genuine science is not the same as 'mechanistic' natural science. The latter is naïve in that it reduces all knowledge to formalistic concepts of weighing and calculating.*

The human animal remains at the deepest level of its nature the same sacrificial animal it has been for countless ages. Given this it should come as no surprise that Nietzsche is happy enough to endorse the logic of sacrifice himself when it suits him. For instance, he can note that 'it has been human sacrifice which has at all times most exalted and elevated man. And perhaps every other endeavour could still be thrown down by *one* tremendous idea [. . .] the idea of *self-sacrificing mankind*' (ibid., 45). The sacrifice contemplated and endorsed here is for human knowledge. As this shows, the idea of giving and thereby exchanging oneself for something greater is, if only de facto, legitimate. The example of the scholar demonstrates that sacrifices are 'needful' even at the most esteemed of levels. Likewise, it is necessary to sacrifice the comforting certainties of life in order to plumb the depths of the nature of values (ibid., 61). Equally, the nobility of soul that Nietzsche so pointedly admires throughout his works is open to being defined by 'the use of a rare and singular standard and almost a madness: the feeling of heat in things that feel cold to everybody else; the discovery of values for which no scales have been invented yet; offering sacrifices that are dedicated to an unknown god [. . .]' (*The Gay Science*, 55). The noble person is like an ancient shaman. Nobility means the creation of new values, the offering up of what one has in the spirit of the most primitive of exchanges to something unknown so that new values, new means of evaluating, may be possible.

What is true for scholars is true for the disciplines they serve. All scholarship and true science carries on in the sacrificial vein of primitive exchange. Science is good for us to the extent that it brings with it a sharp and biting air that unsettles prejudices and leads us to question our convictions (which means none other than sacrificing our faith in things) (*Assorted Opinions and Maxims*, 205). Scientific beliefs, so long as they remain rigorous, are hypotheses, temporary viewpoints that function in each case as a 'regulative fiction' (*The Gay Science*, 344). Thus, science only begins when faith in convictions has been abandoned. Science, in this regard at least, stands against the demands of custom and tradition. However, this sceptical attitude has its origins in the logic of sacrifice: '*To make it possible for a discipline to begin,* must there not be some prior conviction – even one so commanding and unconditional that it sacrifices all other convictions to itself?' (ibid., 344). There is no such thing as a knowledge that is devoid of presuppositions. Knowledge is an expression of an 'unconditional will to truth'. Where the believer cleaves to tradition the person of knowledge challenges tradition by voicing the demand for truth. But this demand at the same time replicates the sacrificial structure of the very conditions it stands against. The desire for truth, the will to truth, means ' "I will not deceive, not even myself"; *and with that we stand on moral ground.*' The desire for truth no less than the desire to cleave to tradition is rooted in sacrificial practice, for it brings with it a preparedness to sacrifice all other beliefs to something ultimate but as yet unknown. People who answer to the demand for truthfulness 'in that audacious and ultimate sense that is presupposed by the faith in science *thus affirm another world* than the world of life, nature and history; and insofar as they affirm this "other world" – look, must they not by the same token negate its counterpart, this world, *our* world?' (ibid.). All desire for knowledge, even that of historical philosophy, is in this sense inspired by the metaphysical systems of the past and echoes the Christian and Platonic belief in the divinity of truth. Say this belief becomes increasingly incredible, what then? Nietzsche's response is simple enough: we could still not do without it. The person who responds to the demand for truthfulness would be prepared to exchange everything in pursuit of the satisfaction of this demand. The logic of sacrifice finds yet another form of expression in the sceptic's urge to question not only traditions but also the very fabric of the everyday world we inhabit.

The above attitude of ceaseless striving should not be confused with the narrower faith that underlies the natural sciences in their most naïve of forms. Natural science, when it pursues a mechanistic explanation of the world, is guilty of presupposing 'a world that is supposed to have its equivalent and its measure in human thought and human valuations – a "world of truth" that can be mastered completely and forever with the aid of our square little reason' (*The Gay Science*, 373). The narrow-minded natural scientist incorrectly sees the world as conforming to 'an interpretation that permits counting, calculating, weighing, seeing and touching, and nothing more'. Such a view would reduce the world to 'a mere exercise for a calculator'. The truly scientific attitude, in contrast, does not wish to strip existence of its ambiguous character. Rather, it seeks to do justice to 'this monster of an unknown world' by affirming the fact that it is so rich in ambiguity that no definitive answer concerning its nature will suffice (ibid., 374). The mechanistic natural scientist is worthy of contempt not because of their employment of calculation, weighing and the like but because of the fetishism whereby they transform these things into conceptual objects supposed to have the status of objective existence. Nietzsche does not wish to worship the unknown at the expense of the calculable. But he does assert the necessity of grasping the limits of our concepts. This means understanding what number, calculation and so forth really signify about humanity. In fact, they are linked to the logic of sacrifice that we have discussed already. Likewise, calculation and custom are also intimately related to one another, as we shall now see.

9. *Human identity itself first appears not as mere collective existence but as a specific kind of collectivism: humankind is an evaluator, a measurer. The name for our kind* ('Mensch': *'measurer'*) *reflects this. We have already seen that the concepts of custom, tradition, sacrifice, and exchange together make up the basis of what it is, according to Nietz-*

sche, which makes us truly human. However, these concepts and practices are themselves only possible in virtue of the presupposition that we can already characterise human beings as evaluators and measurers. Measurement implies a range of skills, practices and conventions that must be adhered to. As measurer, humanity approaches its world equipped to evaluate and thereby control it. Equally, morality is also bound up with this, for morality is a mode of estimation and evaluation and hence presupposes meaning. This amounts to the claim that we are by our very nature economic beings: we think of the world and ourselves in terms of modes of evaluation rooted in the economic estimation of things. This view informs Nietzsche's analysis of promising in the second essay of the Genealogy. *This analysis leads Nietzsche to argue that the relationship between buyer and seller (creditor and debtor) is the necessary condition of all forms of social organisation. It is as measurers and estimators that we become social beings. Our essence is economic.*

Although dismissive of mechanistic interpretations of the world that strive to render it in terms of abstract properties signified by the concepts of number, calculation, weighing, and so on, these concepts are not irrelevant to Nietzsche's conception of human nature. In fact, the opposite is the case: they are central to it. This is because we are, at heart, beings whose essence resides in our ability to estimate. We make values, and this is exemplified in our fascination with numbers, weights, measures and calculation generally:

> *Man as the measurer* [*Messende*]. Perhaps all the morality of mankind has its origin in the tremendous inner excitement which seized on primeval men when they discovered measure and measuring, scales and weighing [*sie das Maß und das Messen, die Waage und das Wägen entdeckten*] (the word '*Mensch*', indeed, means the 'measurer' [*Messenden*], he desired to name himself after his greatest discovery!). With these conceptions they climbed into realms that are quite unmeasurable and unweighable but originally did not seem to be.
>
> (*The Wanderer and His Shadow*, 21)

Our ancestors were creatures dominated by their passions. This is evidenced by the passionate, frenzied response Nietzsche suggests they would have exhibited at the discovery of measuring. There is no such thing as cold calculation; no disinterested contemplation of the world as an object to be assessed objectively by the use of measures and other tools of calculation. Calculation, no less than joy or anger, is passion and compulsion. Measure, measuring, scales and weighing mark the first step on the path to becoming truly human. The act of measuring, in other words, is the self-enactment of human identity that is subsequently identified in the celebration and self-affirmation that adopting the name '*Mensch*' implies.[10] Humanity is, in the essence of its self-understanding at least, Protagorean.[11] Whether they knew it or not, our ancestors elevated themselves to the status of measurers of reality when they became beings capable of calculation. Doubtless, one could add that measuring reality is a means of mastering it. What one does as a measurer, amongst other things, is make the environment one inhabits amenable to control. At the same time, the act of estimating opens up the world not merely as something that can be grasped and manipulated but also as something that can be comprehended in terms of limits and what exceeds those limits. The unmeasurable is only intimated in the light of having grasped what can be measured. The unweighable can only be thought in the context and aftermath of having weighed things. Humanity thereby stumbles into a world that exceeds calculation only in virtue of its ability to calculate and only in virtue of the naïve belief that calculation represents 'things' and 'states of things' that exist independently of the measurer. The naivety of the natural scientist lies in their thinking that weighing is at once both the goal and the standard of thought. But it is rather a means beyond itself. Without the development of humanity *as a measurer* measurement would mean nothing.

Measuring, of course, implies an entire range of related practices and skills. To be a measurer one must be able to identify what is to be reckoned up. One must be able to compare like with unlike. To do that, one must have developed a standard according to which various comparisons can be made. Comparison implies exchange: the means whereby two different things (even different kinds of thing) are attributed a measure of value in common. Approaching its world as a being equipped with measures, weights and scales, prehistoric humanity is from the outset envisaged by Nietzsche as an estimator of values. Ethics, in other words, is entwined inextricably with identification and calculation and lies at the origins of what it is to be human. To be moral is always already to be a being who can count. To observe customs and formulate traditions one must measure time; ritual is repetition according to the concept of measure. Sacrifice presupposes a measure of equivalence such that what is sacrificed is sufficient to pay for what is desired of the gods. Morality presupposes calculating abilities. In the multifarious concepts and routines that accompany that of calculation, an awareness of the fundamental principles of economy is made manifest, for all economy embodies practices of measuring, weighing and calculating. A measuring being is also always already an economic being.

It should come as no surprise, in the light of this, that Nietzsche characterises humanity from the start as resolving the problem of whether to resort to one course of action or another on the basis of a combination of calculation and sensibility:

> What is the cause of a cheerful resolution for action? [. . .] The oldest and most common answer is: 'God is the cause; it is his way of telling us he approves of our intention'. [. . .] When in former times [. . .] anyone who stood in doubt before several courses of action advised himself thus: 'I shall do that which engenders this feeling'. One thus decided, not for the most reasonable course, but for that course the image of which inspired the soul with hope and courage. The good mood was placed on the scales as an argument and outweighed rationality.
>
> (*Daybreak*, 28)

In the hearts of the earliest humans there rests a metaphorical set of scales. The ancient means of deciding on a course of right conduct involved placing a feeling on these 'scales'. It may have been the case that this feeling was irrational, that the outcome arrived at did not in this regard represent a sensible course of action when viewed instrumentally, but the point is that *the means of evaluation* reflect his contention that humans are essentially measuring animals. Today things are no different, we are still dominated by the passions and the dictates of sensibility: '"Create a mood!" – one will then require no reasons and conquer all objections!' In order to evaluate we must think within constraints determined by the notions of weighing and measuring that our forbears endowed us with. We are creatures who cannot but think in this manner, whether it is about others or ourselves. Thus, for instance, 'our respect for ourselves is tied to our being able to practise requital, in good things and bad' (ibid., 205). Self-respect, in other words, presupposes establishing a *balance* between what we receive from others and what we give to them. Self-understanding is the assessment of oneself as a consumer and producer of affects with regard to others according to the principle of calculation. A self is an economic entity.

From the above it should be clear that Nietzsche does not think of our conceptual abilities as existing in isolation from our emotional and animal propensities. There is for him no substantive difference between the realm of evaluations and the realm of feelings. We are beings who evaluate by way of weights and measures, but our ability to conceive of and then respond to such differences is rooted in our sensibility. What leads a person to assess one thing as being heavier than another is not merely the relative difference in weight between individual objects that can then be placed on a set of scales and ascribed a number representative of their heaviness. It is also the propensity to understand the act of measurement itself as having its own peculiar and compelling weight, independent even of the particular objects in question. The act and the propensity it enacts are indicative of what we are. In order to make sense of the world we must evaluate it. But this evaluation is never a crude representation of properties that are thought to reside in an independent nature. Before the world of nature is encountered as such it must be subjected to the demand that it fulfil our evaluating propensities – which does not, of course, mean that it will acquiesce to such a demand.[12]

To make the discovery of measuring a primeval event, a defining moment in our *prehistory*, as Nietzsche does, is to contend that human beings are from the outset economic creatures. Our economic nature is in effect claimed to be prior to all historical experience. Nietzsche develops this notion most strikingly in the second essay of *On the Genealogy of Morality*, which provides an account of the conditions under which humanity emerged from the world of natural beings. In the *Genealogy* Nietzsche argues that the prehistoric conditions of this emergence can be laid out in terms of the problem of how an animal such as we are came to have a specifically *moral memory* made for it (*On the Genealogy of Morality*, II, 1). It is one thing to be endowed with memory, which other animals as well as we have. But a memory that is specifically ethical in significance is another matter. Nietzsche's answer to the question of where this kind of memory came from is to turn for an explanation to the constraints that would have necessarily been imposed upon our forebears by the needs of communal living. Communal life is only possible in so far as every member of a community abides by shared norms. If this is not the case, the community will quickly disintegrate under the stress imposed upon it by its members seeking satisfactions according to their own desires and irrespective of the needs of anybody else. Society, if it is to be any kind of society at all, must therefore be regulated. This regulation, as we have seen in relation to the discussion in *Daybreak*, is linked to the formation of social habits, the adherence to customs and the sedimentation of customs into traditions. Adherence to tradition, moreover, is only possible in virtue of the development of human culture as a sphere of commanding and obeying (*Daybreak*, 9). The primitive human subject is seized by the fear of authority (presented as the superstitious fear of unknowable natural forces, comprehended in the language of the supernatural) and demonstrates their subordination by way of acquiescing to being held in abeyance by traditional observances (customs and rituals). The primitive human being is thereby normalised, that is formed into a creature amongst whose essential features are regular and predictable behaviour, achieved through their being made to adhere to rules, rituals and customs. In the account offered in the *Genealogy* this adherence is likewise achieved through the feeling of fear, that is fear of the consequences of not observing customs, which is where promising comes in. Promising defines the relationship between the individual agent and the communal order of which they are a part in terms of regularised modes of behaviour. The promiser is held to account by promising. Promising is a social bond, a communal glue that regulates all individual relationships by referring them to the needs of the larger social whole. In primitive social forms, Nietzsche argues, a subject is a subject only in virtue of this relationship to the communal whole. This relationship is articulated as one of *responsibility*. The feeling of being responsible, the moral memory that is expressed by promising, derives from the relationship between individuated subject and social body that promising evidences.

For the individual to exist the community must exist. The potentially damaging behaviour of individuals must therefore be curtailed. Our prehistoric forebears achieved this, Nietzsche argues, by unconsciously shaping themselves into beings capable of recognising and respecting authority (our kind's acute sense for power relations and urge to demur to authority might be taken as evidence for this view) and they did so through the imposition of harsh disciplinary procedures. In prehistoric communities, the individual who acted against the interest of the social body had to be prevented from doing so. The means was simple enough: painful punishments.[13] In effect, humans tortured themselves (and one another) into acknowledging the feeling of responsibility. In this way, a moral memory was scalded, stamped and burned into the human mind and became constitutive of its psychology (*On the Genealogy of Morality*, II, 3). The significance of this is extensive. From the point of view of the current discussion, the important thing is that our primitive ancestors were made truly human by an act of labour: their *working upon themselves* was their first genuinely creative act. The manufacturing of a moral memory is thus for Nietzsche a primal event. It is the outcome of a first engagement in an autochthonous world of work, the summation of the 'labour of man upon himself during the longest epoch of the human race, his whole labour *before history*' (ibid., 2).

A labourer from the outset, even from the time of prehistory, humankind is already stamped not merely with the defining characteristic of being the promising animal but is also simultaneously marked out as a creature of economy. Nietzsche's defining of humanity first and foremost as a labourer (as the labouring animal) necessarily invokes accompanying economic characteristics. Centrally, the primeval human is already a creature endowed with an understanding of themselves, others and the community they inhabit in terms of relations of credit and debit. The individual dwells in the safety of the community. He or she is protected by the communal structure from being swamped by the constant tide of dangers sweeping in from the world of nature. As such, any individual always finds himself or herself situated in a specific relationship to the social body: the individual is a *debtor*. The price to be paid in recompense for the protection of society, and *constantly* repaid as a condition of social existence, is the ever-increasing cultivation of the feeling of responsibility and the enactment of this feeling through the observance of tradition, that is adherence to rules of right behaviour. In this way humanity labours upon itself and manufactures its own identity through communal norms and the enforced adherence of individuals to these norms.

The human species, it follows, is defined in terms of its labouring essence, which is made manifest in and as the social domain. The individual dwells in a state of continual debt to the labouring essence of the species in so far as any individual only exists in virtue of the fact that this essence precedes them, both temporally and metaphysically speaking. It precedes them temporally in that without humans already understood as self-manufacturing labourers there could be no society as such. It precedes them metaphysically in that this labouring essence constitutes an essential constituent of the logical definition of what it means to be a person (although Nietzsche himself would probably not have had much patience with this approach to the problem).

I have already argued elsewhere that the economy presented in the *Genealogy* is at the same time also an economy of *violence*.[14] This is evidenced by Nietzsche's emphasis on the role that unrelenting pain and suffering played in the manufacture of the kind of memory needed to prevent individuals committing acts harmful to the prehistoric community (ibid., 3). In turn, this economy of violence is what, for

Nietzsche, grounds the future potential and hence the cultural achievement of humankind. This prehistoric economy is an *economy of violence* enacted in a primeval workplace. Members of the prehistoric social body learned to observe imperatives on the basis of costs and benefits. The benefit of communal life is security, its cost the unrestrained violence turned on the individual who threatens that security. Such horror, Nietzsche argues, receives its justification 'on a grand scale' in so far as this autochthonous violence bestows upon humanity futurity. The ability to promise gives us 'control over the future', Nietzsche argues, because a person who makes a promise is 'answerable for his own *future*!' and must act in accord with this understanding (ibid., 1). In this regard, humanity becomes truly itself only when it is endowed with future potential. This potential is above all a matter of *self-understanding*, that is of self-interpretation in terms of past, present and future. Temporality, in this view, is a matter of understanding: it is an *achievement*. The meaningfulness of making promises presupposes a comprehension of the future as a possible state in which the contract that was stipulated by the promise can be fulfilled. All understanding of promising presupposes an understanding of the past, present and future modalities of time.

As well as serving as the means whereby Nietzsche articulates his concept of human futurity, the model of economy developed from the analysis of promising in the *Genealogy* also represents an extrapolation of the notion of 'man as measurer' first mooted in *The Wanderer and His Shadow*. Promising and all that this entails does not function as a means of ensuring the continuity of the social bond by acting on already fully formed individuals. Rather, it marks out the terrain within which the individual is constituted as a social agent. In order to make a promise one must 'be able to calculate and compute' (ibid., 2). A promising being, in other words, is one who can count, measure, weigh and estimate. Such measuring abilities, in their own turn, presuppose a being (or, as Nietzsche is fond of reminding us, an 'animal') that must first be fashioned and formed according to patterns (norms, practices and the like) characteristic of such abilities. That is, a measuring and estimating animal such as can make a promise is one who has already been kneaded and rendered by communal forces into something '*reliable, regular,* [and] *automatic,* even in his own self-image, so that he, as someone making a promise, is answerable for his own *future*!' (ibid., 2). Our dominant tendency to follow habits in the form of our respect for authority and tradition, sacrificial propensities, need of the concepts of equivalence and exchange, sensitivity to problems of evaluation, likewise our understanding of others, of community and society and, consequently, our self-understanding: all bear the mark of economy. All of them spring from the reliability, regularity and necessarily automatic characteristics that our ancestors cultivated and in turn bestowed upon us. Our psychology is, in this view, our primeval heritage. It is our most abiding inheritance.

The account Nietzsche presents of industrial, economic modernity is at the same time something which both informs and is informed by this conception of the primeval condition of humanity as flowing from economic practices and notions. He may vehemently criticise modernity for being economically driven and, because of this, mundane, instrumental, materialistic and sterile. But the repulsion Nietzsche expresses can only be properly comprehended when it is at the same time set against the claim that economic conditions lie at the heart of the workings of human self-understanding and cultural achievement. So profound is the influence of such conditions, so constitutive of our nature, that culture itself is tied to them. In so far as we are human we are also necessarily traders, dealers and exchangers. Specifically *economic practices*, in other words, mark us out as the kind of beings that we are. For Nietzsche, without such practices there would and could be no such thing as a human being, no such thing as human culture in any shape or form. He makes the point bluntly enough in Section 8 of the second essay of the *Genealogy*: 'Buying and selling, with their psychological trappings, are older even than the beginnings of any social form of organization or association [. . .]'. The point is simple enough. Personal obligation, which comes down to the feelings of guilt and responsibility that characterise a necessary condition of human social life, springs from the most primeval personal relationship that is there, namely the relationship between buyer and seller within a communal structure. Organised human society, in all its manifold manifestations, originates in one essential *form* of interpersonal relationship: the relationship of responsibility that inheres between purchaser and vendor, which is an exchange relationship understood in terms of credit and debit. Creditor and debtor meet in an interpersonal space opened up by the practice of exchanging. It is in this space that 'person met person for the first time, and *measured himself* person against person'. To meet another and understand them as other, that is as a person, means to *estimate* them as such. A person, in this view, is not simply something that is encountered and labelled in virtue of its possessing brute empirical characteristics akin to an object. Unlike any other kind of being (alive or inanimate), a person is *acknowledged*.[15] Likewise, a subject's sense of his or her own identity is entwined with this estimating and acknowledgement. Self and other are the conceptual outcroppings of acts of measurement. What a person is consists in what they are estimated to be *worth*. In this sense, a subject is what it possesses; subjectivity is inextricably tied to the concept of property. In consequence, social hierarchy (a notion of which Nietzsche is always very fond) is a necessary condition not only of modern, complex industrial orders or medieval social orders but of all societies and of the archetype of all societies, the community. All human social arrangements, whatever mode of association one might like to consider, are economically determined realms of possession. In turn, those possessions that serve to define a subject's sense of selfhood can likewise be estimated and ranked. That is why for Nietzsche the most spiritual life is at the same time a life denoted in terms of an aesthetic that concerns the possession of the most refined, rare and hence valuable intellectual and spiritual tastes.

Whichever party initiates the exchange is irrelevant. One party gives something and thereby becomes a creditor. The other at that moment is rendered a debtor and acts on the feeling of obligation to restore the balance by offering something in return for what has been given to them – something that both parties accept has an equivalent value. This primeval condition of exchange is the defining characteristic of civilisation; it exemplifies humankind in its most 'natural' (i.e. spontaneously motivated) state.[16] To the extent that we are 'natural' we are also responsible beings (*Beyond Good and Evil*, 188). We are fundamentally exchangers and, Nietzsche notes, one has still not yet found a civilisation, however lowly, in which something of this exchange relationship cannot be noted (*On the Genealogy of Morality*, II, 8). No surprise, therefore, that human cognitive abilities in general are for Nietzsche inextricably linked to the creditor–debtor relationship. Take the fixing of prices, assessment of values, thinking up of relations of equivalence, exchanging: these practices do not merely signify aspects of thinking but are 'in a certain sense' *what* thinking is, since such preoccupations constitute the oldest activity of humankind and lie at its origins. Likewise, through these practices was bred the oldest astuteness, possibly perhaps our feeling of superiority over other animals. The point Nietzsche has already made in *The Wanderer and His Shadow* (Section 21) can again be hammered home: 'Perhaps our word "*Mensch*" (*manas* [man]) expresses something of *this* self-satisfied feeling: humanity [thereby] described itself as the being that measured values, assessed and measured, as the "estimating animal itself" ' (ibid., 8). Our self-understanding is an extension of our measuring practices and emerges from them.

What we do, in other words, sets the conditions that determine the limits of what we can become. In turn, Nietzsche argues, what became of humanity under the influence of this 'germinating sensation of barter' was that it was transformed by its own actions into a creature capable of formulating and acting according to abstract social notions. Society, in short, got constructed in the manner it did because the communally based creditor–debtor relationship contained concepts and practices that could be extrapolated and formalised. Hence, the notions of duty, right, debt and compensation were taken from the creditor–debtor relationship and given a social and legal dimension, for example, in the form of the idea of legal entitlement to rights and compensation for suffering a wrong. Formalised relationships are in this way rendered open to being regarded as the product of a 'great generalization': 'Every thing has its price: *everything* can be compensated for.' Here lie the beginnings of the most ancient moral of forms

> relating to *justice* [...]. Justice at this first level is the good will, between those who are roughly equal, to come to terms with each other, to 'come to an understanding' again by means of a settlement – and, in connection with those who are less powerful, to *force* them to reach a settlement amongst themselves.

Justice, in other words, is inextricably linked to the conditions underlying exchange: a settling of accounts marks the resolution of disputes and takes place between persons who understand themselves and one another in terms of the equality of value of possessions that the practices exemplifying the exchange principle generate. The notion of equivalence underlies all manner of judgements (ibid., 4). Thus, humans, as creatures of the passions, are beings dominated above all by the feeling for evaluating according to the economic concepts of evaluation.

Today we may be moderns, with all that we have seen this implies for Nietzsche, but modernity is no mere abandonment of a dead past that has simply become engulfed by the tide of a continuous and modish 'newness'. Modernity is, rather, a rearrangement of ancient social elements and forces governed now by the power of capital and industrial production. The overtly economic nature that is made manifest by this power is not in itself something new. No less than custom, tradition, sacrifice and power, the economic itself is a primeval characteristic of human social relations and forms the precondition of these other features of human life, underlying each as a constitutive component. The sacrifice to the social order demanded of the modern worker finds its analogue in the ancient sacrifice demanded by the observance of tradition, which in turn finds its archetype in the sacrifice demanded of the individual in exchange for the protection afforded to them in the ancient community. Not merely the outset of history, but the very opening up of the temporal possibilities of humanity itself are articulations of the fundamental economic mode of behaviour that constitutes our essence. Nietzsche, however, goes further than this in his employment of the concept of economy as a means of elucidating what it is to be human. The economic conditions of human social life are themselves understandable in terms of a 'grand economy' that situates humanity within an even larger framework. It is to this that I turn next.

3
The Great Economy

1. *Nietzsche's account of the emergence of human identity is developed in terms of his narrative account of prehistory. Central to this is his conception of the 'internalization' of humankind. This occurs through the violent colonisation of one primitive community by another. Subjugation provokes in the colonised the appearance of a sense of identity that becomes the self-consciousness characteristic of what we now call the human soul. This springs from what Nietzsche calls the 'bad conscience' and is an enforced reinterpretation of the economically determined relation between creditor and debtor that precedes it. This change is also marked by the formalisation of communal relationships. Community becomes society (replete with state structures, legality and the like). The self, in turn, emerges as a being at war with itself, capable of challenging and overcoming its own inclinations and habits. In the account of internalisation Nietzsche offers an account of human development that invokes the notions of instincts being channelled within a general economy of existence.*

We have seen that for Nietzsche not only modernity but also the most primitive conditions fostering the development of culture are permeated by economic characteristics. Central to this contention is the conception of humanity as measurer. Measuring and estimating abilities are defining features of the emergence of community, social relationships, formal social order including legality and human self-understanding. In the second essay of the *Genealogy*, this conception of 'man as measurer' blossoms into an analysis of human culture as emerging from practices denoted by concepts of exchange, credit and debit. Human nature itself thereby becomes definable by Nietzsche in purely economic terms. The notion of economy that is at work in the *Genealogy*'s second essay covers a multiplicity of domains and simultaneously binds these domains together by way of defining what kind of creatures we are. However, the notion of economy has broader implications even than this. One may approach this issue by briefly considering a further contention Nietzsche puts forward in the *Genealogy*. The contention concerns the nature of the prehistoric transformation from communal social order to something akin to the kind of civil society we live in today and revolves around his claim that this transformation initiated another, which he baptises the '*internalization* of man' (*On the Genealogy of Morality*, II, 16). The notion of internalisation concerns the manner in which humankind has been *spiritualised*, that is endowed with the inner illumination of self-reflective understanding.

Civil society, on the account offered in the *Genealogy*, emerges in a relatively straightforward fashion. Let us envisage Nietzsche's conception of the prehistoric human community. It is a domain governed by norms. Customs predominate, woven together in the form of tradition. Individuals exist in virtue of the shared observance of these norms and relate to one another on the basis of them as economic beings engaged in various practices (exchange-related activity of all kinds, including barter and sacrifice). These practices are all at bottom economic, springing from the creditor–debtor relationship and involving the mutual evaluation of one another (communal hierarchy), or the estimation and putting to use of the environment through measurement and weighing. It scarcely needs to be added that Nietzsche has thereby constructed a narrative account of the development of human beings. He is telling us a story. This is a prehistoric narrative and it is designed to reveal the primitive underpinnings of modern culture, as is revealed by the claim that prehistory involves criteria of evaluation that are present at all times and can hence always erupt into modern society with an overt and uncanny violence (ibid., 9). The idea of 'historical philosophy' first outlined at the beginning of *Human, All Too Human* has in this way borne fruit. The concept of humanity offered here is one that is arrived at in tandem with that of historical development. Nietzsche's historical analysis, in turn, has reached back beyond even itself into the realms of that which constitutes its own precondition. This may produce an account of the past that is, as he himself notices, sometimes obliged to hover in the domain of supposition (ibid., 6), but Nietzsche doubtless feels that his conjectures to be worth more than the empty and discredited metaphysical accounts he himself so forcibly gives us good reason to reject.

There is, one should add to the above, no single human community envisaged at this stage in Nietzsche's prehistoric narrative. The world of prehistory is one in which the basic communal economy that gave rise to humanity has spawned a multiplicity of communities, each going its own way in terms of the norms it adopts and the traditions it develops and therefore becoming culturally distinct. The social order envisaged here remains distinctly communal and primitive. That is, when contrasted with modern societies it may be characterised almost as much by what it lacks as by what is present in it. Above all, the formalisation of social relations into formal law (statute) is lacking, as is a state structure to impose such statutes. The event that triggers both the emergence of civil society and, in turn, the development of a spiritualised humankind is violent colonisation. One community invades another. From the point of view of the colonised, this is experienced as something sudden. Circumstances do not change gradually, as in something akin to an evolutionary development, but suddenly and shockingly as 'a breach, a leap, a compulsion, a fate which nothing could ward off [. . .]' (ibid., 17). Likewise the 'shaping' of the human population, which began with the violence of transferring the human animal into formalised society, also concluded violently in the tyrannical power exerted over the colonised community. The state was thereby born as something terrible. The invaders (the unfairly notorious 'blonde beasts') quite simply subjugated the community they colonised by fair means or foul. What Nietzsche calls 'bad conscience' erupts out of this. Bad conscience is the first characteristic of spirituality. It is the source of human imagination and creative inventiveness. It is also an illness contracted as a consequence of the most tremendous stress that humanity ever experienced (ibid., 16).

Once colonised, the members of the subjugated community found that not only were their natural drives curtailed by convention and tradition (in itself relatively bearable, since the subject of tradition at the same time identifies with that tradition[1]) but by something unrelentingly *other*, foreign and yet unstoppable. Authority and power in this condition come to be experienced as impositions, and the natural drives to which all people are subject are curtailed to an even greater extent than they are by communal life. The creation of a spiritualised being, a person endowed with a soul, is the consequence of the containment of these drives. This is because of the manner in which drives respond to any form of curtailment: all those instincts which cannot be discharged in an outward direction turn inwards. However well contained, the passions constitutive of us (exhibited most tellingly for Nietzsche when humanity discovered measuring, weighing and estimating) vent themselves in any manner open to them. Primitive, communal humanity living under the yoke of oppression thereby unconsciously spiritualised itself in response to the distinctly *un*spiritual behaviour of other (colonial) communal beings. As Nietzsche is careful to point out, the non-spiritual behaviour of one party is a necessary condition of the spiritual and intellectual development of another. The oppressor is, however unconsciously, however brutally, creative in their own way: they manufacture states, they delight in tyrannising and controlling others. The oppressed person reacts by becoming creative in a new sphere capable of escaping the confines of the state tyranny that their rulers have bound them in: that of imagination, fantasy and thought. It is this that marks the moment in which the bad conscience is created.

The sense of guilt that is characteristic of bad conscience is a reinterpretation of the creditor–debtor relationship, the outcome of its transformation (a further transformation of this relationship is what brings about organised religion and, ultimately, monotheism[2]). The feeling of being responsible in the communal context, of being a debtor in relation to the communal body and of relating to others in terms of relations of credit and debit now becomes bound up with a new sense of indebtedness. The creditor, who is originally a being capable of keeping trust, of acting on the basis of good faith (and on the promise of exacting sanctioned revenge if the debt is not repaid), is now given legal status. The creation of state and civil society means that the relationship between creditor and debtor is now marked by formalisation. To be a subject is now to be a dealer with others in the context of private or civil law. It is also to be a debtor in relation to a social body whose dominant creditor is now organised state power. The oppression of the coloniser is oppressive not simply because it is violent and invasive in the sense that the coloniser appears and kills, maims, pillages and the like. Colonial oppression resides most decisively in the construction of the state, in the creation of rules that are experienced by the colonised as a new and ever more invasive mode of oppression capable of colonising even their sense of selfhood. That is why the colonisers can be described by Nietzsche as 'artists of violence', geniuses of power who hew the body and psychology of humanity as a sculptor does a piece of formless rock (ibid., 18). The result is to be found in the victims of colonisation: a soul willingly at conflict with itself, suffering even from its own existence and, as a result, driven to acts of constant self-challenging and self-overcoming. This, for Nietzsche, is the seed out of which all human greatness springs. The account of internalisation developed in the *Genealogy* does not just concern the prehistoric transformation of economically articulated modes of understanding made manifest through practices and the formal imposition of legal and state power. With the introduction of an account of the instincts, of the drives that constitute our embodied existence, Nietzsche also invokes the notion of a general economy of existence. In other words, Nietzsche is also concerned with an economy that is not simply a matter of the contingencies of human psychology, of the way in which we happen to think due to things turning out the way they did. This general economy is outlined explicitly 5 years earlier in *The Gay Science.*

2. *In* The Gay Science *Nietzsche offers an account of the great economy of the preservation of the human species. This economy denotes something both instinctive and collective. It includes not only the so-called 'good' qualities that people have (e.g. selflessness) but also our so-called 'evil' propensities. The qualities associated with dangerous human beings, in other words, are of equal potential value when it comes to the question of human preservation. Nietzsche's formulation of this is expressed in a language permeated by economic notions of credit and debit, costs and benefits. This economy, for example, is one of squandering. Nietzsche's elucidation of it is in part a criticism of modern society: an implied indictment not only of our conformist tendencies but also of our inability to laugh at ourselves. The notion of the economy of human preservation is also resorted to by Nietzsche to explain the human need to endow life with sense. Moral teachings, art and religions are all means of giving life meaning and therefore advancing our faith in life. In this way, our kind's interest in its own preservation is promoted. All manifestations of existence (including the most trivial) can be interpreted in terms of the drive for preservation. Culture is an unconscious expression of this drive. The economy of human preservation is universal, a matter of human nature. Other human practices (including the economic practices of weighing, measuring, estimating and the like) are thereby open to being regarded as manifestations of this greater economic logic. One key aspect of this economy is that it brings the human craving for meaning to the fore. History becomes a parade of teachings of the purpose of existence, coming to be and passing away. The need for meaning is as central to our existence as the requirement for food and raiment.*

The notion of a grand or great economy is introduced right at the outset of *The Gay Science*. It concerns the manner in which all human behaviour can be understood as a manifestation of a general principle. All people, Nietzsche argues, act with one basic aim: 'to do what is good for the preservation of the human race' (*The Gay Science*, 1). This might at first glance seem to be a claim about laudable motives. What good, after all, could be better than the good that benefits the survival of the whole race? However, it turns out that this aim does not have its origins in what most of us might be tempted to think of as 'good' motives, such as that of feeling love for others. Rather, what Nietzsche is discussing here is a deeply ingrained 'instinct' ('*Instinkt*') (hence, something largely unconscious) that springs from our collective nature. The instinctive desire to think and act with a view to mutuality 'constitutes' our 'essence'. A perhaps less polite, but for Nietzsche no less accurate, way of putting this would be to say that we are a 'herd' animal. Our collective nature defines us. As in the account developed in the *Genealogy*, we are above all communal animals. The determining feature of this communal nature is survival, since it focuses individual action towards achieving the general aim of preserving the species.

The communality that Nietzsche has in mind here is, however, not all that one might initially take it to be. Normally, one might think of a communal characterisation of our nature as one that will take us towards a position akin to the philosophy of Marx or some other kind of collectivism. The argument might run: we are communal beings, we have a shared nature, a shared world and hence shared interests. From this it follows that the best approach to answering the question of what kind of life is likely to be best for humanity is the communal life, with its accompanying emphasis upon a person's living their life with the interests of others in mind (selflessness). The best interests of humanity, in other words, are held by this point of view to be collective interests, and beyond the domain of such interests it is impossible to go without entering into a realm of ugly, selfish, destructive, even evil behaviour. Nietzsche does not accept this view. For one thing, he notes straight away, although it may be both tempting and easy to categorise others as good or evil according to their likely effect upon us (i.e. according to how selfish or not they may appear to be), this attitude adopts a small-scale view of human qualities. Nietzsche immediately raises questions about how adequate the defining of others in this small-scale way is: 'in any large-scale accounting, when we reflect on the whole a little longer, we become suspicious of this neat division and finally abandon it'. Categorically neat divisions are not to be trusted just because they look nice. It might be appealing to think of the world as being composed of 'good' and 'bad' people, the one kind worthy and helpful and the other unworthy and dangerous, but what is thereby ignored is the possibility that 'Even the most harmful man may really be the most useful when it comes to the preservation of the species.' What is needed is an account of human qualities that is rather more ambitious and, dare one say it, immoral. In other words, a more perceptive reckoning of what human qualities might be deemed 'useful' or 'good' would need to keep in mind the larger question of the preservation of humanity rather than the narrower issue of the immediate effects that one (possibly very unpleasant) individual's actions might have upon others proximal to them. Those feelings that we are generally inclined to consider bad or downright evil because of the pain they cause or the sense of disgust they give rise to, such as the feeling of hatred, a sense of pleasure at the suffering of others, or the despotic lust to rule and tyrannise, might from this larger vantage point not be altogether bad. A large-scale reckoning up might show it to be the case that harmful humans are at least as valuable from the standpoint of human preservation as are the less harmful ones. The harmful person is a vehicle bearing instincts (sometimes violent, sometimes repulsive) that may actually be necessary to human survival.

Nietzsche is, of course, deliberately rendering problematic the language of good and evil commonly used to distinguish between people of worth and dangerous people. More to the point, he does so by invoking the concept of economy: 'Hatred, the mischievous delight in the misfortune of others, the lust to rob and dominate, and whatever else is called evil belongs to the most amazing economy of the preservation of species [*Ökonomie der Arterhaltung*]'. Human existence, in other words, is maintained by diverse and contrary conditions. Differing and sometimes contrary human propensities gain their meaning from the manner in which they function not merely in relation to one another but by way of reference to the general question of our preservation. The conditions of human preservation, taken together, constitute an economy of relations. Individual propensities (drives, instincts, passions) of all kinds, including those that are of the most sinister nature, do not gain their meaning exclusively from their evaluation by those subject to them (the victim), but from a universal standard that concerns the continuation of life. This is the standard of the economy of human existence. Nietzsche does not shy away from using language that reflects mercantile society in his formulation of the nature of this astounding economy. It is an economy that is costly in the broadest of sense, in that it is both 'expensive' and 'wasteful' (ibid.). It is also consequently a most stupid economy. In other words, from the standpoint of thrift and good housekeeping sense one might assert that the economy of human survival makes little sense. An existence organised along such economic lines does not, paradoxically, economise. But the fact of the matter is on the side of Nietzsche's contention. This is an economy which, he says, can be proven to have preserved our race right up to now.

One should be aware immediately of what kind of economy Nietzsche is proposing here. That it is characterised by a squandering of resources implies it is the opposite of the kind of economy of industrial efficiency characteristic of the commercial world that is catalogued in the *Untimely Meditations, Human, All Too Human* and subsequent texts. That said, it should be recalled that the efficiency of industrial production is, for Nietzsche, illusory. Monetary efficiency, for him, also brings with it cultural squandering, a wasting of human potential in the service of the demands of production. Squandering is a general feature of economy rather than something exclusive to one kind or the other. As the wastefulness of the economy of the preservation of the species suggests, there is also something sinister, violent and amoral at work within it. The economy of human preservation involves a consideration of the potential usefulness of *all* human propensities, not just some selected ones. What is violent, threatening, unsettling and damaging to some individuals may, at the same time, be regarded as representative of drives that are life-promoting, inspiring, creative and nurturing for the species as a whole. Nietzsche's elucidation of this economy is certainly undertaken with a specific target in mind: modernity. Thus, Nietzsche can ask rhetorically and with his spikiest humour, whether we moderns are in any way able to live in a manner that is capable of genuinely damaging the species? 'What *might* have harmed the species may have become extinct many thousands of years ago [. . .]. Pursue your best or your worst desires, and above all perish! In both cases you are still in some way a promoter and benefactor of humanity and therefore entitled to your eulogists – but also your detractors' (ibid.). What, in other words, is one to make of modern humanity in the light of this general economy of preservation? Have we become so normalised, so much mere herd material that we are well enough suited to modern industrial collective culture but good for little else, since the dangerous propensities Nietzsche speaks of are now beyond us? Has the general economy of our preservation worked so well as to have bred out of us the more dangerous, but perhaps life-enhancing, tendencies?

Certainly, for Nietzsche, we increasingly lack one especially dangerous and beneficial characteristic: the ability to laugh at ourselves. Our moral seriousness, in other words our concern to evaluate everything all too carefully in terms of what is beneficial and harmful from the perspective of our immediate fate and the collective social good, has become a guiding principle of life. Doubtless, this reflects the lack in the modern soul that, we have already seen, renders it in Nietzsche's opinion poor building material for future societies. As soon as one takes oneself too seriously, one becomes neurotically engrossed in the fatality of one's own existence and incapable of thinking beyond it. That is certainly modern. That said, 'Even laughter may have a future. I mean, when the proposition "the species is everything, *one* is always none" has become part of humanity, and this ultimate liberation and irresponsibility has become accessible to all at all times [. . .] perhaps only "gay science" will then be left' (ibid.). If we were to acknowledge the economy of the preservation of the species as Nietzsche has outlined it, we would live in a world devoid of guilt. No one would be ultimately responsible for being what he or she was, since every individual would be an articulation of this economy and endowed with inclinations that, whether deemed 'good' or 'evil' from current perspectives, had value from the perspective of their role within the universal structure of preservation. So long as we live without the irresponsibility that the genuine acknowledgement of the economy of the species would bring with it, however, we remain condemned to abiding 'in the age of tragedy, the age of moralities and religions'. This is because we are driven by this economy itself to endow life with meaning, but invariably do so in a manner that finds the suffering inherent within it almost unspeakable beyond words.

In the light of this, much of human life becomes interpretable as a series of unconscious ruses, a trail of tricks played upon the human sense of pride by the guiding economy of its instincts. The person who pens a tragedy may be dealing with what is sorrowful and thereby appear to be affirming a view of the world that is negative, but the tragedian is really expressing something positive because tragic narrative endows existence with depth and significance. Giving life meaning in this way advances 'the faith in life' and thereby promotes the 'interests of the species' (ibid.). The rest of us are no different from the great tragedians in our own much less important ways. We are all of us, from the most refined to the most vulgar, the highest and the most common, dominated by 'the instinct [*Trieb*] for the preservation of the species'. Human culture in all its manifestations (be it art, literature, poetry, philosophy, trading in stocks and shares, designing, building, competing, loving, hating, protecting, taking revenge . . . the list is already long enough) is interpretable as an expression of this drive. In philosophy, as befits the most complex ruminative thought, this drive for preservation may at times look splendid, appearing in the guises of reason or passion. Yet, it remains beneath all this a matter of instinct, of drives; a play of concepts flitting across a landscape where 'folly, [and] lack of reasons' dominate.

The economy of the preservation of the species is the universal principle that bestows a sense of meaning (as *meanings*) in the face of a life devoid of any essential meaning. Two things stand out about Nietzsche's formulation of this view. The first is that the evaluative nature of humanity outlined in Section 21 of *The Wanderer and His Shadow* and subsequently developed in *On the Genealogy of Morality* is presented at the outset of *The Gay Science* as being governed by a larger economic logic. The discovery of measurement, weighing, and our species' act of self-baptism as '*Mensch*' in celebration of it now appear as the expression of something that pertains to universality and is a mechanism of survival. Second, through this mechanism human nature is linked inextricably with the demand for meaning, with the requirement that our lives make sense *for us*. The economy of the preservation of the species endows human existence with possibility not least because it allows for the cultivation of the faith that existence in any possible instance is worthwhile, that whoever you may be, whatever you may go through, your life did not amount to nothing, that it was not devoid of any sense, purpose or value. We are creatures that must find sense in our lives if we are to go on affirming life itself.[3]

History, in the light of this, becomes like a parade of new purposes and meanings passing before us. History, in this sense, is also the history of ethics. If we look back we can note that every teacher of morality has offered a justification for being here at all. In turn, the comedy of history is made manifest by the fact that every teaching claiming access to the eternal has been overtaken by another vision of purposes sooner or later:

> There is no denying that *in the long run* every one of these great teachers of a purpose was vanquished by laughter, reason, and nature: the short tragedy always gave way again and returned into the eternal comedy of existence [... but...] human nature has nevertheless been changed by the ever new appearance of these teachers of the purpose of existence: It now has one additional need – the need for the ever new appearance of such teachers and teachings of a 'purpose'. Gradually, man has become a fantastic animal that has to fulfil one more condition of existence than any other animal: man

> *has to* believe, to know, from time to time *why* he exists; his race cannot thrive without a periodic trust in life – without faith in *reason in life*.
>
> (Ibid.)

If we could but stand back and laugh at ourselves, our sense of tragedy would pass away; tragedy itself would pass away as a meaningful genre of expression.[4] But life, for us, *must make sense*. This is the demand humanity brings to bear upon existence. It is the ultimate meaning of the fairy tales that we weave around existence in the attempt to enrich it. Such stories allow us to continue in the firm faith that whatever happens to us, however much we suffer from the arbitrariness of states of affairs, the ill will of others or even from ourselves, the events that go to make up life are ultimately meaningful.

The systems of belief that reassure us, that shore up this sense of human pride, come to be and pass away in the context of the general economy of the preservation of the species. They, as much as the desires for food and raiment, satisfy a fundamental need, a condition of human life: life must be accounted for, there must be a reckoning up of some sort. Moral and metaphysical beliefs are therefore subject to the rule of economy: they have their day; the various purposes of existence wait to be taught, are formulated, communicated and go stale and become devalued. One thing this implies for Nietzsche is that the time may come when the kind of teaching that he favours can have its day, too. He, too, may have his chance to put forward reasons for us to place our trust in life. The time may come when humankind possesses the right ear and sensibility for *Zarathustra*.

3. *Recognition of the economy of human preservation brings with it the demand for a reassessment of values. Nietzsche does not propose an inversion of values, so that what was once deemed 'good' would now be frowned upon, but a re-balancing of them. The So-called 'evil' qualities can be positive, they can rekindle our passion and interest in life and in this way encourage its continuation. The 'evil' people Nietzsche has in mind here are those who challenge accepted norms: Socrates, Buddha, Caesar. Such people preach or perform the virtue of pursuing what is new. They also desire mastery of the world around them. The conception of history that this implies is cyclical. Societies move between long periods of custom and brief, explosive episodes of turmoil and change. The imagery used in his discussion here (of conventions marking out land, ownership, cultivation and the constant need for renewal and re-ploughing)*

> *invokes notions of labour and ownership: a system of production, an economy, forms the template upon which this view is developed. Nietzsche compares his approach to that of utilitarianism. The latter, with its emphasis on pleasure and displeasure, is naive. The general household budget of the affects is not limited in scope to the consideration of such factors.*

Nietzsche's formulation of the view that we are governed by a tremendous overarching economy, and that this economy allows for the affirmation of a diversity of human characteristics in turn allows him to urge a reassessment of the terms according to which qualities are deemed 'good' or 'evil'. What today counts as the normal moral attitude, the view that has normative force, needs not so much to be turned on its head as on its side. It is not a matter of rejecting what now count as good qualities in favour of the so-called 'evil' ones and producing thereby an inverted model of the virtues. The point, rather, is to count *all* human propensities as being situated within the general economy of our preservation, not just some of them. This, however, is perhaps more shocking than the alternative strategy just mentioned since its very inclusiveness blocks the critic from adopting the relatively straightforward path of attacking Nietzsche for overtly favouring only 'bad' things. For Nietzsche, it is a matter of taking what look to be 'evil' propensities and examining the manner in which they no less than the 'good' ones can be reckoned as having positive value within the context of this overarching economy. Thus, he contends that humanity has been impelled forward not by those usually deemed moral beings but by the 'strongest and most evil spirits' (*The Gay Science*, 4). These preservers of the species are like inflammable substances: they always serve to rekindle sleeping passions in humankind and challenge it to respond to life and, in turn, continue living. Who are these people? They are those who by various means have challenged norms. They are those who have overturned the prehistoric preconditions of human existence outlined in both *Daybreak* and the *Genealogy*, that is the dominance of custom and tradition. Wherever we look for them in the past, such people aroused

> the sense of comparison, of contradiction, of the pleasure in what is new, daring, untried; they compelled men to pit opinion against opinion, model against model. Usually by force of arms, by toppling boundary markers, by violating pieties – but also by means of new religions and moralities. In every teacher and preacher of what is *new* we

> encounter the same 'wickedness' that makes conquerors notorious, even if its expression is subtler and it does not immediately set the muscles in motion.
>
> (Ibid.)

It is not merely a matter of making us re-examine what we think is good and what is evil. We need, also, to re-examine *who* might be counted as such. The argumentative Socrates, the contemplative Buddha and the conquering Caesar all count in their different ways as challengers and preservers, spurring humankind to re-engage with existence. All, however differently, provoke a response in others: they give rise to passion and thereby generate the desire for meaning. Equally significant is the contention that teachers of morality are always harbingers of what is *new*. They are, in keeping with Nietzsche's comments in Section 18 of *Daybreak*,[5] from the normative standpoint of their time open to being regarded as *evil* because in preaching the new they stand against tradition and render themselves prey to the ferocity of its adherents should they fail to triumph. One might be tempted to think that Nietzsche here shows himself to be, by his own lights, irredeemably modern in his praise of the new. But what separates the modish character of the modern's worship of the new from the bringing to light of the new that every great teacher of morality performs is the relationship both have to convention. In modernity the fetishism of the new has become a convention, one word for it being 'fashion'. There is nothing risky about such newness, for it is produced in accordance with the demands of industrial mass culture. Such newness is, from the outset, tamed, managed and targeted by the servants of dominant social interests. It is not regarded as an end but as a means of maximising profit. In contrast, the newness that the great teacher of morality brings is shocking, destructive to the status quo and seeks to set itself in place as the dominant guiding force of convention and tradition. The new here is that which wants to be taken as an end, not as a means. It also thereby betrays the desire to possess humanity. Whether conscious of the fact or not, the teacher of a new morality or religion desires to seize hold of the world around them and make it pliant to their vision. The religious and philosophical mind wants conquest no less than a Caesar. Indeed, the results of such teachings are no less concrete than acts of political colonisation. Great teachings redefine social relationships: the boundary stones of old are knocked over, as are the old virtues with them. Hence, for Nietzsche, both the spiritual and the material relations that constitute culture are open to being refashioned by new moral discourses.

History, as the history of the teachings of the purpose of existence, takes on a cyclical aspect. It is a movement from the steadily increasing staleness of relative stability, the carrying on of everyday life under the presumption of one kind of truth, to times of upheaval and loss of faith followed by reinvention and the return to everydayness. 'The good men are in all ages those who dig the old thoughts, digging deep and getting them to bear fruit – the farmers of the spirit. But eventually all land is exploited, and the ploughshare of evil must come again and again' (ibid.). The story of the cycle of values coming and passing away is narrated in terms of possession, property boundaries and the investment of labour. The property delineated by the boundary stones of a culture is worked upon and exhausted. In the wake of such exhaustion the ploughshare comes in the form of a new teaching of the meaning of existence. That such 'evil' teachings and teachers are here transformed by metaphor into agricultural implement and implied labourer bespeaks the economic character Nietzsche takes as underlying human existence. A ploughshare is itself the product of labour and implies labouring on the land, overturning and replenishing the soil for new crops. It is also the archetypal symbol of non-nomadic culture, of the cultivation of land, the fixing of abodes, the establishment of a delineated world and the building of civilisations. In this way, Nietzsche presents us with a vision of a world of diverse cultures constructed on the ground of a grand economy, a universal system of production that constitutes the ground of all systems of production that germinate, thrive and finally die upon it.

Nietzsche contrasts his approach to history and ethics with alternative accounts of morality. In *The Gay Science* his prime target is that 'profoundly erroneous moral doctrine that is celebrated especially in England', that is utilitarianism (Section 4). The utilitarian believes that the moral worth of any action can be evaluated by way of reference to whether it produces the greatest happiness of the greatest number of people (the 'greatest happiness' principle, or 'principle of utility'). What is called 'good' in this view is what has pleasant and, in consequence, beneficial consequences for humankind as a whole. Actions deemed 'bad', on the other hand, are those that have unpleasant and hence harmful consequences. The erroneousness of this view, Nietzsche argues, lies in its ignoring of the fact that many 'unpleasant' things can be deemed to have consequences that preserve the species. The point is that their role with regard to such preservation is 'merely different' (ibid.). Acts of covetousness or colonial aggression may be unpleasant (to put it mildly) if you happen to be on the receiving end of either, but the qualities that such acts express should not be so easily dismissed. Caesar and Napoleon may be monsters, but monstrosity is no less human than saintliness and no less valuable.

The utilitarian ignores the general economy of human existence, which constitutes the ensemble of the so-called 'pleasant' and 'unpleasant' sensations. This ensemble is a totality within which the question of usefulness is not a matter of 'pleasant' or 'unpleasant' qualities but the general economy of human drives. This general economy cannot be grasped in terms of individual actions understood in terms of their more or less immediate consequences. The consequences of any action are far too multifarious to be amenable to this simplistic approach. A note drafted in the last active year of Nietzsche's life both reinforces and clarifies the point:

> The value of an action must be judged according to its consequences – say the Utilitarians: – they measure according to its origins, implying an impossibility, namely, *knowing* these. But one knows the consequences? Five steps away, perhaps. Who can say what an action excites, agitates, arouses against itself? as stimulant? as percussion spark perhaps for an explosive substance? . . . The Utilitarians are naïve . . . . And anyway we must first *know what* usefulness is: and here, too, their gaze reaches only five steps away . . . . They have no concept of the great economy, of the evil that cannot be dispensed with.[6]

The 'great economy' is the totality of human attributes, good or evil. It is, in other words, what we, as a species, are. The naivety of the utilitarian, a naivety that reflects the narrowness of the mechanistic account of the world proffered by some of the modern natural sciences[7] and whose approach is quintessentially 'modern' in the pejorative sense of the word,[8] lies in their ignorance of the essential value of these attributes. These attributes no less than any others define what it means to be human. What is proposed here against the kind of view espoused by consequentialist thought is couched in terms of necessity: what is sometimes deemed 'evil' cannot be done away with or cleansed from the totality of dispositions that make us human. We need to consider the dizzying possibility that 'even the affects of hatred, envy, covetousness, and the lust to rule [function] as conditions of life, as factors which, fundamentally, and essentially, must be present in the general economy of life [*Gesammt-Haushalte des Lebens*] (and must, therefore, be further enhanced if life is to be enhanced) [. . .]' (*Beyond Good an Evil*, 23).[9]

To use the language of morality, 'evil' is necessary to existence. This necessity is, moreover, like the budgetary requirements governing the income and expenses of any household. Human life, in this way, is rendered in terms of the concepts of credit and debit, but here writ large.

4. *The great economy reveals human nature to be a combination of attributes, the arrangement of which, relative to one another, is fluid. Humans are, it follows, open to being fashioned. We are a manifold of affects, some of which can through norms and culture be emphasised at the expense of others. Another way of putting this is to say that our nature is yet to be fixed in place. That is why enhancement (the pursuit of what Nietzsche calls 'higher men') is possible. It is also why we are more prone than any other being to come to grief. Human existence is in this way revealed to be akin to an economic balancing of costs and benefits. To contemplate the rich diversity of human possibility that this economy bestows is to experience a feeling of awe at the sight of all humanity (good or evil). The plethora of possible human types is an indictment of the normative desire to censure humanity in all its dangerous diversity. Although such a censorious attitude is dubious, the paradox is that at the same time all life involves judgement and censure. Our measuring essence means that we cannot escape from the need to evaluate, since this need constitutes a necessary aspect of our existence. We cannot be like nature, in so far as nature does not judge.*

Nietzsche's articulation of the great economy opens up a gulf between the assumed everyday meaning of ethical beliefs and the sense these beliefs are endowed with when taken in their wider context as enabling conditions of human existence. One must not mix up ends and means here. The great teacher of a new ethical system is prone to taking the teaching itself to be the purpose of life, just as the teaching's adherents do. But from the point of view of the larger economy, such teachings are a mere means, an articulation of the economy of drives that must be vented in order for human life to be renewed again and again. There is no easy teleology to be generated from this view, however. Although the grand economy stipulates the terrain of human nature, it at the same time reveals that nature to include not only a diversity of attributes but also openness to being fashioned. The 'evil' drives and the 'good' drives taken together, the equality of value of *both* given due recognition, indicate the reality of a humanity that consists of a multiplicity of inclinations. This is why 'man is the *as yet undetermined animal*' (ibid., 62).

We each of us are an assemblage of drives: a welter of inclinations and wants organised in relation to one another. The implications of this are easy enough to extrapolate: there is no guarantee that things will turn out one way or another for us. Our destiny is not our responsibility. Likewise, the greater the complexity of a person's personality the greater the chances that he or she will suffer for it. That is why 'higher men' are more likely to be the victims of this economy than its beneficiaries. The more refined a person you are the greater your chances of coming to grief against the harsh realities that constitute the conditions of human existence: 'the higher the type of man that a man represents, the greater the improbability that he will turn out *well*. The accidental, the law of absurdity in the whole economy of mankind [*das Gesetz des Unsinns im gesammten Haushalte der Menschheit*], manifests itself most horribly in its destructive effect on the higher men whose complicated conditions of life can only be calculated with great subtlety and difficulty' (ibid.). Nietzsche here conjoins the language of law-like behaviour with chaos. The rule of senselessness may be utterly devoid of rationality, but it is a form of governance nonetheless. In the same way as a household is run according to the requirement that the books be balanced at the end of every month, so the balance that makes human life possible must be struck. It just happens to be the case that the balance characteristic of the economy of human life is one that does not bestow advantages on those endowed with the qualities that typify 'higher' individuals. The conditions of the household management of humankind do not distinguish between 'higher' and 'lower' in this sense. What matters is the *diversity of affects* that make up the canvas of human tendencies, irrespective of the terrible possibilities (in all senses) that mark out the terrain of our existence. Human economy is characterised by a range of universal tendencies that may be observed but are at the same time impossible to master and steer by way of any methodology. Within this economy of human nature, individuals necessarily fall by the way. Failure is the necessary precondition of a few successes. The absurd budget of the universal human household must be balanced. Suffering, in other words, is an inevitable consequence of being human.

Open to suffering, undetermined in our individual natures, yet governed by a universal economy of possibility, humanity is viewed by Nietzsche as embodying possibilities of such rich diversity that contemplation of it is humbling. As he notes, it is common enough to be overwhelmed when contemplating nature, but reflection on humanity, too, should inspire this feeling of unworthiness: 'once or twice, when I have intimately observed all that is human, all its abundance, strength, tenderness, complicatedness, it has seemed to me as though I had to say in all humility: "*man* too is beautiful for the man who reflects on him!" [...]' (*Assorted Opinions and Maxims*, 342). By 'man', Nietzsche adds, he does not mean only the moral man, but each and every one. To contemplate the beauty of humankind is to contemplate something of such richness that even what is taken to be a socially inferior or objectionable kind of person, the so-called 'evil' human being, inspires the feeling of awe. The invocation of the economy of humankind in turn allows the suspension of moral judgement. This means taking a stand even against one's own prejudices concerning what is palatable and what is not. There is a plethora of types of person, a delightful 'wealth of types' (*Twilight of the Idols*, 'Morality as Anti-Nature', 6) and one ought to celebrate this wealth of abundance and encourage it: 'More and more, our eyes have opened to that economy which needs and knows how to utilize all that the holy witlessness of the priest [...] rejects – that economy in the law of life [*Ökonomie im Gesetz des Lebens*] which finds an advantage even in the disgusting species of the prigs, the priests, the virtuous' (ibid.). A compelling hidden logic allows us to make sense of even the people most repulsive to us, of the most dreadful and unsightly manifestations of human behaviour. All kinds of humanity have their uses. Nothing and no one is dispensable.[10]

The economy of human preservation thereby maps onto the world of absolute morality as its nemesis. There is no moral meaning to existence, no universal court of moral arbitration applicable to all the different forms of life. Yet, at the same time, life itself demands judgement. Existence hangs upon this seemingly contradictory condition. It may not, from the point of view of the great economy, be legitimate to demand of humanity that it be such and such a kind of being, that it live according to *one* set of moral precepts, but in order that we may live at all we must judge. We are in our essence measurers (*The Wanderer and His Shadow*, 21) and in the discovery of measurement lies the unveiling of the human essence. Hence, although he rejects the absolutism of Christian moral doctrine, Nietzsche at the same time remains critical of anyone who expresses the desire to escape from evaluating. The Stoics, for instance, may wish to live according to the precepts of nature. But, Nietzsche argues, this is fantasy: 'Imagine a being like nature, wasteful beyond measure, indifferent beyond measure, without purposes and consideration, without mercy and justice, fertile and desolate and uncertain at the same time; imagine indifference itself as a power – how *could* you live according to this indifference? Living – is this not precisely wanting to be other than this nature? Is not living – estimating, preferring, being unjust, being limited, wanting to be different?' (*Beyond Good and Evil*, 9). Life, in short, is judgement; but all judgement is condemned to being partial, incomplete, the expression of a point of view. We are not 'pieces' of nature in the sense that our individual constitutions passively mirror the world of nature. We are, rather, all expressions of the grand, overarching structure of the economy of our species' preservation, which demands judgements, and consequently acts, of all kinds.

5. *The notion of economy pervades all aspects of life. It can be resorted to as a means of understanding the inner life of the soul, which is a system governed by the economical distribution of the drives. The drives themselves are presented by Nietzsche as being akin to economic consumers engaged in a search for sustenance within the household of the soul. The self becomes analogous to a system of production and consumption. It is a socio-economic world in microcosm. The philosopher's psyche is no exception to this rule. Philosophers are defined by the organisation of their spiritual economy. In line with this, Nietzsche uses imagery of wealth and luxury to invoke the philosopher's soul. Likewise, his conception of the development of philosophical language reflects this economy of relations. Language is the passing on of a conceptual and grammatical endowment. The history of language and its grammatical rules is also the history of the spiritual household from which it emerged. These rules can, in turn, be read as reflecting the environmental conditions under which different cultures came into being. Language thereby mirrors the grand economy of the primitive conditions of human life (its normative field of habits and customs). Language is also presented by Nietzsche as a part of the capital accumulation that sums up the legacy of human culture – and which awaits the squandering talent of the artist.*

Nietzsche perceives this economy at work in many aspects of life. It is the hidden logic, the covert structure of relationships, upon which human existence is worked out in things great and small alike. Economy is a central metaphor, but not only a metaphor, for understanding human nature and its conditions of preservation. We are intellectual and spiritual beings only in so far as we are already economically determined beings. The operation of our spiritual life must always accede to the demands of economy since it constitutes a precondition of all spirituality and thought. The passage between cleaving to one set of beliefs and another, for example, sometimes requires intermediate ideas in order to make the transition palatable. This obeys the demands of our spiritual economy (*'geistigen Ökonomie'*) (*Human, All Too Human,* 227). The fact that 'the highest and most cultivated spirits and the classes that pertain to them' are seldom fruitful in the ordinary sense (that they do not tend to be married, have a lower sexuality than normal, etc.) is likewise 'essential to the economy of mankind [*der Ökonomie der Menschheit*]' (*The Wanderer and His Shadow,* 197). Such cultivated spirits, although exceptions and to be prized, are nevertheless often unstable since they have reached 'the outermost point of spiritual evolution'. Their inner life is a world extended beyond the normal boundaries of everyday understanding, consequently their mental world is more perilous and prone to internal disruption. It is not a good idea to hand such propensities down to one's descendants, especially given the chances that such propensities could become increasingly exaggerated. Consequently the economy of humankind ensures that such unfortunate outcomes are unlikely by enforcing a system of checks and balances: the greater the spirituality the lesser the inclination to express sensuality. Those who are summits of humanity are hence disinclined to leave lesser outcrops in their wake.[11]

The economy of human preservation is expressed not merely in the panoply of human dispositions, 'good' or 'evil', but also in the inner life of the soul. For Nietzsche, the soul is like a 'primeval forest' (*Beyond Good and Evil,* 45) that reflects the ancient conditions of humanity's emergence from the world of natural beings.[12] Each one of us, in turn, is an assemblage of drives, and these constitute an inner economy of personal identity. The relation between these drives makes us what we are. One can turn to one of Nietzsche's discussions of the inner life of the mind in *Daybreak* to illustrate this point in more detail. However much self awareness a person may have, he argues here, such knowledge never manages to encompass 'the totality of drives' that constitute his or her identity (*Daybreak,* 119). However spiritual it may be, however much a matter of intellect, the life of the mind is an embodied one. Being a person means being someone endowed with a physical identity; we are collections of biological drives and psychological attributes. Yet, these features remain consistently hidden from us. With regard to our drives, it is more or less impossible to name even the coarsest of these and elucidate 'their number and strength, their ebb and flood'. Above all, the 'laws' governing the 'their *nutriment*' remain invisible to us. Some drives are 'starved', 'stunted', others overfed. We can, on this basis, engage in the thought experiment. Suppose that 'a drive finds itself at the point at which it desires gratification – or exercise of its strength, or discharge of its strength, or the saturation of an emptiness – these are all metaphors –: it then regards every event of the day with a view to seeing how it can employ it for the attainment of its goal [. . .]' (ibid.). Using metaphors, and reminding us of this, Nietzsche personifies the drives: they are like little people, mini desires seeking satisfaction through the experiences offered to them by the self. If no 'food' is available to satisfy its need, a drive vents itself in other ways. Evidence of a frustrated drive can be found in dreams. Dreams are *compensatory* strategies designed to make amends for the absence of the 'food' desired by a drive for its sustenance during our waking hours. In turn, the problem of how the same stimuli can give rise to different dreams is resolved by the fact that from one night to the other a different drive is making its frustrated demands felt. Nietzsche uses this account of the drives to question the assumed priority of consciousness in human life. We may like to think that when awake the capriciousness of interpretation that makes our dream-world so quixotic is lacking. But when conscious no less than when asleep our drives are at work, pursuing their needs, seeking out their nutrition, making their living. There may, it follows, be no difference in kind between the mental states of sleep and wakefulness. Is it not possible, Nietzsche asks, to conclude that consciousness itself may be 'a more or less fantastic commentary on an unknown, perhaps unknowable, but felt text?' (ibid.). The self, an embodied being consisting of conscious and unconscious elements, is envisaged in this section of *Daybreak* as being analogous to a social space populated by crude entities (drives) seeking gratification of their needs. They respond to what is offered in the way of the experiences of the day, experiences that constitute their sustenance, as consumers. They are agents whose unwitting behaviour betrays an economy of relations.

The self is in this way envisaged as being akin to a system of production in miniature. It is an entity that gleans the raw material of experience from its environment and then manufactures 'experiences' out of them that are, in turn, distributed for consumption through networks of nerves to be picked up and fed upon by the drives. We are the creatures of manifold desires, desires that relate to one another on the basis of the supply and demand at work within our psychical household. The self is an economy. The world of unconscious dreams fits together with the world of conscious thought to form this economy. Together, unconscious and conscious elements constitute a totality that ought not to be separated from one another: 'What we experience in dreams [. . .] belongs in the end just as much to the over-all economy of our soul [*Gesammt-Haushalt unsrer Seele*] as anything experienced "actually" [. . .]' (*Beyond Good and Evil*, 193). The soul operates according to the dictates of budgetary requirements. Like any socio-economic order it needs to be viewed as expressing a totality of relations; it is something that cannot be grasped adequately unless it is comprehended as a complete system, a domain whose activities consist of in-goings and out-goings, credits and debits, incurred costs and accompanying compensations.

The philosopher himself or herself is no exception to the rule of economy in the soul of humanity. The difference between the 'philosophical animal' and other types of person lies not in them having a soul that is different in kind from anyone else's, but in the organisation of its dominant characteristics – its economy. The philosopher's soul, Nietzsche notes, is like a sumptuous household stocked with riches; it is a voluptuous economy (ibid., 204) overflowing with nobility and valuable wealth. Like any one else's, the philosopher's soul is an assemblage of drives, a realm of competing, scavenging consumers of feelings and experiences elevated into something admirable. Nietzsche himself is no exception to this rule. In a discussion of pity, his own inner life[13] is presented as an economy closed off from the understanding of others (*The Gay Science*, 338). This, in many ways, encapsulates the problem of pity. We are each of us isolated from one another in the profoundest of senses in that we are as unable to comprehend the suffering of others as they are of understanding ours. The feeling of pity tramples over this sensitivity to the intensely private nature of inner experience, 'it strips away from the suffering of others whatever is distinctly personal'. Likewise, the evaluation of greatness, of being up to the task of offering a critique of society and culture, is rendered by Nietzsche in language that is not merely to do with determination, with acts of *will*, but as a matter of economy.[14]

The proclamation of the philosopher as an expression of the great economy of human existence finds its justification in the most hidden and yet everyday of places. Notable amongst them is language in general and philosophical language in particular. All life is credit and debit; it is a matter of what is passed on with costs and benefits in equal measure. Language, too, is inherited and this inheritance speaks in the most ancient of terms: however arbitrary their appearance may seem to be, philosophical concepts develop in harness with one another. Nietzsche is happy to represent such concepts as being akin to natural kinds in the conditions of their development in that they all 'belong just as much to a system as all the members of the fauna of a continent [. . .]' (*Beyond Good and Evil*, 20). Listened to with the right ear, one sensitive to form and tone, one hears in the ordering of words, the mutation of nouns or the conjugation of verbs the resonant after-effects of an inherited world, of our history. Every language is a system that stipulates relationships between concepts and their use (rules of grammar). Philosophers, in so far as they must be users of concepts, are prone to think by way of these rules like everyone else and are just as prone as everybody else to take them for granted. We do not notice the conditions that guide the path of our thoughts. In this regard, philosophical journeys are 'in fact far less a discovery than a recognition, a remembering, a return and a homecoming to a remote, primordial, and inclusive household of the soul [*Gesammt-Haushalt der Seele*], out of which these concepts grew originally [. . .]' (ibid.). The household in question is, in turn, established by way of physiological value judgements and 'racial conditions'. Language is envisaged as emerging in virtue of the primordial economy that governs the human soul because it is the master of the body. All language speaks in terms of this economy, elucidating, however unconsciously, the relationship between environmental and bodily constraints and cultural milieu. In this way, language is, in all instances, the current summation of a history. One can, in consequence, reject the empiricism of a thinker like Locke as epitomising 'superficiality', for his account of the origins of ideas ignores the larger comprehension of the conditions under which ideas are fashioned and used.

Language reflects the general economy of the primitive conditions of human life outlined in both *Daybreak* and the *Genealogy*. Both texts take communal living conditions as the decisive conditions governing the emergence of humanity from the realm of natural beings. It is out of this communality, Nietzsche notes in *The Gay Science*, that language springs. We are self-conscious beings only to the extent that our ancestors were social creatures driven by the conditions of their existence to enhance their communicative abilities (*The Gay Science*, 354). The need for communication gave rise to an ever-increasing reliance on signs (words), and the use of signs in turn stimulated an intensified consciousness. To this extent, 'the development of language and the development of consciousness [. . .] go hand in hand'. Reason, notably, is to be excluded from this analysis. The origins of reason do not lie in consciousness. The latter is better regarded as the becoming self-conscious of a rationality that is already at play in the governance of life and the body, of a mastering sense of self-hood of which the conscious 'I' is but a feeble expression and after-effect.[15] Nietzsche is often tempted to regard everything that can be linguistically (that is to say, consciously) expressed as signalling a potential diminution of individuality, since what is linguistic must always at some level concern our 'herd nature'. Yet at the same time he notes that our communicative abilities are akin to a storing up. Language feeds into the development of culture and becomes an integral part of the capital accumulation of humanity's potential as something that has been gradually amassed and is now awaiting an inheritor. This inheritance lies in wait for those capable of taking it and using it up, wasting or squandering it. This is a domain of expertise reserved for the so-called 'artists', always '"late born" every one of them in the best sense of the word', and, as aforesaid, essentially tending towards being wasters of what has been stored up for them. Art, in this sense, is an expression of the economic conditions that abide in all culture in the form of language.

6. *Nietzsche's critical analysis of the emergence of Christian morality is also linked to his conception of the great economy. The account of noble and slave morality in the* Genealogy *is articulated in terms of a struggle between competing interests, initially between different types of noble: the chivalric aristocrat and the priest. The priest is inward, spiritual, resentful and, because of political impotence, poisonous. It is their great unconscious achievement that, because of this resentment, they contributed most to the development of the human intellect. Priestly values become identified with slave values because of common cause against the active, aristocratic noble. This initiates the conflict between moralities, which thereby springs from an economically determined field of relations consisting of possessors and possessions. The noble, as possessor, is also endowed with the ability to name and thereby bestow value. They name themselves as embodiments of the 'good' and baptise the slave as the embodiment of what is 'bad'. The slave reacts against this, deeming the noble to be 'evil'. Estimation originates in social division, which also presupposes a division of labour rooted in the unequal distribution of goods. The creditor–debtor relationship that characterises the primitive human community is in this way re-articulated in a formalised ethical language denoting different modes of self-consciousness (noble-active-affirmative; priest/slave-reactive-negative). Modernity dwells in the aftermath of this struggle, which has culminated in priestly victory. Given the negativity and impotence of the priest how is this possible? This question can be reformulated in terms of the ancient problem of impiety. Impiety occurs when the weaker overcomes the stronger (Protagoras's argument about the existence of the gods). It is a problem that occurs when ontological absolutism is asserted. Nietzsche resolves this question by way of the notion of economy. The human race is maintained by the cultivation of average and*

normal beings; such beings have one strength: tenacity, springing from collectivism. Regularised individuals are the least likely to be dangerous to the social body; their existence thereby fosters human preservation. Ironically, 'strong races' are the least fit for answering the requirements of preservation. Strength, when vented, is destructive. The strong human is a being of strong affects, a creature of the passions. Hence, the 'evil' inclinations Nietzsche sees at work in the great economy of human preservation are both necessary, as stimulants to life (in that they provoke the generation of meaning and answer the demand for a sense of purpose that we need in order to have faith in life) but ultimately decimate it. Great ages are, in this sense, always paid for. High cultures, composed of strong human beings who are 'evil', are squanderers of the capital accumulation bequeathed to them by customs and traditions. Normative moral codes, in turn, are taken by Nietzsche to have an instrumental significance. The average person is the precondition of the 'higher'. The latter inherits the accumulated wealth of the former and discharges it in celebratory excess – creativity, culture at its most supreme. Values, in turn, become a means of ensuring such average regularity is achieved – they form the basis of the unconsciously articulated economy of relations that governs human life and makes possible self-overcoming and transformation. Morality, in this sense, is a necessary narrowing of life, a means of simplifying existence (the forms of life) in order to ensure conditions of survival. Merely living, as such conformity requires, does not give sufficient reason to affirm morality as an end. On the contrary, it is only a (unconscious and immoral) means to the unconscious goal of human enhancement. The general economy of life shows itself here as an amoral arrangement masquerading in ethical garb.

Significant as art may be, however, it is Nietzsche's concern with morality that is perhaps most telling with regard to his conception of the grand economy of human nature. As we have seen in *The Gay Science*, this economy is foremost one of preservation: it is what ensures the continuation of the species. We are normative animals, and this fact means any questions concerning our preservation must also be questions that concern the kinds of norms that dominate us – and the kind that ought to. Nietzsche is notorious for his vehement exposures and denunciations of Christian morality, perhaps most tellingly formulated *On the Genealogy of Morality*, *Twilight of the Idols* and the *Antichrist*. In the *Genealogy* he proffers an avowedly historical account, situating the emergence of Christian morality (or 'the morality of pity') in the context of ancient struggles in an attempt to render problematic our common-sense understanding about the origins of the concepts 'good' and 'evil'. In the first essay, the origins of 'good and bad' talk are contrasted with the origins of 'good and evil' talk. Both are articulations of interest. Talk in terms of 'good and bad' evidences an aristocratic form of evaluation. The noble's initial positing of value is one of self-affirmation: 'I (the noble) am good.' Only then, after casting his or her eye around the social milieu, does the noble judge what is to be deemed ignoble or 'bad'. In contrast, the value system that considers the world in terms of 'good and evil' has its origins in the slave's resentment of their master. 'Good and evil' talk emerges only as a distorted variant of the initial noble evaluative postulate. The slave, a victim of noble domination, resents their oppressor and baptises them as 'evil' – the assertion by the slave of themselves as 'good' being only a kind of after-effect of powerful feelings of resentment. These two ancient evaluative ideologies unsurprisingly end up locked in a struggle for domination. This struggle, however, would be nothing if it were not for one specific kind of human being: the priest.

What happens, Nietzsche asks, in a community in which, as tends to happen due to the need to appease the gods and sacrifice to them, priests become dominant and form at least part of the noble class? In such a context it is easy to see how 'contrary valuations could become dangerously internalized and sharpened, precisely in such an aristocracy at an early stage [. . .]' (*On the Genealogy of Morality*, I, 6). The customs of priests are from the beginning, Nietzsche says, 'unhealthy'. By this, he means that their customs involve a turning away from action, that is an antagonistic attitude towards the senses and the body (e.g. 'Brahminism [. . .] the Buddhist yearning for nothingness'). At the same time, 'Priests make *everything* more dangerous [. . .] with some justification one could add that man first became an *interesting animal* on the foundation of this *essentially dangerous* form of human existence, the priest, and that the human soul became *deep* in the higher sense and turned *evil* for the first time [. . .]'. This is important because these two features (depth and evil) constitute the basic conditions of human superiority over animals. However, if the priestly mode of evaluation splits off from the 'chivalric–aristocratic method', it is easy to see how it will turn into its opposite (ibid., 7). A dispute over the spoils of war can give rise to this. In such a situation, a dispute arises between the sheer 'physicality' of the chivalric–aristocratic form and a powerless priesthood. The very fact of their powerlessness means that the priestly caste has to express its power differently. 'Out of this powerlessness, their hate swells into something huge and uncanny to a most intellectual and poisonous level.' Priestly revenge is an intellectual and spiritual act. It is also, as such, constitutive of our fullest potential ('The history of mankind would be far too stupid a thing if it had not the intellect [*Geist*] of the powerless injected into it [. . .]' (ibid.) – a point that will be returned to in Chapter 5). What looks like an ancient *class* dispute between values (between haves and have-nots) is as much a power dispute between competing noble interests.

The noble method of evaluation expresses the sense of power, above all the sense of self-possession, characteristic of a ruling tribe or class (be it chivalric or priestly). This, Nietzsche argues, is made manifest in the act of giving names, for naming is always evaluating. Thus the noble's feeling of power is possibly nothing less than 'the origin of language itself', since their act of naming is an expression of power over someone or something, a taking possession of something by identifying it linguistically (ibid., 3). In this regard, the communal origins of language discussed in *The Gay Science* (354) are at the same time thinkable only in the context of relations of power and social division. Naming, of course, presupposes an array of practical conceptual abilities. Above all, as an expression of evaluation, the uttering of a name is already a measurement of something: it delineates the terrain of the relationship that inheres between the designator and the designated. The central thing to note, however, is that the relationship between baptiser and named as it is expressed here is not a relationship between an abstract consciousness and an environment of passive 'things'. There is no epistemological starting point posited here on the basis of which one might be tempted to construct a systematic account of knowledge. What is identified and evaluated, measured and differentiated, are *other people,* and they are distinguished by virtue of social standing. In other words, the struggle between values that Nietzsche envisages as being played out in the ancient world is an articulation of the prehistoric logic of social differentiation exhibited in the creditor–debtor relationship discussed in *Genealogy* II. The struggle between interests that characterises Nietzsche's account of the development of noble and slave morality rests upon this basic condition of sociality. Without primitive economic differentiation there would be no historically articulated social differentiation between classes and hence no struggle to be gone through. To put the matter slightly differently: to the extent that the most primitive humans were always already exchangers (whether engaged in bartering or buying and selling), social hierarchy is merely one expression of the 'natural' condition of their existence.

If there is one thing that the *Genealogy* is absolutely clear about when it comes to the history of the struggle between evaluative regimes it is that one side of this struggle in particular has come off best. In surveying the historical conflict between noble and slave morality 'we', Nietzsche tells us, must fit our understanding in with the facts of the matter: the 'people' have been victorious (alternatively, you can call them 'slaves', 'rabble' or 'herd') (ibid., 9). All thought, even that of the freethinker, is permeated by this victory. The 'poison' of priestly values has passed 'through the whole body of mankind [and] seems unstoppable'. Who, Nietzsche asks, could be a freethinker without the Church? In any case, opposing the Church is not the same as opposing its poison: 'We loathe the Church, *not* is poison . . . ' The text thereby sets itself in the context of achieved priestly dominance over all matters spiritual and intellectual. It is because of this unsightly matter of fact that Nietzsche is compelled to consider the significance of the priestly attitudes. Given the grand economy of human preservation and given the fact that priests, on his account, epitomise a turning away from life, an incarnate indictment of their own embodiment and hence of the very essence of what it is to exist, how come the priest has won out?[16]

One could phrase the last problem in terms that take us back, via the writings of Jean-Fran François Lyotard,[17] to the thought of Plato. In this sense, the question that Nietzsche poses about priestly dominance in the *Genealogy* is also an ancient problem. This is the problem of impiety. Briefly, impiety is an inversion in an order of discourse that undermines accepted presuppositions made within it concerning the nature of reality. If one takes two opposing arguments, it ought to be the case that the stronger argument wins out over the weaker. The triumph of the weaker argument (when it happens) constitutes a gesture of impiety, since what ought to be the better argument has come off worse. The claim (usually attributed to Protagoras) that it is impossible to know if the gods exist due to lack of time and demonstrable proof and the Homeric depiction of the gods as fallible beings who are deceivers (something which Plato famously castigates in the *Republic*) are instances of such impiety. According to Lyotard, the problem of impiety crops up as soon as any form of ontological absolutism is asserted. The ontological issue turns, for him, on the question of identity, according to which the ontological truth of any sentence (Being) is a moment of revealed self-identity.[18] In the mystical poem of Parmenides, for example, Being speaks from the position of both addressor and referent: what is spoken about speaks and thereby enunciates the unmediated truth about itself. The thinker of Being, as its mere mouthpiece, in this way articulates something that is pure and unmediated, a revelation of the true nature of existence. However, as soon as the sentence is asserted, mediation occurs, since another sentence is needed to link with it in order to testify that the ontological assertion has happened. The authentic voice of Being is thereby rendered the referent of another sentence and subordinated to it. In this way the unity of addressor and referent demanded by the ontological sentence is shattered. What one speaks about and in virtue of (Being) is subverted by an impious act. The true (which is that which is unified, self-identical and the condition of speech) is subverted by speech itself. The weaker (speech) overcomes the stronger (that in virtue of which speech exists, Being).[19] In the case of his concern with the victory of slave morality, Nietzsche has his own concern with impiety, one which turns precisely on the question of how something weak can turn out to be capable of defeating something strong. The context of this victory and defeat is the grand economy, human life itself.

A note written in 1888 makes the point: 'Reflection. – It is nonsensical to assume that this whole victory of values is anti-biological: one must seek to explain it as an interest of life.'[20] Humanity, Nietzsche writes, is in effect *maintained* through a kind of methodology that involves the dominance of an almost overpowering weakness and under-privilege. To put the matter in terms more faithful to the account of the normative nature of social order offered in *Daybreak* and the *Genealogy*, human life seems best preserved by the propagation of average promising animals. Such beings are disinclined to break with the dominant social codes of their time and place. The fostering of their existence is the best strategy for preserving the social stability and leads to a greater chance of future survival. At the same time, such people are not, for Nietzsche, to be lauded for simply being there. Tenacity is a virtue, perhaps, but it is a limited one. The ability to survive is one thing, but what characterises humanity most essentially in terms of its potential is the high cultural achievement of the kind whose demise at the hands of modern commercialism is lamented from the *Untimely Meditations* onwards. The great economy of human preservation is, in this sense, for Nietzsche rendered meaningful as a *means to an end*, that is, the end of human enhancement. The notion of the 'overman' (discussed in the following chapter) represents an attempt by him to confront the issue of such enhancement.[21] The problem is that the fostering of an enhanced type of humanity, that is a more cultured and dangerous one that is not likely to rest content with merely getting by and paying the bills, seems at the same time for Nietzsche to be 'disastrous for the conservation of the species'. Why is this the case? If we examine the history of 'strong races', one thing stands out about them: they have a tendency to mutual self-decimation, a lust for war, power and adventure. They almost literally rub themselves out of existence under the influence of each other. In the simplest terms, 'their existence is expensive'. Their strong affects are destructive, and in their wake there is wastefulness, since the strength that is built up by everyday culture is now no longer capitalised on. Nietzsche concludes that there is always a payment levied for the existence of 'great ages'. Deep weariness and slackness ensue in the aftermath of strong human beings, even the strongest kinds of person are enfeebled by them, made more absurd, weaker than the norm over whom they dominate. *Squandering* races are, it follows short-lived. They lack the durability required for the construction of cultures. As the writer and artist is to language, namely its inheritor and squanderer (*The Gay Science*, 354) so the enhanced kind of human being is to human existence in general. One might, it follows, prefer a longer-lived and more durable ideal of humanity, a humanity that is capable of preserving itself for as long as possible. But durability, for Nietzsche, is *not a measure of value*. One might, he muses, well prefer a briefer but more 'worthy', that is a '*richer* form of existence' to one that is merely stable and enduring. The question is how to address this issue:

> It would remain to be proved that such a richer return of value is itself achieved in the case of the shorter existence, i.e. that man as summation of strength gains a much higher quantum of domination over things, things being what they are . . . We stand before a problem of economy.[22]

The problem of the enhancement of human life through high culture, of the development of humanity into something capable of attaining the 'highest potential power and splendour' affordable to it (*On the Genealogy of Morality*, Preface, 6), is essentially tied to the notion of economy and beckons to be resolved in such terms.

The question of economy as it is articulated here invokes the notions of preservation and squandering, of a kind of capital accumulation and its outpouring in a moment of celebratory excess. What is also implicit is the view that social orders generally and morals in particular are amenable to being grasped in such terms. All values hitherto have, in this view, been selected with an eye cast towards their economic suitability. Societies, whether under the influence of a lawgiver or as a consequence of their dominant instincts, operate in such a way that the ideals they pursue have the function of serving to ensure 'regularity in performance'.[23] Moral codes, in other words, have the role of establishing criteria of selection and cultivation when it comes to dominant modes of behaviour that serve social utility. Questions of happiness are never at stake here. Sometimes rather painful or individually destructive practices are valued in a culture (witness the example Nietzsche gives in *Human, All Too Human* of the young man who burns himself out in the pursuit of 'duty'). The point of ideals is to overcome such feelings of pain by introducing 'value-ideas' such as those of 'right', 'duty', social identification (e.g. nationalism), selflessness and the like: 'That one should like to do disagreeable things – that is the object of ideals.' Questions of what is useful and what is harmful are, it follows, only meaningful when they are situated within the context of the great play of social forces. The provinciality that characterises all morality, with its notions of what is harmful and useful, is in this regard perfectly rational and has its own good sense. Morality is a native social adhesive, 'the necessary perspective of society, which is able to survey only the close and closest in regard of consequences'.[24] But what is also needed is the larger perspective, exhibited by the extra-moral way of thinking that states and politicians employ habitually (and probably thoughtlessly) due to their having to deal with commercial and other unpredictable factors. They 'have to reckon with a much greater complexity of effects'. Within such a calculation moral perspectives simply fade away into insignificance. Imagine, Nietzsche says with a prescience that must resonate in an age of global awareness, the possibility of a 'world economy [*Weltwirtschaft*]' governed by 'such distant perspectives that all its individual demands might seem unjust and arbitrary at the moment'.[25]

7. *Given the instrumental nature of morality as Nietzsche conceives it, it follows that it stands in need of justification in non-moral terms. Nietzsche begins to experiment with the notion of an economic justification of the virtues. Normative constraint and conformity becomes in this way the precondition and means of attaining a high culture of 'strong' human beings capable of affirmation. A notebook entry from 1888 shows this conception of constraint translated into a mechanistic terminology that reflects the realm of modern economic industrial practices and processes. The virtues become 'machine virtues': tools that create the conditions whereby something more valuable than the average human being will be created. The ancient normative structure of habit, custom and tradition becomes reflected in modern industrial social forms. The*

> *very aspects of modernity of which the young Nietzsche is so critical thereby return to haunt his later thinking. The great economy of human existence therefore finds itself open to being situated in relation to the social world from which it is articulated. Social orders, in turn, become understandable for Nietzsche as the local economic organisation of the universal economy of human affects. The affects are thereby rendered elements within a system of distribution determined by our economic essence. Human culture becomes a matter of the unconscious regulation of expenditure of the passions. The storing up of the effects (their economising) envisages humanity as eternal worker creating the conditions of its own self-overcoming. From the most sovereign to the most humble, all human beings are living testimony to this. All are trapped within a universal economy of capital accumulation and expenditure and conceived as expressions of it. Human identity is more a matter of the cultural endowment of the affects that preserve certain forms of life rather than the genetic inheritance of propensities in a struggle for existence. Social structures are structures for cultivation and the need for preservation explains normativity – it also explains the suspicion of the individual who stands outside the norm.*

The implication of this is that there is no truly 'moral' perspective, no unified moral standpoint from which to look down upon and judge reality. The virtues, such as they are, thus stand in need of a new mode of justification. The *Genealogy* in part attempts this justification not only through its analysis of the economic conditions that gave rise to community and culture, but also in its extolling of the independence of the 'sovereign individual', a being attained as the direct consequence of the calculating and violent prehistory of our forebears. The essential feature of sovereign individuality lies in the degree of compulsion and normative control that is required to create such a personality. Out of constraint comes freedom.[26] Nietzsche thereby does not object to the view that what is necessary in the development of humanity, today no less than in past millennia, is its *regularisation*. Only when normative constraints have been imposed is it possible to envisage the flowering of true culture. The question is what form can such regularisation take? A notebook entry from the late 1880s makes the point plainly enough:

> I attempt an *economic* justification of virtue [*eine ökonomische Rechtfertigung der Tugend*].– The task is to make man as useful as possible and to approximate him, as far as possible, to an infal-

> lible machine: to this end he must be equipped with the virtues of a machine (– he must learn to experience the states in which he works as the supremely valuable states [. . .]) [. . .] The first stumbling block is the boredom, the monotony, that all mechanical activity brings with it. To learn to endure this – and not only endure it – to learn to see boredom enveloped in a higher charm: this has hitherto been the task of all higher schooling. This is why the philologist has been the educator *as such*: because his activity provides the model of sublime monotony in action; under his banner the young man learns to 'grind': first prerequisite for future efficiency in the fulfilment of mechanical duties (as civil servant, husband, office slave, newspaper reader, and soldier). Such an existence perhaps requires a philosophical justification and transfiguration more than any other.[27]

The virtues, in other words, receive their *justification* from the notion of economy. The grand economy of human preservation is not merely a complex consisting of relations and drives (some of them 'good' some of them 'evil') that together constitute the basis for our continued survival. No less important is the role within the grand economy played by a cultural conditioning just as compelling in its power as prehistoric communal norms. Such conditioning is viewed here as being implicit in the cultivation of what Nietzsche considers the necessary conditions for the fulfilment of human potential – the rights of labourers of all kinds are not his concern. Virtues, like those into whom they must be inculcated, are mere tools, no more than means for creating the conditions that will facilitate the emergence of something more valuable. Their justification, in short, becomes *instrumental*. The 'machine-virtues' stand in need of cultivation because they are not spontaneous. No one greets the prospect of getting down to the kind of work described here with joy. They must be given other compelling reasons for doing so, their habitual responses to their environment must be formed for them. Such virtues are simply habits, cousins of the prehistoric customs that crystallised into the traditions that shaped our nature in dim and distant eras past. What is interesting is that in their presentation here virtues at the same time reflect the very modernity in which, we have already seen, Nietzsche finds himself immured. Virtues become allied with machines, with the system of mechanical production that characterises industrialised society. The world of scholarship ('philology') no less than that of the factory requires swotting and sweating to be taken as worthy in themselves. This may appear to stand in sharp contradiction to the radical (and probably romantic) form of individualism that one could attribute easily enough to Nietzsche. But, it needs to be recalled that the sovereign individual celebrated in the *Genealogy* is the outcome of the most rigorous compulsion. The enhancement of humanity is not something that involves the cultivation of admirable forms in a politely and kindly managed garden. To use a metaphor Nietzsche himself uses with relish, things that grow, including things that are cultural rather than natural, that require 'manure'.[28] Likewise, the 'making smaller' of humanity must, in Nietzsche's view, be considered for a considerable time to be the only goal any society aspires to. The reduction of human beings in general, their being mastered at the hands of forms of regulation, is a prerequisite of a stable existence. It is, moreover, the means whereby a foundation upon which a 'stronger' kind of human being can stand is laid. Without this foundation, without what is from some points of view lowly and contemptible, there can be no possible flowering of a higher humanity.[29]

Nietzsche thereby finds himself drawn to the conclusion that a humanity defined as 'moral' only in the sense of being habitual, customary, normative is amenable to being considered both in its treatment of the world and itself in the most profoundly *immoral* manner. Morality is a kind of masquerade, a masking of powerful but ultimately amoral forces and interests. That is why 'there are *only* immoral intentions and actions'; and also why all the so-called 'moral ones' need to be both recognised for what they are and allocated their role as *immoral*.[30] Value oppositions (such as good versus evil) in this way become amenable to being conceptualised in terms of relations of force, degrees of power that differentiate differing instincts by situating them within 'temporary orders of rank' that either keep them in check or put them to work. The conclusion again follows: '*Justification* of morality: economic, etc. [. . .]'.[31] The dislocation of morality that Nietzsche performs from *Daybreak* through to the *Genealogy* thus brings with it the embracing of regulation, form and severity as means to fulfilling the highest potential power and splendour proffered by the existence of humankind. The attainment of this potential means putting to work *all of the affects*, that is all of our propensities, whether 'good' or 'evil', as appropriate.

The grand economy of human nature hence transcends moral discourse. All of the affects are useful. In some cases this usefulness may appear direct and simple enough to work out; in others, the opacity of the relation between an affect and its usefulness makes it impossible for anyone to allocate it a firm place within a value sequence.[32] But in all cases there is a mode of evaluation that invokes the larger-scale relationship in that one can reckon things up economically: 'in economic terms [*ökonomisch gemessen*] the forces of nature are one and all good, i.e., useful [. . .]'. That so much dreadful and irrevocable disaster comes from them, too, Nietzsche does not doubt. But he can, in the same breath, assert his own knowledge concerning what the most valuable affects are and thereby affirm the realm of nature. This is not something to be resolved in terms of qualitative distinctions (the distinction between 'good' and 'evil' is, on the face of it at least, such a one) but in quantitative ones that refer to degrees of power. The most valuable affects are the most powerful, and the affects with the greatest degrees of power are the greatest possible sources of strength.

Nietzsche views social order as a matter of the local economic organisation of a universal economy of the affects (human nature). Any society is an arrangement of the affects, a system of distribution whose limits are set by our economic essence; they are economic structures that abide by the larger economy of principles that operate in the preservation of our kind. Such affects are subject to procedures of distribution or curtailment, use or suppression according to cultural needs. Human culture is, in this sense, governed not merely by a great economy but also, in virtue of this, by a grand rationality that operates according to the logic of a capital accumulation (investment) and expenditure of forces/affects. Every society is, in this way, a large-scale storing up of human potential. This is because the mastery of the affects does not imply their eradication. As with the story told in the *Genealogy* concerning the '*internalization* of man', social control and discipline, grinding labour and cramming of all kinds, focus the affects inwards. This focussing has the consequence of constituting both the individual and the social milieu in tandem, creating the conditions whereby some affects are stored up, some encouraged through habituation and some depleted. A type of human being is thereby fashioned. In this sense, all social orders stand as domains of the investment of labour, of the self-labour of humanity, unconsciously fashioning itself as a living kind in a manner akin to the way it has done since time immemorial. How, for Nietzsche, could it be otherwise, given that humanity has always been essentially a labourer, a creature whose world is an outpouring of meaning generated by the most primitive investment in itself through work?[33] Every individual, from the most sovereign to the most humble, stands as a living testament to the economy of costs and benefits that governs human preservation:

> In general, everything is *worth as much as one has paid for it.* This does not hold, to be sure, if one takes the individual in isolation; the great capabilities of the individual are utterly out of proportion to what he himself has done, sacrificed, and suffered for them. But if one considers his family history, one discovers the history of a tremendous storing up and capital accumulation [*Capital-Sammlung*] of strength through all kinds of renunciation, struggle, work and prevailing. It is because the great man has *cost* so much and *not* because he appears as a miracle and gift of heaven and 'chance' that he has become great: 'heredity' is a false concept. One's forebears have paid the price for what one is.[34]

Here, the economic exchange principle that underlies human relations is taken as constituting the possibility of enhanced human achievement. What one gives for something determines its value: the more that is given and the longer the time over which it is given the greater the return. In cultural terms, and in line with the account of the emergence of the individual in the second essay of the *Genealogy*, the greatest return that springs from culture is to be found in the achievements of the individual. An individual may thus be endowed with great abilities, but this endowment is an inheritance. In other words, one cannot make oneself into any kind of person just by simply willing and creating oneself as if out of nothing. It is on the basis of this exchange principle that we can draw a distinction between inheritance and heredity. Human identity is not so much a matter of heredity, of the genetic passing down of specific tendencies and abilities between the generations (the affects), as something that concerns what has been endowed (handed down) by way of the fashioning of the individual through social forces of habituation, custom and tradition that transform the affects by constituting them as social functions. The policing of the individual, it follows, is at least as decisive as his or her 'natural propensities' in making them who they are.

Societies, it follows, are necessarily domains in which an unconscious calculation of the kind of conditions that will perfect a certain kind of person (or, more accurately, persons) is constantly at work. Calculation encapsulates both the essence of human self-understanding (as revealed by our ancestors' self-baptism with the word *manas*) and is an essential principle underlying social order. The domains of practices and customs, the traditions that licence their being followed, all take their place within the economy of social order. The point, to repeat, is *regularisation*, the normativisation of subjectivity with a view to the regulation of individual behaviour. In this way, conditions of social order are enhanced by the containment or re-focussing of the affects. This is also one reason why extreme individuality is a dangerous exception, something that does not fit in well with the smooth organisation of a community. To recall *Daybreak* (Section 18), Nietzsche notes that anyone who challenges the dominant norms of their time must either become a new source of values or they are doomed to being designated as 'evil'. From the point of view of the community, the individual is always a potential danger. That is why any means (especially violent ones) have been resorted from the time of prehistory in order to bring the individual's anti-social inclinations under control. Exceptions to the norm are discouraged by normalisation. The struggle against 'great men' within any society, Nietzsche tells us, is thereby 'justified on economic grounds'.[35] Such beings are, from the standpoint of social utility, dangerous and coincidental, they are like 'thunder storms' in that their presence even is sufficient to cast doubt on what has been slowly built up and established by the labour of civilised society, i.e. adherence to norms. The basic instinct of civilisation is, it follows, to seek out a means whereby such thunderous explosives may be harmlessly discharged or, even better, prevented form originating in the first place. Social structures are economic, it follows, in that they are domains of cultivation in which the resources of the human affects are nurtured or discouraged in order to further the structure itself. The central concern of cultures is the self-preservation characteristic of the economy of the species. All elements within them are, it follows, organised according to this demand. Education, for example, takes its place as a means of social conservation.[36]

8. *Although normative beings, humans are nevertheless at the same time endowed with the ability to transcend their own normative limits. This potential for transcendence springs from the norm itself. Norms create internal contradictions as a side effect of their formation of the individual. The conquering and suppression of the affects is achieved, but temporary. Nietzsche's discussion of the 'aristocratic polis' in* Beyond Good and Evil *demonstrates the manner in which he considers conformity to be a means to individuality. Environmental conditions dictate the polis' value system. The individual is forged within this. Environmental conditions change, the normative constraints lose their power and the individual dares to be different. Culture flowers. The notion of ethical systems as organisations for the capital accumulation of the affects is revealed here at its most stark. The consequences of such flowering are also articulated*

by Nietzsche in a manner that reflects the economy of capital: after boom comes bust, the exception gives way to the return of the mediocre and average. The norm, once it has born fruit, withers only to return with the passing of the fruitful season. The latter becomes the justification of the former, articulated in economic terms. Normative humanity is, in turn, open to being interpreted as a scattering of fragments and parts, shards of an incomplete whole that is only intimated by the exceptional human being that escapes the norm. This incompleteness is reflected in its need to feel that goals exist independently of it.

What fascinates Nietzsche is the manner in which the economic conditions that gave rise to humanity have at the same time endowed it with the potential to be more than merely 'average'. The norm, in other words, is for him the necessary precondition of its transcendence. The 'thrift' which is evidenced through human life, the great reason that underlies fatalism,[37] at the same time creates as an unconscious side effect the kind of accumulation of potential that gives rise to the very thing it seems designed to suppress. All social arrangements are struggles with the affects. In the same way that colonisation and political repression in the distant past gave rise to the inner nature out of which wells up human imagination and creativity, so even now the imposition of norms is like an act of containment that plays with explosive materials. In the short term, the affects are conquered. But their suppression does not automatically entail their dissolution or eradication, it merely means that they are forced into new ways of venting themselves just as they have been since prehistoric times.

Under social constraints a kind of human being arises, a type 'becomes fixed and strong, through the long fight with essentially constant *unfavourable* conditions' (*Beyond Good and Evil*, 262). Take, by way of example, an aristocratic polity, such as Athens or Venice. A polity of this sort is, says Nietzsche, an 'organisation' for cultivating or breeding. The type of being thereby formed is the product of a demand that springs from the need of the community to preserve itself and thrive – the alternative is probable extinction at the hands of neighbours or under environmental duress. The type is rendered, cut straight like a suit of clothes that are manufactured to conform to a design and in this way made 'durable' through 'its very hardness, uniformity, and simplicity of form'. *Conformity* is the byword here. Such a being is a regulated and regularised social and cultural creation. It is endowed a few very strong characteristics, and these are 'fixed beyond the generations'. Thus, cultural inheritance supervenes over genetic heredity. What Nietzsche envisages next in the story of the polity is significant. A turning point in history arrives: the harsh conditions of the life of the polity change and all of a sudden life gets easier. Because of this, 'the old discipline' ceases to have the value it once did, since the usefulness that formed the power of its tradition has evaporated. The terms under which the economy of preservation operates have altered. The very constraints that cultivated the type are suddenly lifted and individuality burgeons forth. This is envisaged in the most naturalised of terms. A tropical forest-like upward growth and soaring ensues, 'a kind of *tropical* tempo in the competition to grow, and a tremendous ruin and self-ruination' in which 'savage egoisms' now unable to take guiding knowledge from the morality that formed them struggle with one another 'for "sun and light"' (ibid.). Their morality may have been outlived, but it was this very morality that made possible such striving by hoarding up tremendous strength, like a bow bent to a frightening degree and waiting release. The disciplining of the type bred in the *polis* now pays off in the form of a kind of being capable of experimental living. Thus, out of the rigours of harsh conformity comes diversity. Likewise, there comes crisis. For the flowering Nietzsche describes (which is the flowering of the culture of Ancient Athens and of the Renaissance) is also a swan song. A fateful coincidence of 'spring and autumn' coalesces and all forms of expression abound, including the most corrupt and destructive. As with all systems in which capital accumulation is pursued, after boom and luxury comes bust and depression. What, Nietzsche asks, 'will the moral philosophers of this age have to preach now?' The answer is they must praise the virtues of the 'mediocre', the average person who now stands as the only kind left able to withstand what will come. '"Become mediocre!" is now the only morality that makes sense [. . .] But this morality is hard to preach: after all it may never admit what it is and what it wants [. . .] it will find it difficult to conceal its irony. –' (ibid.).[38] Cultures are, in this view, modes of hoarding and preservation. Mores serve to make an accumulation of potential possible. They are a means to an end which is realised in their destruction and the springing up of a short-lived, but intense, creative and rich form of life. If the Renaissance proves anything at all it is that 'the empire of the "individual" can only be brief'.[39] This is because the costs of such self-expression are high and cannot be borne for long: 'The squandering is too great; the resources themselves are lacking that can be gathered, capitalised upon, and exhaustion follows. They are times where everything is *spent*, where the strength itself is spent with which one accumulates, capitalises, piles up riches upon riches . . . '[40] Even those who stand in opposition to such cultural movements end up squandering themselves and so become exhausted, written-off and barren. In this way, Nietzsche effectively envisages societies as operating through a dialectical unfolding in which the storing up of affects gives rise to contradictions in the shape of forces which, when their chains are severed, spring forth with a degree of energy that would not otherwise have been possible.

The norm is therefore the means of its own transcendence and the normative structure that gives rise to it a kind of social greenhouse in which energy is stored up that may subsequently be released in the form of an explosion of creativity and culture. 'A culture of exceptions, of attempts, of danger, of nuance – a *hothouse-culture* for the exceptional plants has first a right of existence when strength enough is available so that henceforth squandering itself becomes economical[ly possible].'[41] Prior to that, so long as a culture's main concern has to be the maintenance of the conditions of its preservation, every exception, every going beyond the norm, will appear from the dominant perspective of communally held values to be 'sickly', 'isolated', 'a sort of squandering of strength'. As soon as chance makes the time ripe, however, the flowering of culture may ensue. History, in this way, becomes a cyclical storing up and squandering of cultural energy, a capital accumulation followed by an extreme and almost foolhardy expenditure. But it is the expenditure that justifies the accumulation. It is no good saving and hoarding for its own sake. For Nietzsche, all ordering, controlling, shoring up and accumulating (in short, all the daily, average, everydayness which makes up the lives of most of us) lacks reason and justification when viewed on its own terms. The averageness of life, its everyday patterns, joys and tribulations, needs a reason for being here at all. What, for him, is the point of the average, of the norm if it is not something that leads in some manner beyond itself? What, to phrase the matter differently but in a better known form, is the point of 'good and bad' or 'good and evil' (normative structures of action) if they are not to be overcome, if it is not possible to consider modes of human existence that are *beyond good and evil*? The lacuna that haunts the average and the everyday is characterised by a lack of universality. Taken as a whole, as the great mass and norm, there is no such thing as an overarching purpose for humanity's having been here at all: 'mankind as a whole has *no* goal' (*Human, All Too Human*, 33).[42] One thing that defines the indifferent mediocrity of the 'typical' person is his or her very lack of an understanding of this. The average has a tendency to see in itself the meaning and purpose of things.[43] By the same token, such a person does not understand as necessary 'the reverse side of things'.[44] By this, Nietzsche means that the average person recoils in the face of the great economy. When faced with evils, the usual attitude is to struggle against them as if they were inconvenient and unnecessary obstacles to the smooth, and above all painless, passage of existence. The point for Nietzsche is that every development and *growth* of humankind is marked by a necessary degree of pain: for every benefit there is a corresponding cost.

The kind of humanity that most embodies the opposed and conflicting character of human existence would be, for Nietzsche, 'its glory and sole justification', but the average person is incapable of such a terrible embodiment of contradictions. For the average person, in a manner that fittingly reflects the primitive conditions under which humankind was constituted in the image of a regularised promiser, life must be as managed and regulated as they are. In this regard, most of us are condemned to being mere fragments, parts of an invisible whole that would be the sum of all of the human affects. The 'ordinary' human being is akin to a little corner or cranny of the larger totality that is our species' 'natural character' – 'one has to add them up for a complete man to appear'. The same goes for entire eras or even peoples. This fragmentary feature of human existence may, however, be a matter of necessity. It belongs perhaps

> to the economy of human evolution [*Ökonomie der Menschen-Entwicklung*] that man should evolve piece by piece. But that should not make one forget for a moment that the real issue is the production of the synthetic man; that [...] the tremendous majority are merely preludes and rehearsals out of whose medley the whole man appears here and there, the milestone man who indicates how far humanity has advanced so far.[45]

Considered 'en masse' people are little more than individuated instances of types. Their uniformity testifies amply enough to their lack of uniqueness. In line with this Nietzsche constructs a telling overview of existence: it is a realm where the 'overall aspect' is of 'a vast experimental workshop, where a few succeed scattered through all the ages, and unspoken complete failures; where all order, logic, connection, obligation are lacking...'.[46] Humanity's lack of a goal bespeaks it lack of a genuine identity, the random instance of success indicting the uncountable failures. Humankind's being situated at the same time within an immense depersonalised and naturalised system of production bespeaks the economic as being inextricably entwined with its essence. We are all creations of the vast economy of our kind's preservation.

We are all, in this regard, subject to the rule of its caprice. Like the forces that govern the financial districts of a world economy and those living in them, the parts operate with a relative autonomy that is in an uncanny and unconscious harmony. Parts are manufactured, assembled, distributed and consumed. This much constitutes a necessary precondition of the economy of any system of production. But what parts, when and how many of them are questions determined by contingent factors that no one can predict with certainty. All that is known is that much of what is similar is and will be made. Much is created and much is consumed, while unutterable amounts of energy wasted and squandered in the pursuit of regularity.[47] Then, if and when enough surplus energy has been stored something truly individual happens.

9. *Nietzsche's use of the notion of economy in this way betrays a deep ambivalence in his thought. His opposition to the world dominated by commercialism that he lives in, its invasion into the spheres of thought and scholarship, is a consistent feature of his thinking. Yet, at the same time, as we have seen, his own thinking is invaded by the language of economy to such a degree that it becomes constitutive of his philosophy as such. By way of example, the framing of the question of the psychology of 'the good human being' in* Ecce Homo *renders such a person as being susceptible to an economic evaluation, to being grasped in terms of costs and benefits. This is also the case in the Preface to the* Genealogy. *Culture becomes a matter of the evaluation according to a logic that he himself spurns. This contradiction can be read as something fruitful. Industrial society may become the normative means to the production of exceptional human beings. Its mechanical nature may become the most efficient means of inculcating the social regulation needed to cultivate exceptions to the rule. The horror of mechanised life expressed in the earlier works (e.g.* Human, All Too Human) *gives way to the celebration of the possibilities offered within the 'culture-complex' of modern life.*

This kind of presentation testifies to a deep ambivalence with Nietzsche's work concerning the very economy he perceives as underlying human development. Culture and economy are so intimately tied together as to be unthinkable without the other. Yet the economic conditions of the preservation of human life become translated easily enough into the economic conditions of production that characterise the modernity which Nietzsche rails against from the time of the *Untimely Meditations*. Towards the end of his active life, Nietzsche says of his second *Meditation* (on history) that it

> brings to light what is dangerous and gnaws at and poisons life in our kind of traffic with science and scholarship [*Wissenschaft*] – how life is made sick by this dehumanized and mechanical grinding of gears, the 'impersonality' of the laborer, the false economy of the 'division of labour'. The aim is lost, genuine culture – and the means, the modern traffic with science, *barbarized.*
>
> (*Ecce Homo*, 'The Untimely Ones', 1)

The risky, life-gnawing and poisoning sort of scholarship-business that reflects the division of labour in contemporary society may be brought to light here. However, at the same time, Nietzsche can never separate himself entirely from this world and its language of evaluation. Thus, when he considers 'the psychology of the good human being' with a view to establishing its value he frames the possibility of the resolution of such a question in the following way:

> To estimate what a type of man is worth, one must calculate the price paid for his preservation – one must know the conditions of his existence. The condition of the existence of the good is a *lie* [. . .] To consider distress of all kinds as an objection, as something that must be abolished, is the *niaiserie par excellence* and, on a large scale, a veritable disaster in its consequences, a nemesis of stupidity – almost as stupid as would be the desire to abolish bad weather – say, from pity for poor people. In the great economy of the whole [*In der grossen Ökonomie des Ganzen*], the terrible aspects of reality (in affects, in desires, in the will to power) are to an incalculable degree more necessary than that form of petty happiness which people call 'goodness'.
>
> (Ibid., 'Why I am a Destiny', 4)

It is worth bearing in mind here something that has already been quoted: 'I attempt an *economic* justification of virtue'.[48] In the *Genealogy*, too, the 'good man' of Christian virtue is rendered an object of criticism through the invocation of a language of costs and benefits. What, Nietzsche asks, if as a result of this ideal being pursued 'the present *lived at the expense of the future*?' (*On the Genealogy of Morality*, Preface, 6). Likewise, here in *Ecce Homo* the virtues are rendered as being susceptible to economic assessment. They and the bearer of such virtues are constituted and held to account by the great economy of preservation that makes us what we are. A person's 'worth' is worked out by reckoning up what his preservation *costs* are in the face of the great economy of 'good' and 'evil' affects that make up the panoply of human nature. Such a checking of figures is implicit in the economic model that Nietzsche here effectively presupposes as being adequate for the assessment of a person's value.[49] But it is also characteristic of the very attitude that he himself notes with approval to be lambasted in the second of his *Untimely Meditations*. Nietzsche himself has made *culture* a matter of the mere reckoning up of figures, of something that he avowedly despises. His desire to promulgate a rank-ordering of humanity, to promote an assessment of our virtues in terms of our affects and their enhancement for creative purposes drives him to resort to a language of quantification that the impetus of much of his thought nevertheless states itself to be inexorably against.

Nietzsche's ambivalent use of economic language and concepts is rooted in his view that fruitful contradiction is an inherent constituent of economy. We have already seen this view expressed in his discussion of the aristocratic *polis* (*Beyond Good and Evil*, 262). Likewise, in his notebooks, he muses over the possibility that increasingly economical consumption of people and humanity coupled with an ever-more solid entwining of the ' "machinery" of interests and services' will of itself yield a 'counter movement'. He can now designate this counter-movement as '*the secretion of a luxury surplus of mankind*: it aims to bring to light a stronger species, a higher type that arises and preserves itself under different conditions from those of the average man. My concept, my metaphor for this type is, as one knows, the word "overman" '.[50] The precondition of the emergence of this luxury product is nothing less than the 'inevitable' total control of the earth enabled through the possession of its common commercial and industrial administration.[51] In such a world and in the service and conformity to this 'vast mechanism', average humanity will find its best sense, its greatest chance of discovering something like a meaning for its own existence. It is against such a backdrop that human greatness might flower:

> In opposition to this dwarfing and adaptation of man to a specialized utility, a reverse movement is needed – the production of a synthetic, summarizing, justifying man for whose existence this transformation of mankind into a machine is a precondition, as a base on which he can invent his *higher form of being*. He needs the opposition of the masses, of the "levelled", a feeling of distance from them! he stands on them, he lives off them. This higher form of aristocracy is that of the future. – Morally speaking, this overall machinery, this

> solidarity of all gears, represents a maximum in the exploitation of man; but it presupposes those on whose account this exploitation has a meaning. Otherwise it would be nothing but an overall diminution [...] a regressive phenomenon in the grand style. It is clear, what I combat is economic optimism [*der ökonomische Optimusmus*]: as if increasing expenditure of everybody must necessarily involve the increasing welfare of everybody. The opposite seems to me to be the case: *expenditure of everybody amounts to a collective loss*: man is *diminished* – so no one knows what *aim* this tremendous process has served. An aim? a new aim? – *that* is what humanity needs.[52]

The notebooks thus exhibit the workings of a profound shift in Nietzsche's thought. The social and economic dimensions of life that concerned him so deeply in the *Human, All Too Human* books and *Daybreak* are, from the time of *The Gay Science,* increasingly undermined by an ever more instrumental and naturalised conception of socio-economic relations. What is presented in *Human, All Too Human* as the horror of modern production, with its diminishing of human dignity and dwindling cultural returns, here becomes a mere (albeit painful and unpleasant to behold) means of establishing the conditions for the higher humanity celebrated in the form of the 'overman'. Nietzsche's desire to endow humanity with a purpose and thereby with an identity generated from a common pursuit settles on a vocabulary that fuses the account he offers of the primitive economic origins of humankind with modern industrial systems of production. The notebooks reveal a name for the domain of interest stipulated by this fusion: the 'culture-complex'.[53] This is a domain in which modes of social differentiation and identification (marriage, property, language, tradition, tribe, family, people, state) are taken as 'continuums' of low and high orders. These orders are governed by an economy that operates according to the logic of balancing the advantages gained by using organised labour against the expenses incurred by its maintenance.[54] In other words, Nietzsche is here beginning to consider societies as complexes consisting of hierarchical networks that exist independently relative to one another but are governed by a common economic logic. The great economy of human preservation thus finds its analogue in the envisioning of a grand economic system of production with the potential to give rise to a humanity capable of the kind of excellence Nietzsche so values when he contemplates ancient Athens or Renaissance Venice. Out of economic regulation comes sovereign individuality and thereby the justification for human prehistory and history alike. That said, the great economy announced at the outset of *The Gay Science* no more finds its fullest flowering in these notebook entries any more than its implications are exhausted by the rather unsettling implications these ruminations may have. Nor is it confined in its impact to the explorations of the second essay of the *Genealogy*. As Nietzsche himself says, it is in the form of the overman that we find his conception of the 'luxury surplus of mankind' most forcefully expressed. Let us take the hint, therefore, and turn in the next chapter to a consideration of *Thus Spoke Zarathustra*.

4
Zarathustra and the Economy of the Overman

> But tell me, my brothers, if humanity still lacks a goal – is humanity itself not still lacking too?
>
> (*Thus Spoke Zarathustra*, 'Of the Thousand and One Goals')

Laurence Lampert has offered some helpful comments about Nietzsche's *Thus Spoke Zarathustra*. *Zarathustra* is, he argues, 'the only book that affords entry into Nietzsche's essential thought'.[1] In other words, and leaving aside the fact that he had another three productive years left after writing Part IV of *Zarathustra*, the work can be taken as representing the definitive expression of Nietzsche's philosophy.[2] For Lampert, *Zarathustra* is a work whose underlying intention is to clarify both why the kind of teaching concerning human excellence Nietzsche extols is required and what this teaching is. The work, says Lampert, begins by offering the 'provisional presentation of an unfinished teaching' in which Zarathustra develops his idea of the *Übermensch* (the 'overman' or 'superman') and finds disciples who may serve to prepare for this (Part I). It then moves to an exposition of the teaching that will lead to the overman – a teaching which, it turns out, leads to Zarathustra abandoning his disciples (Part II). The teaching is then fulfilled in the announcement of eternal recurrence and will to power in Part III.[3] Part IV of *Zarathustra*, Lampert persuasively argues, 'violates the ending of Part III', which is in fact the genuine conclusion of the text.[4] Part IV, he points out, was not intended for public consumption at the time of writing. Nietzsche tried to retrieve the few copies he had printed for private circulation, but publication nevertheless occurred in the aftermath of his mental collapse. Thus, we have three completed parts plus a fragment. Leaving aside the question of the relation between whole and fragment, on Lampert's reading what we are proffered in

Thus Spoke Zarathustra is a teaching which envisions the highest human potential as residing in our ability to overcome ourselves. This ability leads to the transfiguration of humanity into something greater than it currently is in the form of the overman.

Lampert sees the Nietzsche of *Zarathustra*, the essential Nietzsche, as a kind of prophet promulgating a new vision of the future. Many of Nietzsche's earliest English-speaking audience greeted him in similar terms.[5] Such a view has justification from Zarathustra himself when he says, for example, 'I, too am a soothsayer' (ibid., 4, 'The Cry of Distress'). Moreover, as befits a prophetic voice, Zarathustra's speeches are oriented towards the central question of futurity. As will be seen below, however, rather than expressing visionary or prophetic thought, the teaching that Nietzsche advocates in *Zarathustra* needs to be comprehended in terms of the great economy that constitutes the basic condition of human development. This, in turn, allows for a clarification of precise nature of Nietzsche's vision of the overman.

1. Zarathustra *begins by invoking an image of Zarathustra's spiritual labour. The fruits of this labour need to be distributed. This need is driven by an inner necessity akin to an instinctive drive, the logic of which reflects the conception of 'internalization' later to be developed in the* Genealogy. *Zarathustra first tries to bestow his spiritual riches on the masses. His speech in the marketplace invokes a vision of human enhancement deriving from self-overcoming – a feature of all living beings. The question of what it means to be human is thereby raised. We are, contra Kant, means not ends. This means–ends account is reflected in the* Genealogy's *conception of the subject emerging from normatively designated practices within the prehistoric community. It is humankind's future potential that Zarathustra really loves – the fact that we can be a means to something greater. We must, Zarathustra tells the crowd in the marketplace, sacrifice ourselves to attain the greater goal of the overman. The value of humanity, in other words, can be estimated in terms of its ability to go beyond itself.*

Having reached the age of 40, Zarathustra quits his solitude in the mountains and goes on a journey. The reason for this journey is given by way of a comparison between Zarathustra and a star: 'You great star, what would your happiness be had you not those for whom you shine?' (ibid., I, 'Prologue', 1). The star bestows light upon those below it. This light is a gift that expresses the star's wealth of energy, its abundance of resources. Zarathustra, likewise, has his own light and wealth to bestow. He wishes to make a gift to humanity. It is a gift that testifies to his abundance born of the arduous labour of a lone spirit. Like anyone who has toiled, Zarathustra is tired. His exhaustion, however, does not relate to the spiritual labour he has undergone so much as the burden of carrying the fruits of this labour alone. He is overloaded with what he has managed to collect: 'I am weary of my wisdom, like a bee that has gathered too much honey; I need hands outstretched to receive it.' One is struck in this passage by the naturalised image of the labourer as a bee,[6] which is, after all, a toiler and gatherer whose behaviour is essentially instinctive. The labour that Zarathustra has engaged in, which is a labour of the intellect or spirit, brings riches that only realise their true worth through distribution. Wisdom needs to be shared out. How is it to be shared and with whom?

The nature of Zarathustra's compulsion to distribute his wisdom is revealed soon enough. Zarathustra's gift, he tells another solitary whom he meets on his descent, is an expression of his love for humankind (ibid., 2). Like the bee driven by the hidden force of instinct in its search for pollen, this bestowal is guided by an unconscious inner necessity, by a 'must' that can only be acknowledged and acted upon, not questioned: 'I must *go under* – go down, as is said by man, to whom I want to descend' (ibid., 1). As the worker bee is overburdened by what she has collected, so Zarathustra needs to be relieved of what he has garnered. In this, Zarathustra's compulsion reflects the general tenor of Nietzschean psychology. Drives, desires and feelings lacking means of expression are stored up in the world of the soul until the point arrives when, refashioned into things new and strange by their containment, they engender transfigured modes of expression. Zarathustra's solitude is a means of achieving the inner communion of his spirit. Solitude damns up thought and emotion, directing the internalising tendencies of human nature into increasingly intense levels of self-expression. The point arrives when such forces demand to be released. In Zarathustra's case, this release is achieved through the act of communication. He must give voice to what he knows.

In the first instance Zarathustra finds himself driven to speak to pretty much anyone. In the marketplace of the nearest town he assumes the role of orator to the masses:

> *I teach you the overman.* Man is something that shall be overcome. What have you done to overcome him? All beings so far have created something beyond themselves; and do you want to be the ebb of this great flood and even go back to the beasts rather than overcome man?
>
> (Ibid., 3)

Straight away, this speech invokes a humanity whose nature is envisaged in terms of progression. Human being is defined by way of its ability to pass beyond itself. Zarathustra urges his marketplace audience and thereby his readers to rethink what it means (or perhaps *ought* to mean) to be human. Take, by way of comparison, a thinker like Kant.[7] Kant endorses the view that we are ends not means. For him, humans are capable of being rationally defined. In virtue of such knowledge we can attribute to any person properties that endow him or her with the moral right to be treated as an end and the obligation to treat others in a like manner. Kant's conception of the subject as a nexus of rights and duties is rooted in the extrapolation of universal rational principles. It is rule-based. The rules are transcendental conditions without which the concept of a human subject is, strictly speaking, unthinkable. Nietzsche, always unforgiving when it comes to what he regards as Kant's moralising stance, takes the contrary view. For Nietzsche, we are every one of us not an end in ourselves but a means to something greater. If we think of the second essay of the *Genealogy*, it is clear that there a subject is not defined through the invocation of universal conditions but through the elucidation of practices that emerge out of structures dominated by the economic logic of exchange (creditor and debtor). Means, not ends, define the manner in which the subject is initially constituted by communal practices and is subsequently driven to create an 'inner' self as a consequence of still later political colonisation. The essence of the 'animal man' is to be found in the futurity that springs directly from the primitive violence of communal and colonial life. It is its futurity that makes humanity worthy of admiration. Zarathustra's love of man, in other words, is love of its potential derived from this understanding of its emergence:

> Man is a rope tied between beast and overman – a rope over an abyss [. . .] What is great in man is that he is a bridge and not an end: what can be loved in man is that he is an *overture* and a *going under*. I love those who do not know how to live, except by going under, for they are those who cross over [. . .] I love those [. . .] who sacrifice themselves for the earth, that the earth may some day become the overman's. I love him who lives to know, and who wants to know so that the overman may live some day. And thus he wants to go under. I love him who works and invents to build a house for the overman and to prepare earth, animal, and plant for him [. . .] I love him who justifies future and redeems past generations: for he wants to perish of the present.
>
> (Ibid., 4)

The repetition of the word 'love' in the speech serves to emphasise what Zarathustra holds to be worthy of the highest possible praise. The kind of humanity that Zarathustra loves is exemplified by the capacity for *self-sacrifice*. However, the kind of self-sacrifice spoken of here is not to be confused with the selfless sacrifices that a person can make to his or her fellows – including what would generally be regarded as the ultimate sacrifice of dying for another. Neighbour love is far from Zarathustra's thoughts. What Zarathustra loves about humankind is summed up in the dual images of rope and bridge. It is when considered as a willing *means of crossing over from him or herself* that a person becomes worthy of love. The person who thus 'crosses over' sacrifices themselves, willing their own down-going and with it the down-going of humanity. The 'love of mankind' that motivates Zarathustra is thus from the outset focused on what humanity could be rather than what it is. Likewise, although he is speaking to a crowd it is notable that the focus of Zarathustra's love is already concentrated upon individual action. It is the will of the solitary agent that is appealed to here. Moreover, the agent's will is appealed to not in relation to how their agency relates to others who exist *now* but in so far as what is done concerns a more radical form of future 'Other', a being-beyond-the-human: the overman. *Thus Spoke Zarathustra* cannot be properly comprehended without bearing this in mind: what humanity is worth resides in its ability to will its own demise in the pursuit of something greater. The value of the human, in short, can be set according to what it is the precondition of, and what it can be exchanged for.

2. *Zarathustra's talk of sacrifice invokes the principle of exchange. The exchange here is one of sacrificing what we are now for what our kind could become. By participating in this exchange we render ourselves labourers who serve the fulfilment of a higher purpose. Labour, sacrifice and human futurity are thereby conjoined. Labour is at the same time an instrument that fashions the earth, transforming it into a resource suitable for the overman's use. Zarathustra's vision of human enhancement therefore presupposes an entire world of organised production – an industrial society. The self-sacrificer must act on trust. What is trusted is the exchange principle, which guarantees that the labour bears future fruit. The crowd in the marketplace are uncomprehending. They welcome, in contrast, Zarathustra's nightmare vision of the 'last man' – the self-satisfied conformist who craves normativity as the surest means of safety.*

Zarathustra's love is the love of a specific form of sacrifice. To talk of sacrifice, of course, invokes the most primitive exchange principle.[8] But where the material exchange characteristic of communal social existence involves getting one thing for something else, whether through barter or purchase, the mode of exchange brought to the foreground by Zarathustra is knowingly mythological. Exchange as sacrifice is the trading of something one has for something else through the medium of a mysterious equivalence that comes to fruition only in the promise of what (it is in some manner believed or at least hoped) will be the case. It is not a matter of the merely material exchange of like for like, be it even one commodity for another, or of an exchange that crosses boundaries between heterogeneous but coordinated elements (such as the receiving of money in exchange for time). The sacrificial logic of equivalence that Zarathustra extols here involves sacrificing the present for the future, the current human self for the radical otherness of the overman, what we know of ourselves for what our kind might become. The self is what is at stake here. And the sacrifice urged upon us is one that demands we regard ourselves as, at best, preparatory beings; mere labourers, like the bees of a hive, governed by the larger purpose that at the same time must remain tantalisingly distant and at the limits of our most fanciful imaginings.

It is notable that Zarathustra's speech conjoins the notions of sacrifice and futurity with labour. The kind of person who Zarathustra praises sacrifices himself in a very specific manner: the person Zarathustra loves is the labourer, a willing instrument capable of subordinating their own humanity (and individuality) to the larger task exemplified by the overman. A labourer of this kind is the willing means to an end that transcends them. But as well as this Zarathustra also envisions labour in the form of the work that will fashion the earth into a dwelling place suitable for the overman.[9] The world here is envisaged as a place standing in need of preparation. It is a standing-reserve[10] (consisting of soil, mineral resources, and the uses to which animal and plant may be put) awaiting supra-human exploitation. The world is to be fashioned so that it will be replete with the cultivated resources of nature that this supra-human futurity will need. What should not escape us is the fact that an entire world of organised production is implied here. The world awaits future exploitation, but such exploitation cannot even be so much as imagined if there are not already the conceptual and practical means of exploitation. A world of command, of division of labour that is commanded, of modes of distribution and consumption is presupposed by the invocation of the task of humankind to prepare for the overman. Thus, an incomplete and preparatory humanity enacts itself as labourer within a world governed by an exchange principle beyond which it is not permitted to see but which must be taken on trust as a given. Individual existence, in its own turn, becomes justified by *labour*. Zarathustra's love of humanity thereby reveals itself as the love for anyone who contradicts the dominant tendencies of what he sees as the incomplete and unfulfilled present by acting with a will to a future that in its completeness will justify the whole human past.

The *present*, of course, is what Zarathustra from the outset stands against. The present must be overcome. As with Nietzsche's understanding of himself, Zarathustra, too, is in this sense 'untimely'. This is confirmed in the text by the uncomprehending silence that greets Zarathustra's speech in the marketplace. Responding to this, he tries a different approach and tells the audience of the 'last man'. If the vision of the overman provokes thoughts of the sublime, that of the last man is sure to provoke disgust, for the last human exemplifies lack of futurity. Unable even to feel self-contempt, the last man sees life as a means to comfortable living: '"We have invented happiness," say the last men and they blink [. . .] One stills works, for work is a form of entertainment. But one is careful lest the entertainment be too harrowing. One no longer becomes poor or rich: both require too much exertion' (ibid., 5). The last man exemplifies mass culture. His world is one dominated by the desire to ease the travails of life. It is a world of minimal pain, little effort and small sins, a world dominated by the trite mass entertainment of self-indulgence. In the realm of the last man, human labour has ceased to denote genuine effort. Consequently, the vision that the last man encapsulates leads nowhere. Presented with this, Zarathustra's audience, however, laughs and applauds. For the masses the last man is preferable. They have misunderstood Zarathustra's irony and thereby show themselves to be unworthy of the teaching he has to offer. Clearly, Zarathustra concludes, he has no message for a mass audience. Individual disciples must be sought to receive his teaching (ibid., 9).

3. *Zarathustra's turning away from the masses is reflected in a shift in emphasis in his subsequent speeches. They are increasingly addressed towards the individual and towards questions of self-exploration. The three metamorphoses of the spirit occur in this context. They analyse the progression of the spirit from asceticism, to attaining the ability to question even the most sacred of values (the overturning of faith in norms) to realising a state of creative freedom and innocence. This progression mirrors a form of spiritual investment and the reaping of its benefits. The spirit moves from being a labourer (camel-like, a best of burden) to a coloniser and possessor (lion) to a state of innocent self-possession*

> *(child), a spirit that is capable of willing itself and winning its own world. The creative spirit is a world-maker, a self-coloniser. Autonomy as it is presented here is sublimated colonial consciousness. This conception is reflected in Nietzsche's monological aesthetic (developed in* The Gay Science*). Creating involves an essential forgetting in its amorality and innocence. Nietzsche's formulation of this in the three metamorphoses harmonises concepts of forgetfulness and possession, which is cleansed thereby into self-possession (cleansed because as 'spiritual' self-possession the concept of ownership is shorn of its historical and social meaning).*

Zarathustra's turning away from the masses is followed in the text by his discourses, or 'Speeches'. These take up the rest of Part I of the work. The discourses cover an array of concerns: there is an initial account of the life of the self-overcoming spirit, there are criticisms of theology and the state, discussions of marriage and femininity, analyses of the nature of value and meaning. All elucidate aspects of Zarathustra's teaching. Many, moreover, cleave to the logic of exchange that governs both past human development and its future potential as Zarathustra has already outlined it in the speech just discussed. They also display a shift in emphasis from the approach of the speech in the marketplace. That speech urges the masses to forget themselves, to become workers concentrated on the task of achieving the conditions that may make the overman a reality by forgetting their individuality. Turning his back on the masses, Zarathustra now addresses a very different audience and, reflecting this, his emphasis shifts to the cultivation of individuality. The journey to the overman is now, at the same time, a journey that involves exploring the self and its fate.

'Of the Three Metamorphoses' (*Zarathustra*, I) presents its readers with a parable telling of 'how the spirit becomes a camel; and the camel, a lion; and the lion, finally, a child'. What is first presupposed in this parable is a person who has already attained a specific level of intellectual or spiritual development. This is the spirit 'that would bear much', a person of reverential disposition. Such a being is like a camel in so far as he or she is compelled by an inner drive to seek out spiritual burdens. The central characteristic of such a being is an overwhelming desire to carry spiritual/intellectual burdens. This desire becomes realised concretely: desire becomes ability. Intellectually transformed, the camel-like spirit continually seeks to act in a manner apparently contrary to its best interests.[11] In simpler terms, a spirit who has become a beast of burden has begun to live an intellectual life centred on the principles of reverence and self-denial. In contrast to the last man, who seeks above all comfort and freedom from trauma, the weight-bearing spirit scorns mental and bodily ease. The camel, in other words, is symbolic of asceticism. Only when the spirit has first been an ascetic, Zarathustra is saying, can the journey he wishes to embark upon begin.

Asceticism of this unrelenting kind leads to loneliness – hence, the camel wanders laden into the 'loneliest desert' of its own making. The spirit thereby attains solitude and it is in such a condition that it now becomes capable of an act of self-overcoming. To attain the right to understand the teaching Zarathustra wishes to communicate it is a necessary but not sufficient condition for the spirit to be fashioned by the discipline of self-denial. Having fled into solitude, the spirit needs to become capable of challenging and destroying even the cherished belief in self-denial that took it to its inner desert of loneliness. The reason for this is that the spiritual journey Zarathustra is describing has individual autonomy as its goal. What is celebrated here, in other words, is the desire for freedom. The spirit metamorphoses into a 'lion' because freedom (at least as Nietzsche understands it here) and reverence do not mix. Where the camel signifies schooling in discipline, asceticism and self-abnegation in the face of something perceived to be greater than individual self-interest, the lion stands for self-assertion, the elevation of self-interest to a guiding principle. The lion's essential characteristic is summed up in the phrase 'I will.' In the guise of a camel the spirit submits to the discipline of moral imperatives and thereby is both fashioned by and comes to an intimate understanding of the words 'thou shalt' (personified in the text as a dragon). Morality tells us, 'All value has been long created, and I am all created value.' Against this, the lion-like stage of the spirit challenges the negation of the will that morality requires. As in a medieval romance, the dragon must be slain. Such an assertion of will, however, is no mere negation of asceticism. Only because it has been trained in the discipline of denial can the spirit turn on its own most cherished beliefs and subject them to ruthless questioning: 'He once loved "thou shalt" as most sacred: now he must find illusion and caprice even in the most sacred, that freedom from his love may become his prey [. . .]'. The assertive willing of the lion-like aspect of the spirit is, it follows, a variant and extension of the ascetic drive to deny. Questioning doubt is a form of denial. In an act of doubt, all that has been taken as sacred by the spirit in a state of reverence is rendered suspect. Morality is found wanting, as are the theological beliefs that support it. Values are thereby spirited away by the desire to take hold of 'the right to new values'. Ultimate negation destroys the sacred and in doing so prepares the way for affirmation and creativity. Creativity, as

Nietzsche esteems it, is a beginning afresh and requires innocence. The spirit metamorphoses into a child: 'The child is innocence and forgetting, a new beginning, a game, a self-propelled wheel, a first movement, a sacred "Yes" [. . .] [T]he spirit now wills its own will, and he who had been lost to the world now conquers his own world.'

The metaphorical metamorphoses of the spirit exemplify an intellectual journey whose destination is the embracing of a creative aesthetic of freedom. At the same time, in each of its metamorphoses the spirit exchanges one thing for something else: one characteristic is swapped for another complementary characteristic. The first stage itself epitomises a kind of spiritual investment. The camel is a labourer – ultimately the bearer of intellectual goods into the desert of scepticism. Through asceticism the spirit learns the value of veneration. In turn, veneration imparts the value of willing, for without revered beliefs to kick against there can be no possibility of autonomous willing. Only when once obedient thought is let loose on what it hitherto esteemed can the soul reap the benefits of asserting and willing. Thus, what the camel invested the lion can exploit, annul and simultaneously preserve in the unbridled pursuit of possession and mastery. As lion, the spirit 'would conquer his freedom and be master in his own desert'. Where the spirit was camel-like it was once colonised by what it revered. Now, as a lion, it becomes the coloniser. Driven by the instinct to dominate, the lion-like stage of the spirit exemplifies the ruthless self-assertion needed for the possibility of freedom. Only with the innocence of the final child-like stage, however, is that freedom realised. In seeking freedom the spirit destroys values. But life for humanity is not possible without values of some kind. The spirit, therefore, must forget how it got to where it is and in doing so reinvent itself. As it exchanged its weight-bearing visage for territorial instincts, so it must now exchange the rampant, colonising visage of the lion for the open fascination expressed by a child's face. The freedom won by the lion is now a space of creative possibility. The innocence of the child-like, the sacred 'Yes' of affirmation that follows the profane 'No' of the lion's reviling of the sacred, is characterised by Nietzsche as pure self-possession. In a moment of hermetically sealed self-identity when the need to search for exterior causes and effects evaporates like an empty question, it is asserted that the spirit 'wills his own will'. In the child-like stage of spiritual development the self now realises its potential through a clean break with the past. Separation prefaces the conjoining of thought and act. The spirit may have been broken off from the world by its lion-like aggression, but in exchange for this final transformation it also wins its 'own world'. The spiritual life reaches its goal in self-creation. Like the artist, the child now is a world-maker. The child is also the *possessor* of its world. Its self-assertion is the unselfconscious affirmation of a possessive individualism. The life of the spirit is envisaged as having its greatest expression in the security of a homeland of its own making.

Innocence, it follows, is the purest form of self-possession. Just as its will is the product of self-assertion, so its world is the outcome of an internalised self-colonisation. In the guise of the child the spirit returns to itself *as itself most purely*: the spirit is now uncontaminated by memory and responsibility (the camel), nor by the negation and sacrilege that prepared the way for its innocence (the lion). The metamorphoses are guided by the goal that the image of the child represents. 'Autonomy' here signifies a sublimated form of colonised consciousness, the same consciousness whose emergence from primitive communalism is charted in the *Genealogy*. Here, though, consciousness returns to itself as something complete: it and its world are essentially indistinguishable. 'Affirmation' and creation, it follows, are strictly unthinkable without the innocence of forgetting.

This forgetting exemplifies Nietzsche's creative aesthetic. It is, to speak in terms outlined in Section 367 of *The Gay Science*, a *monological* aesthetic. A dialogical aesthetic presupposes an audience, a shared realm for the creative act. An audience is a second and third and fourth party: it is diverse, yet pertains to a collective dynamic that cannot be mastered by a simple act of assertion. Others, when they are there, are always prone to question and even resist one's acts of assertion. *The Gay Science* draws the distinction between the monologial and the dialogical starkly and informatively enough. There are, he says, two kinds of creating that relate to 'All thought, poetry, painting, compositions, even buildings and sculptures.' The first kind is monological and involves a work unfolding according to an inner necessity for which the gaze of the viewer is irrelevant. The second is dialogical. Dialogical creation takes place in the presence of 'witnesses'. The witnesses can be real or imaginary (thus the religious person remains locked in a relationship with their God). What is central to this distinction is the inner *orientation* of the creative act, its trajectory. Creativity, in other words, is defined for Nietzsche by the *attitude* adopted by the thinker, poet, writer, painter, sculptor or designer from the moment of the work's inception. It is defined in this way because, Nietzsche argues, what is at stake in the work is the selfhood of the artist: when an artist 'looks at his work in progress' he looks 'at "himself" '. The work (be it a thought, poem, sculpture, painting or building) and the creator are one and the same: there is no distinction between the doer and the deed. Creation, whatever its mode, is always a kind of self-creation. For this reason the attitude of the creator designates whether creation occurs in the freedom of genuine solitude or under the gaze of a moderator and judge. Monological thought pertains to a freedom that dialogical thought cannot begin to attain. This is because all monological creation 'is based *on forgetting*; it is the music of forgetting'. The innocence, solitude and freedom of forgetfulness are essential to what Nietzsche would consider to be authentic creativity.

The child in the metamorphoses of the spirit, we have already seen, exemplifies such characteristics. Yet these alone do not encapsulate Nietzsche's conception of the creative act. Forgetting, which to recall the *Genealogy* is no passive 'letting-go' but an active repression of memory, at the same time involves the retention of the things attained in a world of possession and property, only shorn of their historical and social significance. Nietzsche here takes forgetting and harmonises it and its attributes with the cleansed notion of ownership. Solitude, freedom, repression of memory and self-possession are conjoined. Their association is rendered indelible. The journey of the spirit through its various incarnations leads to an affirmation of possession in its apparently purest of forms. The image of a colonised and cultivated desert transformed by the spirit's journey to creativity shows Nietzsche conceiving of the inner life of the soul in a manner akin to socially constituted relationships based upon the very principles of ownership that are dominant in the world he inhabits. No less than the colonised spaces of the natural world, which become codified as territories, so the soul has its form of territorial possession gained at the price of a painful exchange whose memory is erased by forgetfulness. Once forgetting has occurred, the world now willed and thereby owned becomes a terrain open to free exploration, a realm that can be passed through, returned to, cultivated, fashioned, refashioned and played in like a well-loved garden (a piece of territory) filled with unexplored and surprising nooks and crannies.

4. *The spirit remains a vague notion unless conceived in terms of embodiment. The 'afterworldly' believers denigrate body and earth. Their reality is not monological but dialogical. The belief in afterworlds is rooted in the concept of exchange. Present misery is compensated for by the promise of eternal bliss. Beliefs of this kind betray physical exhaustion. The afterworldly person's compensatory benefits are paid for by the acceptance of what is false as true. The exchange value of beliefs means that you reap what you sow. You can spend your belief unwisely, squander it on false-*

hoods or you can be thrifty and keep faith with the earth and the world of experience. The spirit utters the desire for metaphysical compensation but is not the source of this desire. The source is the embodied self. Through belief in the metaphysical world the 'I' seeks to escape from the condition of its suffering embodiment. Even as it raves against it this condition is acknowledged. The body is a hierarchy. Its nature cannot be comprehended through the mere analysis of consciousness (the 'I' of Cartesian philosophy). Its embodiment is best comprehended in terms of its being an assemblage of heterogeneous elements and their co-ordination. The self's essence is found in its activity. Its activity is summed up by the notion of command. The 'I' is the slave of its commander, a mere part of a larger community, but it believes itself to be the master of this community. The self is, it follows, a kind of synthetic unity, but not one that can be articulated in terms of the model of consciousness. Its unity resides in unity of action. Nietzsche does not, however, seek to denigrate consciousness. His view is that we have misunderstood it and in consequence imprisoned ourselves in metaphysical illusions. Properly understood, the self is an economically articulated structure of relations. It is the object of a mode of production: culture.

The three metamorphoses of the spirit may tell us about the creative potential that Nietzsche here urges us to accept as the goal of the human soul. However, the nature of the self that persists throughout these spiritual transformations remains vague if we are left with no more than this parable. For Nietzsche, spirit cannot be spoken of without also speaking of the body. Hence, Zarathustra's parable of the metamorphoses of the spirit is followed almost immediately by an attack on those who proclaim metaphysical belief in an afterlife that is combined with an account of the embodied self (*Zarathustra*, I, 'On the Afterworldly'). The 'afterworldly' mentality criticised by Zarathustra can be contrasted directly with the affirmative attitude denoted by the metaphorical metamorphoses of the spirit. Believers in afterworlds see the world of experience as an illusion, says Zarathustra.[12] They cannot think of reality in a genuine way. For them, living always involves a witness: God looks on as the ultimate beholder of the events he has instigated. The believer's reality is dialogical since for them solitude is impossible. Afterworldly beliefs are powerful for very specific reasons: it was 'suffering and incapacity that created all afterworlds'. Through the believer, suffering speaks as metaphysics and in doing so takes on a spiritual aspect.

Afterworlds are the product of an exchange. They gain their distinctive power by virtue of the fact that suffering *here and now* is compensated for by an imaginary future cleansed of discomfort. For Zarathustra, the body that has wearied of itself is responsible for leading us to metaphysics. The believer is cajoled into metaphysical faith by physical exhaustion: 'a poor ignorant weariness [...] created all gods and afterworlds [...] it was the body that despaired of the body [...] it was the body that despaired of the earth and heard the belly of being speak to it'. The bodily exhaustion of the sufferer forces them to seek metaphysical comfort to counter what they cannot endure otherwise. Zarathustra here invokes a framework of compensatory satisfaction wherein the sufferer gains solace at the cost of accepting false beliefs. For Zarathustra, integrity of belief is a kind of currency. Beliefs have an exchange value, and you get what you pay for. You can spend your belief unwisely, just as you can exchange your money for narcotics or burgers in search of the short-lived comforts they afford. Or, like a person who has made themselves sick of sweetmeats to the point where they are sick of themselves, you can learn to be thrifty with your beliefs and cultivate good spiritual health. It is 'the healthy body' that 'speaks of the meaning of the earth', says Zarathustra. In other words, being a sceptic and unwilling to accede to any form of faith too easily is a sign of being well turned out and bespeaks the kind of sense that makes life worthwhile.

Afterworlds have their origins in us, but are themselves 'inhuman' and sterile. That the desire for metaphysical consolation comes not from disembodied spirit but has its origins in the body points to something important concerning the nature of spirit itself. The 'I' is the source of the *articulation* of metaphysical, compensatory thought. However, the linguistically codified utterer who says 'I' is not the motivating force and wellspring of belief. The 'I' enunciates, but what speaks through the 'I' is something other and greater. This entity that so speaks is the self, an entity that is at the same time the body:

> Indeed, this ego [*Ich*] and the ego's contradiction and confusion still speak most honestly of its being – this creating, willing, valuing ego, which is the measure and value of things [...] speaks of the body and still wants the body, even when it poetizes and raves and flutters with broken wings.
>
> (Ibid.)

When the 'I' speaks, it necessarily acknowledges its embodiment. Those with other-worldly yearnings seek to deny the reality of their embodiment, but they are driven to assert its reality even in order to hold what they do. Other-worldly 'realities' are fanciful projections instituted within the subterranean realm of bodily demands. They are wish-fulfilments that depend for their possibility upon the insurmountable primacy of the body.[13] The body is a complex totality and an ordered hierarchy (*Zarathustra*, I, 'Of the Despisers of the Body'). Although we are usually tempted to think of the mind as the highest expression of complexity and abstraction, for Nietzsche the body is greater than our greatest imaginings of complexity. It is 'a great reason, a plurality with one sense, a war and peace, a herd and a shepherd' (ibid.). Thus, the body combines the socially and hierarchically distinct roles of ruler and ruled in the shape of a greater (and predominantly instrumental) rationality. The diminutive reason of mind is a mere 'instrument' of this superior rationality.

The self is not a collection of mental attributes that can be encountered and classified by the kind of self-conscious introspection characteristic of Cartesian philosophy. The self is a multiplicity, an assemblage of heterogeneous elements that are summarised by the word 'body'. At the same time, this contention does not make Nietzsche a classical empiricist. The body is not to be reduced to a collection of sensory impressions any more than it can be reduced to the mode of abstract self-consciousness called 'mind' or 'intellect'. The empiricist thinks of the self as a passive receptor of bodily sense impressions, but Nietzsche thinks of the relationship between *cogito*, body and self in a rather different way:

> 'I', you say, and are proud of the word. But greater is that in which you do not wish to have faith – your body and its great reason: that does not say 'I', but does 'I'. What the sense feels, what the spirit knows, never has its end in itself [. . .] Instruments and toys are sense and spirit: behind them still lies the self. The self also seeks with the eyes of the senses; it also listens with the ears of the spirit. Always the self listens and seeks: it compares, overpowers, conquers, destroys. It controls, and it is in control of the ego [*Ich*] too. Behind your thoughts and feelings [. . .] there stands a mighty ruler, an unknown sage – whose name is self. In your body he dwells; he is your body. There is more reason in your body than in your best wisdom [. . .] Your self laughs at your ego and its bold leaps. 'What are these leaps and flights of thought to me?' it says to itself. 'A detour to my end. I am the leading string of the ego and the prompter of its concepts'.
>
> (Ibid.)

The self is a 'body'. Its embodiment, in other words, is something without which it could not be what it is. Yet, at the same time, one cannot define the self in the same manner as is appropriate when one indicates something that is a mere 'body at hand', such as when one refers to a stone, a pen or a table. The self is an entity and because of this it must be embodied, but the notion of embodiment alone does not capture it satisfactorily. Bodies are of different kinds. They can be akin to stones, pens or tables. Entities such as these have things happen to them – they are the victims of accident or will: the stone just sits where it happens to have ended up; the pen lies where it has been forgotten; the table is sat at without a thought. But the self is an entity in a sense that is different from this. The self is a doer. Its essence is its activity, not mere existence. This activity, moreover, is characterised by relationships of power that make the entity what it is. The 'I' that thinks (the consciousness of which we are so proud) is an abstraction and puppet of the greater reason of the self.

The self hovers over the 'I' like an arch-surveyor – its watching and listening denoting the superiority that accompanies command. Without this greater self and the relations of power it embodies there would be no 'I', for the 'I' exists to satisfy the demands of the self. The self is a provider of aims and maker of reasons, the senses and the mind tools and playthings subordinated to its commandments. The 'I', in short, is a kind of slave, the self the master that determines what the slave shall endure or enjoy. For the 'I' the self is not an object of everyday awareness. Zarathustra's characterisation of the self as simultaneously unknown and wise succinctly expresses its power over the 'I'. It is a 'mighty ruler' that is all the more resplendent because of its invisibility – just as the God of the Old Testament has power of such divinity that prohibits His being looked upon or represented. This invisibility of the self at the same time denotes a structure. We can think of this in terms of the façade of a building. Just as the building's façade conceals its structure, so the 'I' taken at face value conceals the relations of hierarchy that constitute the self. The self is a structure of which the 'I' is but one component. How, though, are we to articulate this structure?

Part of the answer to this last question is to be grasped in terms of the consciousness that characterises the 'I'. Consciousness is situated by Zarathustra's speech in the context of a hierarchy. The 'I' is akin to the member of a community who does not realise that they are subject to the rule of a superior force when they follow conventions. The 'I' is like a fool unaware of the laughter being had at his expense behind his back. Consciousness wishes to fly in thought, but the experience of thought as freedom is a flight of fancy. The 'I' cannot escape from the conditions and environment necessary to its continued existence, however much it entertains fantasies of doing so. The self is an embodiment of power. The relationship between intellect and self is in this way always already a political and social structure, albeit in microcosm. The 'I' is a form of subjected subject, one who experiences, thinks and deliberates only in so far as these activities are the result of the unperceived promptings of its ruler. Zarathustra portrays the subjection of the 'I' to the ruling self starkly enough. When told by the body to feel pain the 'I' does so 'and thinks how it might suffer no more – and that is why it is *made* to think'. Likewise the feeling of joy betrays the same relationship: when the 'I' celebrates it does so only at the prompting of its despotic monarch. Suffering, celebration: neither of these are, for Nietzsche, spontaneous acts of consciousness. The spontaneity of conscious thought, which can be taken as symbolic of its freedom, is here rendered an illusion. At heart the self is an unconscious despot dictating to the 'I' what feelings and beliefs it may have. That the body makes demands and calls upon our little argumentative reasons to sanctify its big reasons is true spontaneity: 'I' with its diminutive reason must trail in the wake of its commandant. It is on the basis of this view that Zarathustra can then turn to those who despise the body and argue that their contempt for it evidences a kind of self 'that wants to die and turn away from life'. What speaks through the afterworldsmen's contempt for the worldly is the self-loathing of their bodies.

Five features emerge from Zarathustra's discussion of the self when he challenges those who despise the body. First, the self is embodied and unthinkable without embodiment. Second, it is always superior to consciousness. Third, it is characterised in terms of relations of power. Fourth, the self is a kind of unity, although at this juncture we are not told what kind. Certainly, its unity is not the sort of conceptual unity that words like 'stone', 'pen' or 'table' denote. The unity is in fact linked to the fifth characteristic: notions of activity and creativity sum up the self. It is this creative and productive feature which, for Nietzsche, accounts for the origins of intellect and all else that accompanies it: 'The creative body created the spirit as a hand for its will.' In spite of appearances, however, the point of Zarathustra's teaching is not to denigrate the 'I'. Consciousness may be, strictly speaking, a derivative phenomenon, yet Nietzsche esteems and venerates consciousness. That we suffer and are conscious of this suffering, that our suffering drives us to create meaning, is what makes us remarkable. The problem for Nietzsche is not that the 'I' is the helpless victim of a despotic ruler and that freedom will only be secured by liberation from this ruler. The problem is that in thinking of consciousness as independent and superior, as the 'other' of the embodied self, we have imprisoned ourselves in metaphysical illusions just as despotic as any absolute ruler. The self is a hierarchy of relations, a social order in miniature, a system of production and consumption – in short, an economy of relations. The miraculous nature of the 'I' is only properly grasped in the aftermath of this insight and such understanding is itself liberation for Nietzsche. The 'I', in short, has a history. It emerges from the activity of a body shaped (often violently) by procedures of valuation – procedures that operate on the basis of the fundamental exchange structure that characterises the primitive economy consisting of custom, tradition, creditor and debtor out of which human beings emerge.[14] In slightly blunter terms, one can say that the 'I' is the object of a specific mode of production called 'human culture'. It is a commodity, the value of which rises or falls accordingly with increased or decreased investment in its future. The greater the investment, the greater the future return on that investment.

Although Zarathustra's attack on those who despise the body initiates the sustained account of the self that Nietzsche provides in the text, Zarathustra's comments at this stage leave us with questions that need to be answered. If the self is not simply the 'I', then commonly held conceptions of personal identity ought not to be invoked to characterise it. The self is not 'I' or 'You', but what gives rise to these notions. It is creative, but its creativity is not of the kind associated with the conscious willing of a reflective mind. It is to Zarathustra's discussion of values that one must turn to begin to understand Nietzsche's articulation of the self and the economy that leads down the road to the overman.

5. *Values are needed for us to live. Different cultures assert themselves by embracing different values. Their source does not reside in the self but in normativity. The self emerges from this normativity. The 'I' is the most recent of human creations to be esteemed. Esteeming itself points to our measuring essence. The assertion of the 'I' springs from the great rationality of the self, an organised structure of command, as an extension of the demands of that structure. Thus, the 'You' preceded the 'I' as its precondition. That is why saying 'I' has always been tainted by the twinge of bad conscience. Nietzsche's aim is to allow the affirmation of the 'I' in pure innocence. Values, it follows, are a necessary precondition of there being selves. They are also an expression of the human desire for mastery over its environment. Assertion of values is an assertion of principles of measurement and economy.*

Valuation is a necessary condition of human existence: 'No people could live without first esteeming [. . .]' (*Zarathustra*, I, 'On the Thousand and One Goals'). We simply could not be here if we did not live according to the terms signified by values. This does not mean that our values are the straightforward 'causes' of our beliefs, however. There is, says Zarathustra, 'no greater power on earth' than what is summarised by the words 'good' and 'evil'. But the power of these words springs from a peculiar causal necessity. Living means evaluating, but even more than this it means esteeming things that are different from what others esteem. The causal necessity underlying the esteeming of values is one that springs from the external relations between peoples and cultures. Crudely, living means being different: if a nation wants to conserve itself it 'must not esteem as [. . . its . . .] neighbor esteems'. To value the same things as someone else is to be like them. Even worse, perhaps, it means to be colonised by them. Different societies have different customs and different conceptions of good and evil because every social order is driven to differentiate itself in order *not* to be swallowed up by those nearby. A community needs to evaluate, but it is equally necessary that the community esteems different things from those valued by its distant neighbours on the other side of the mountain range or deep down in the distant valley. Your distant neighbours are different from you and from those close to you. This difference maintains the identity of the neighbour no less than your community's own. Values cultivate and preserve both you and your neighbour as similar and yet different from one another. This simultaneous similarity and difference means that values must be understood as expressions of both the vicissitudes of human relationships and what these relationships are based upon. The meaning that values have thus resides in us, nowhere else. They are expressions of a creative need intrinsic to human life – a need analysed within Nietzsche's conception of the 'great economy' in *The Gay Science* (Section 1 – and discussed in Chapter 3 of this book). Values are necessary for peoples to be peoples, a condition of the shared cultural identity that defines nationhood. As peoples, we are united in our ability to make and esteem values but separated by what we happen to esteem.

If the source of values is humanity, it is by the same token the case that this source need not be understood in terms of the selfhood that defines the 'I'. For Nietzsche, since values are normative they cannot have their origin in the individual: it is the other way round. In order for the 'I' to exist, values and the conventions that embodied them as concrete practices were first needed. Individuated consciousness is the creation of the collective mode of human association that takes the form of the most primitive human community. The individual's origins lie in the generation of meaningfulness on the part of peoples and communities, and of the manifold events that have overrun them. Values have a human face and a human sense:

> Verily, men gave themselves all their good and evil. Verily, they did not take it, they did not find it, nor did it come to them as a voice from heaven. Only man placed values in things to preserve himself – he alone created a meaning for things, a human meaning. Therefore he calls himself 'man', which means: the esteemer. To esteem is to create [. . .] Esteeming itself is of all esteemed things the most estimable treasure. Through esteeming alone is there value: and without esteeming, the nut of existence would be hollow [. . .] First, peoples were creators; and only in later times, individuals. Verily, the individual himself is still the most recent creation.
>
> (Ibid.)

What comes out starkly in Zarathustra's comments here is the newness of the 'I'. To call oneself 'Man' is to baptise oneself as a creator and bestower of values. As with *The Wander and His Shadow* and the *Genealogy* to be human is to be a measurer, that is a creature endowed with economic characteristics. But 'creation' and 'bestowal' here do not signify personal acts. They are the products of an unconscious, automatic and impersonal mode of behaviour characteristic of the species. The 'I' arises out of this only after primitive communities have already first existed and developed. The 'I' arises as a consequence of something internal to the dynamics of communal life. The significance of this should not be underestimated with regard to the question of how we should understand the embodied self that, Zarathustra argues, is concealed behind the conscious 'I', the affirmation of which opens the path to the overman. The embodied creative self, the commander and despot that rules the realm of thought and feeling which the 'I' inhabits, does not denote anything like an individual 'subject', a *cogito*. It is, rather, the manifestation of what must be regarded as a primitive and collective rationality. The self, as Nietzsche thinks of it here, is not a 'person' in the sense that we might usually understand it. It is not a form of self-consciousness that can point to its own body and say 'I!' and thereby define it through an apparent description that resonates with the desire to command. The 'great reason [*Vernunft*]' of the self, the agency lurking behind the 'I', does not inhabit a discrete 'body' to which subjectivity is coincidentally attached, like a pendant dangling around the neck of its wearer. To take this view would be to replicate the essentials of the Cartesian thought, which thinks of the 'I' and the body as being distinct because they are made out of different kinds of 'stuff'.[15] The issue for Nietzsche does not concern kinds of stuff but modes of organisation. The self is a *structure of command* that is first made manifest as an *organised social body* – the community – and only subsequently as an organised, *socialised* and thereby individuated body (the debtor subject of *On the Genealogy of Morality*). The structure characteristic of communal relationships is passed on to the individuated 'I'. The interior world of subjective thought is not merely shaped but actually constituted by this communal structure. This command structure (this hierarchy) is a necessary feature of any entity that can be called a 'person' – the 'I' cannot be thought of without reference to it. The 'I' is not in any sense additional to this structure but is, historically speaking, the extension and development of the organisational demands of that structure.

The greater, embodied self that the 'I' serves is none other than a shared sense of selfhood without which there would be no thinking subject. This shared characteristic that defines human identity emerges, for Nietzsche, in different cultural contexts *irrespective of which culture*. It is the universal pattern of subjectivity that comes from the similar creative propensity characteristic of diverse peoples. All peoples, it follows, are culturally distinct. Their different estimations of what is valuable can be opposed – what one people deem 'good' is regarded by another people as disgraceful (ibid.). But the *valuing* of each people, their active desire to endow the world around them with a moral sense, is possible only in virtue of the impersonal, shared structure of selfhood from which the bestowing of value flows and, in turn, from which flows the subjectivity of the subject. Encountered first only as a social body, the self preserves itself in microcosm as the individual designated by the word 'You'.

The wisdom of the body created the 'I' as its servant and slave out of the necessity imposed upon our human forbears by the demands of communal existence. I have already discussed the issues of community, creditor, debtor and the formation of the 'I' in relation to the *Genealogy*, and there is no need to repeat those points here. It is sufficient to note that much prehistoric development prepared the way for this late invention – with the 'You' preceding the 'I' as its precondition – and that the text of *Zarathustra* draws these same conclusions. Zarathustra tells us: 'The *you* is older than the *I*; the *you* has been pronounced holy, but not yet the *I*: so man crowds toward his neighbor' (*Zarathustra*, I, 'On

Love of the Neighbor'). To put the matter slightly differently, the 'You' already has the benefit of normative respectability. What 'You' designates already has collective agreement and the inestimably powerful authority of age to give it currency: 'delight in the herd is more ancient than the delight in the ego [*Ich*]; and as long as the good conscience is identified with the herd, only the bad conscience says: I' (ibid., 'On the Thousand and One Goals'). The point for Nietzsche is to learn to say and do 'I' in a state of joy untainted by feeling the twinge of bad conscience. Only this will prepare the way for the innocent affirmation of the overman. We are thereby urged to engage in the journey of a spiritual metamorphosis that will result in our abandonment of ourselves in the hope of making an investment in the future.

Values are the precondition of selfhood. They are also inextricably linked, for Nietzsche, to our desire to master our environment through the imparting of meaning. This desire for mastery is always situated in the context of the relationships extant between peoples. The announcement in the text of the inextricable connection between values and will to power stresses the role that such relationships play in establishing values: 'A tablet of the good hangs over every people. Behold, it is the tablet of their overcomings; behold, it is the voice of their will to power [. . .] Whatever makes them rule and triumph and shine, to the awe and envy of their neighbors, that is to them the high, the first, the measure, the meaning of all things' (ibid.). What is esteemed by any nation as denoting the highest, the first and the sense of all things is so esteemed because it separates them from other cultures by articulating their feeling of superiority over these others. The desire for power that is present as a characteristic of all peoples speaks as values. This desire is the evaluative drive, the dominant feature of all living things, Zarathustra will go on to say when announcing the principle of the will to power (cf. *Zarathustra*, II, 'On Self-Overcoming'). But it is to a discourse of economy that *Thus Spoke Zarathustra* turns when it unfurls an account of the nature of values. To this we can turn next.

6. *Value is conjoined by Zarathustra with a special kind of virtue that is apparently far removed from the world of economics and commerce. However, the gift-giving virtue that bestows value is articulated from the outset in terms that refer back to principles of monetary exchange: gold is taken as its paradigm. Gold is esteemed because of its rarity – its scarcity marks its being what it is. This esteeming translates into use-value (money) and the fetishism of the entrepreneur, or into the kind of valuing Zarathustra advocates. Zarathustra wants to celebrate the gift-*

giving virtue as it is epitomised by the person who wishes to become a sacrifice to the earth and the future of humanity. They wish to give themselves, and this is their bestowal. Prior to bestowal, however, acquisition is needed. The person who desires to be a bestower goes to the realm of values and seizes hold of them acquisitively and selfishly. This selfishness is not like that of the spiritually impoverished, who out of resentment wish to take from others what they lack. These Zarathustra indicts on the basis of his account of identity as springing from embodiment. Poverty in body and poverty in spirit are one and the same: resentful desires express a 'diseased body' and a 'degenerate sense'. Zarathustra, in contrast, advocates a sense that is uplifting and celebratory of bodily existence. Its selfishness is not self-seeking but, in its seizing of values, strives to transcend self-interest in the pursuit of something greater than the self as it is currently known. Values are parables of elevation and self-transcendence, expressions of the great reason of the self in its desire to be self-overcoming. They are allegories of the self's journey through history. History, therefore, is not to be understood as a series of events that happen to a body or bodies. It is, rather, the self's temporal unfolding told in the allegorical language of values. Values tell of the self's struggle with its environment and its becoming what it is – stages of becoming being marked by differing value systems coming to be and passing away. The decoding of values as parables of the self's overcoming indicate its future possibility of enhancement. Values are the body's expression of rapture, its creative urge realised as esteeming. The 'I' speaks and rejoices in the body's creativity in rapturous incantations of celebration, affirming the fact of the self's embodiment and its grasping of its world and mastering of it as values. All virtue bespeaks this desire for power and creative self-overcoming. It is realised, through values, as culture. The honest account of this creativity spurns metaphysics and the desire to see the origins of rapture as coming from another (divine) realm. Embodiment is the sense of the self's rapturous inspiration. The creative body demands celebration through recognition.

It is in the last of his speeches in Part I that Zarathustra addresses his disciples on the nature of value (*Zarathustra*, I, 'On the Gift-Giving Virtue', 1). He begins by asking what looks like a relatively straightforward question about origins. It is a question that takes us back to the question of the body and the self as we have already encountered it.

> Tell me: how did gold attain the highest value? Because it is uncommon and useless and gleaming and gentle in its splendor; it

> always gives itself. Only as the image of the highest virtue did gold attain the highest value [...] Uncommon is the highest value and useless; it is gleaming and gentle in its splendor: a gift-giving virtue is the highest virtue.

Zarathustra is here eulogising a very special kind of 'virtue'. This virtue bestows upon others, it is a form of generosity that flows from the bountiful wealth of the giver. Those that receive the products of this virtue do not in any way solicit them. They come to the recipient as a surprise. This virtue is something that is itself beyond all estimation of value as might occur in the world of commerce. As Zarathustra is wont to say elsewhere, he is not (at least apparently) interested in the world of the marketplace: 'Let the shopkeeper rule where all that still glitters is – shopkeepers' gold' (ibid., III, 'On Old and New Tablets', 21). In other words, small-minded, acquisitive people have their domain and are welcome to it, for it is illusory. Yet, in his use of the word 'gold' in introducing us to the gift-giving virtue, Zarathustra nevertheless invokes the very world of commerce he spurns in order to capture the nature of the kind of virtue he endorses. Gold is like the gift-giving virtue in the manner whereby it comes to be highly esteemed. Claiming that gold's value is derivative of the 'highest virtue' because its being so valued reflects rather than exemplifies esteeming does not completely expunge this link once it has been established within the text. The gift-giving virtue is alluded to in the first instance in terms that invoke the realm of monetary exchange, and this invocation makes that realm difficult to ignore (unless one does so wilfully). The underlying reasons for esteeming are common with respect to the grocer and Zarathustra alike. Even if what they esteem is different, the manner and *basis* of their esteeming is shared.

Gold is primarily valued because of its rarity. Gold is, in this sense, a kind of bestowal: we value it because it is what it is, not because of its use-value. This can be true for the grocer whose love of gold approaches fetishism no less than for Zarathustra. In this sense, estimation is a necessary precondition of use (although this need not commit us to the view that estimation must precede use in a temporal sense). We esteem gold for being gold and it thereby gains a use-value that can be translated into commercial terms because this initial evaluation renders such a translation possible. This kind of esteeming, shorn of its commercial resonance, epitomises Zarathustra's initial discussion of the gift-giving virtue. 'Verily, I have found you out, my disciples: you strive, as I do, for the gift-giving virtue.' The person who strives to embody this virtue wishes to become a sacrifice and an offering to the world. They are consumed by the burning desire to *give* rather than take. Such a person wants to be a living gift, and for this reason desires their soul to be a repository where 'riches' can be stored up. A virtue of this kind does not always look particularly virtuous. For one thing, it 'must approach all values as a robber'. It is in this sense *selfish*, yet 'whole and holy I call this selfishness'. In this sense, Zarathustra praises a kind of virtue that could be taken as running contrary to the common understanding of what is virtuous. Normally, it would not be contentious to say, selfishness is held to be a bad thing. Being selfish means being a self-seeking person with little or no regard for the interests of others. Actually, and in spite of his comments about the necessity of our acquisitive and 'evil' instincts making up part of the great economy of human life,[16] Nietzsche has no time for this kind of selfishness either. The selfishness which gazes with 'the eyes of a thief [. . .] at everything splendid', which regards the world around it 'with the greed of hunger' and 'sizes up those who have much to eat', is not praised by Zarathustra but rejected with scorn. This is because there is no giving in this kind of selfishness.

The latter kind of bad selfishness is presented in the text in terms that replicate social divisions: it is the desire of those with little for what is owned by those with much. Nietzsche has no favourable opinion of the have-not's covetous desire for what the wealthy possess. His reasons for this are interesting, for they take us back to the embodied self and thereby demonstrate the essential connection he holds to pertain between selfhood and values. Covetous, selfish desire is not a socially constructed phenomenon for Nietzsche. For him, there is no neutral, a-temporal body of the dispossessed that is subsequently acted upon by socially constituted power relations that happen to take the form of an unequal distribution of wealth. The social agent is not different in kind from what he or she does and hence from the conditions of their embodiment. To put it another way, the self-seeking person's disenfranchisement is not innocent, nor is it an excuse. Being poor in body and poor in spirit amount to the same thing, Zarathustra tells us. The self-seeking person's desire itself bespeaks a 'diseased body' that enacts a 'degenerate sense [*entartende Sinn*]'. Such a degenerate way of thinking wants everything only for itself. The sense that leads Zarathustra and his disciples, in contrast, draws them aloft. It expresses a selfishness that is not a self-seeking but a seeking of self-overcoming: 'Upward goes our way from genus to over-genus.' This attitude does not see the world as a matter of 'Everything for me.' For Zarathustra, 'our sense', our way of thought, 'is a parable of our body, a parable of elevation. Parables of such elevations are the names of the virtues. Thus the body goes through history, becoming and fighting.' Our concepts, in other words, are expressions of our embodiment. Our ideas and values are instances of the 'I' responding to the demands that make up the great reason of the self and thereby articulate our identity. The intellect fulfils its role as the body's puppet – the 'I' responds to the demands made upon it by its ruler, the self.

But values are a very specific kind of expression of embodiment: they are 'parables' of our elevations; that is, they need to be understood *allegorically*. It is worth recalling here that for Nietzsche the body and the self are one and the same. The intellect accompanies the embodied self on its historical journey as the herald and good friend of its travails. History here is effectively defined as the temporal unfolding of the self through a narrative whose key elements are the allegories we call values. Another way of putting this would be to say that history is not some kind of story about what happens to bodies endowed with a biology that exists independently of the story – as if history was simply an account of events that flowed over and around pre-defined entities called 'bodies'. Rather, these events *are* the body's story, its becomings and struggles with itself and its environment. Historical events, for Nietzsche, are the articulations and self-overcomings of the primitive rationality that Zarathustra has already identified as constituting the basis of the self in primitive communal life. History is the story of the body and its great reason; hence it is the narration of the becoming of the self as made manifest through values, which in turn need to be decoded and thereby cleansed of their allegorical aspect. History, in this sense, does not happen *to* the body any more than it happens *to* us. Still less is history a battle of abstract ideas. The body *makes history*: history is a product of the body's activity, an expression of the identity of the active, embodied self voiced in different social forms and thus different systems of evaluation. Values are the coded evidence of this 'great reason' of the self as it journeys onwards. The fact of different values helps justify Zarathustra's claim that the self is a becoming and a fighting since the coming and passing of different moral customs is the *evidence* of this bodily progression. If moral customs were fixed eternally, the body could not progress: history would simply be the passing of events over a fixed self untainted by temporality. But, if this were the case, metaphysics would be right and historical philosophy (which, we have seen, Nietzsche extols from *Human, All Too Human* onwards) would have to be rejected.

To be properly comprehended, the historical progression of the self needs to be decoded: 'All names of good and evil are parables: they do not define, they merely hint.' Values are not definitions. What people value needs to be taken as something akin to a wink or a gesture in the direction of what is really going on in domain of esteeming. To put the matter more bluntly, only an idiot would think it possible to get genuine knowledge *out of* values. There is no such thing as a 'science' of values in this sense. If used as the *source* of our knowledge, morality would create only illusion and ignorance. This is why values must be treated as allegories. When the spirit speaks in the language of values it speaks 'in parables'. But these allegorical musings are themselves indicative of something greater: they point to the self-overcoming that is the special possibility of humankind. They point, in short, to the possibility of human perfectibility (human enhancement) that is essential to Nietzsche's faith in futurity and exemplified by the metaphor of the overman.[17]

The times when our intellect speaks in parables, Zarathustra says to his disciples, indicate moments when the 'body is elevated and resurrected: with its rapture it delights the spirit so that it turns creator and esteemer and lover and benefactor of all things'. This is nothing less than the *origin of our virtues* – the basis upon which gold is esteemed for being what it is, the reason that the diverse virtues of many cultures have been formulated and celebrated by humankind. In all these cases the body dictates to the 'I' that it celebrates. The 'I' responds with joy to the demands of its master. The hierarchy of the self outlined in Part I of *Zarathustra* ('On the Afterworldly') now comes into full play in the text as Zarathustra envisages the intellect driven by the body to murmur incantations in praise of its ruler's rapturous ecstasy at its own embodiment. This celebration is not an arbitrary exercise. It is not irrational and unfounded, for the 'great reason' of the self – the collective rationality that defines the emergence of the animal man – is at play here, working through its own internal logic of exchange.

The origin of virtue is at play in all self-overcoming. When the intellect feels love for its world; when it is overfull with expressive outpourings; when it spurns its own comfort for a greater sense of achievement than mere physical ease can ever provide; when it feels itself irresistibly pressed in one direction and responds to that necessity by calling it freedom: at all of these times the origin of virtue speaks. In order to remain authentic, self-overcoming must nevertheless cleave to the source from which it is nourished: the earth (ibid., II, 'On the Gift-Giving Virtue', 2). The great reason of the self is the distinctly human achievement of culture. But to remain true to itself this great reason must spurn the desire to flee into the illusory metaphysical comfort that comes from bodily torment. The great reason of the body did not have its origins in pure rationality. The debit side of this is that the self's source can give rise to madness and unreason also: 'Not only the reason of millennia, but their madness too, breaks out in us' (ibid.). To resist this, Zarathustra says to his disciples, we must follow the path of our intellect and our virtue when they bid us to embrace the earth and love it. The body is essentially creative; thus, Zarathustra urges those who listen to him to follow the path of creativity. This is the love of man Zarathustra declares at the opening of the text, pure and simple, for in all creation there is futurity. Creativity means letting the intellect speak the rapturous language of celebration that comes from the spontaneous overflowing of the embodied self. In Part III of *Thus Spoke Zarathustra* we are presented with an example of this spontaneous expression of the self. It is to this that I turn next.

7. *Zarathustra now offers his own parable. He has a dream in which the self has spoken to him allegorically. The dream concerns our ability to bestow value. It is presented in terms of the economic language of measurement. As parable, the dream expresses the combination of self and intellect, the body and its 'I' in fruitful conjunction. The great reason speaks. There are no infinite worlds. A world of limitless becoming is, at the same time, one open to the creative estimation of the self. A conceptual schema is imposed upon it and it is thereby rendered something that can be mastered. Valuing, as measuring, determines limits; Zarathustra's wisdom mocks the false infinity of other-worldly transcendence. Number becomes mistress of reality in virtue of greater force as Zarathustra brings his scales to the world, holds them over the open ocean of becoming and weighs and measures. The world and its meaningful limits are delivered over to us in this manner. The world itself is thereby revealed as something amenable to our economic abilities of measuring, comparing, weighing, evaluating and putting to use. Zarathustra then places the three most evil things on his scales. The evil attributes, variants of the evil propensities that are discussed in terms of the economy of human preservation in* The Gay Science, *are shown to be both dangerous and rich in unfulfilled potential. Weighing, the principle of comparison according to the logic of equivalence, reveals this divergent potential. Thus, some may be tortured and controlled by the lust for power, but others can be transfigured by it. It is the same for sex and selfishness. In selfishness, especially, the rich potential of self-celebration, the affirmation of one's own existence as itself 'virtuous' and, in turn, the rendering of the world as meaningful in the light of this is celebrated. The world is thereby revealed as plastic, amenable*

> *to the mastery of will, the old 'evils' capable of recuperation as pure gold. The overman stands as the epitome of this glorious selfishness. He is the luxury surplus of human achievement. In this way, parallels intrude into Zarathustra's vision: the world managed, cultivated and prepared for the overman is, at the same time, a world that is plundered by the efficient organisation of economy and production. The freedom celebrated as self-possession in this way teeters dangerously on the verge of becoming a bogus market-oriented, consumerist world dominated by the illusion of 'free choice'. The redemption of humanity that Zarathustra seeks is therefore compromised.*

In 'On the Three Evils' (ibid., III) Zarathustra offers a parable. He has a dream, he tells us. In other words, his imagination and intellect have communicated with him in allegory. In his dream Zarathustra is standing on some hills looking down on the world about him. He then does something remarkable: 'I stood in the foothills today – beyond the world, held scales, and *weighed* the world [. . .] Measurable by him who has time, weighable by a good weigher, reachable by strong wings, guessable by divine nutcrackers: thus my dream found the world. [. . .]' (ibid., 'On the Three Evils', 1). The content of the speech concerns the ability to estimate, to divine value. Moreover, it is presented in the very terms of measurement (i.e. economic terms) that we have already seen Nietzsche use in Section 21 of *The Wanderer and His Shadow* to characterise something essential about human self-understanding. The point of Zarathustra's vision-like dream is to offer a parable of the estimation of value. The dream demonstrates Zarathustra's great reason communing with his intellect – and it communes in a specific manner. There are, says Zarathustra, no 'infinite worlds' in this dream. The world as estimated in his vision is the world established as *finite*. Recall that this is a world that is, at the same time, one of limitless becoming. Bearing this in mind, one must note that a limitless world rendered finite is a world rendered malleable: in order to be rendered finite it must accede to the constraints of the *conceptual scheme* that imposes the finitude upon it. Such finitude is imposed upon the world in order to master it. The dream confers upon Zarathustra the power to grasp reality by evaluating it through the use of *measurement*. Valuing is about *determining limits*. Valuing is measuring, it invokes the finitude of counting numbers rather than the infinity of number itself, that is of determining positions within an infinite series of becoming, rather than invoking the bogus, other-worldly, non-specific infinities of metaphysical thought. This is why Zarathustra can talk of his 'laughing, wide-awake day-wisdom' as one that 'mocks all "infinite worlds"'. It rejects the idea that infinity is a matter of somewhere else, of a metaphysical beyond on the other side of life. This wisdom then speaks in the most definite terms: 'Wherever there is force, number will become mistress: she has more force.' Measurement, in other words, the economic ability to estimate, is a means of attaining mastery over the world of becoming. It does so without imposing upon it the false infinity of an existence bounded by the absolute concept of being. Rather, it measures, weighs and in doing so determines the limits of the world available to us.

Clearly, then, Zarathustra's wisdom presents him with a 'finite world' capable of being valued by number. Significantly, the beholding itself is in its turn presented in the text as a *grasping*. It is communicated by way of imagery that invokes physical control of the world. The world is offered up to Zarathustra, like a gift that celebrates itself in terms of its openness to someone's use:

> How surely my dream looked upon this finite world, not inquisitively, not acquisitively, not afraid, not begging, as if a full apple offered itself to my hand, a ripe golden apple with cool, soft, velvet skin, thus the world offered itself to me; as if a tree waved to me, broad-branched, strong-willed, bent as a support, even as a footstool for one weary of his way [. . .] as if delicate hands carried a shrine toward me.

The world grasped in this manner is 'a humanly good thing'. It is a world at once inviting and open to human questioning, yet sufficiently challenging and mysterious to provoke such questioning in the first place. Above all, Zarathustra's dream reveals the world as amenable to the economic ability to measure, compare, evaluate and put to use. In spite of the contention that no taint of possessiveness can be found in the attitude conveyed by the dream, Zarathustra's enraptured vision nevertheless affirms by its use of them the view that our economic abilities are the essential precondition of revealing and mastering the world. The world is measured. It is evaluated only because it is something that can be measured according to economic principles of exchange.

This last point is hammered home by what follows immediately in the text. The explicitly stated point of the dream, says Zarathustra, is to 'place the three most evil things on the scales and weigh them humanly well'. In other words, hitherto denigrated human attributes can be examined and assessed by way of the basic economic practice that can be found at work in every marketplace since time immemorial: measuring on a set of scales. The three things to be so measured are sex, lust for power and selfishness. In other words, the so-called 'evil' attributes that Nietzsche includes as essential components within the great economy of human preservation outlined at the beginning of *The Gay Science* here likewise receive their due and praise in economic terms. In order to assess the value of these three attributes Zarathustra says he 'will hold the scales over the rolling sea'. He thus proclaims *his* ability and right to fix values in the face of infinite instability and change. The sea of becoming rages on, but the sea of doubt is stilled, 'the scales are balanced and still'. Now the right can be exercised and the true value of these evils determined.

The image of the scales in this section of *Zarathustra* serves as the paradigm for determining value by weight through equivalence. On the one side of a set of scales the thing to be weighed can be placed, on the other are placed the units of measurement whereby the weight is determined. It is no different in Zarathustra's dream: on the one side of the scales lie 'the three weighty questions' and on the other lie their equivalents in the form of answers. In order to offer his answers Nietzsche invokes the fundamental principles of exchange and equivalence. A discourse is thereby constructed which will give assurance of the actual value of these hitherto denigrated human propensities. According to this discourse of equivalence, in order to be true the answers must be equal to the questions posed. In other words, the truth of what Zarathustra says is asserted by the correspondence (the 'balance', which presupposes the notion of a *standard* whereby such a balance can be struck) between question and answer. What is at stake is the correspondence between propensity and possibility, disposition and potential. The 'evils' that Zarathustra is talking about are actions that have become the objects of (negative) judgement. In themselves, these judgements express nothing; but when it comes to the issue of what kind of humanity we want Nietzsche thinks that such judgements are crucial.

The answers to these questions are straightforward enough, but only on the face of it. *Sex*, Zarathustra tells us, tortures those who despise the self because the positive pleasure it affords confounds their contempt for the body. Likewise, the rabble suffers from its own uncontrollable nature in the face of sex. For those with a positive attitude to their embodiment, however, sexuality is 'the future's exuberant gratitude to the present', likewise 'the happiness that is the great parable of a higher happiness and the highest hope' (ibid., 2). Rightly regarded, sex is an affirmation of the body; its joys indicative of the perfection that an enhanced humanity might aspire to. In its turn, *lust for power* is a torture for those victims unable to overcome its baser aspects. It can be a 'rumbling, grumbling punisher [. . .] the lightening-like question mark beside premature answers'. Like sexuality, the desire for mastery can control us. It can be that 'before whose glances man crawls and ducks and slaves and becomes lower than the snake and swine, until finally the great contempt cries out of him' that demands nothing less than self-destruction. Yet, desire for mastery, too, can be transfiguring. When the lust for power touches 'the pure and lonely', the longing for control is neither sick nor self-destructive. Just as the mountain descends to the valley or the wind rolls from high down to lowland areas, so the longing for power drives the solitary to share his or her wisdom with others. So transfigured, such lust and longing can be dignified with a new (but for readers of *Zarathustra* by now familiar) name: it is the ' "Gift-giving virtue" – thus Zarathustra once named the unnameable!' The virtue that bestows upon others is the advocacy of the selfishness of the 'mighty soul' that has much to give and is thereby driven to share in the same way that Zarathustra himself was driven out of his solitude at the opening of the narrative. Following on from this, the third evil, *selfishness*, is also not what common wisdom holds it to be. As soon as the selfishness in question is not the petty self-seeking behaviour characteristic of mass culture but is the great-souled selfishness of the solitary creator, its significance alters. The evil becomes transfigured into a good. The lone creator Nietzsche extols exemplifies an existence that belongs to 'the high body, beautiful, triumphant, refreshing, around which everything becomes a mirror'. Such a body, such a *self*, celebrates its own existence through the spontaneous overflowing of rude health: 'The self-enjoyment of such bodies and souls calls itself: "Virtue". ' Thus, the 'blessed' selfishness of the supreme soul creates its own virtue as the by-product of its self-celebration. The world about it becomes mirror-like because it is rendered *meaningful* by the expression of the creative spirit's rejoicing: it mirrors celebration (pathetic fallacy).

Subjected to Zarathustra's dream of revaluation, the world reveals itself as essentially plastic: as capable of being modified according to our will. The world is in this way shaped and endowed with sense by the gift-giving virtue. This, for Nietzsche, encapsulates the endowment of life with *sense*. The scales of comparison Zarathustra wields are tipped in favour of the three evils because it is they and they alone that foster what the gift-giving virtue promises. The so-called 'evils' allow us to venerate the 'I' in a manner that accords with its true potential. In line with his conception of the great economy, Nietzsche thereby urges us to embrace a transformation of what we regard to be good and evil. That he holds the 'I' to be 'wholesome and holy, and selfishness blessed' is what marks

Zarathustra as the prophet of this transformation. Affirming the 'I' in this way affirms the great reason of the self. Such affirmation does not praise the abstracted and emptied selfhood that praises just consciousness. Rather, what is praised is the embodied great reason of our kind in the shape of its fullest potential. In this way, the journey from animal to human animal is rendered a prelude to the greater journey that entails the overman.

The overman stands as the metaphorical representation of the most gloriously selfish creator-spirit. We should perhaps recall here a section from *The Will to Power* cited in Chapter 3. Here, Nietzsche holds that the more economically structured human life becomes the more inevitable it is that a 'counter movement' emerges. This movement is the 'luxury surplus of mankind' which is summed up by the metaphor that is presented with the word 'overman'.[18] The more integrated and uniform modern humanity becomes in the service of this grand system of economic administration, the more we each of us are rendered helpless cogs in its machinery, the greater the need for a humanity that will come and justify existence for us. Economic subordination, the mastery of human and environmental resources alike, is in other words the precondition of the overman's emergence. The economic estimation of gift-giving on the scales in Zarathustra's dream of virtue finds its precondition in a corresponding social reality consisting of the efficient organisation of the factory floor in harmony with the road network and labour supplies, the maximisation of yields and a world of supply, demand and above all *surplus*. The overman thereby becomes a metaphor for the pursuit of self-possession in a world dominated by production and consumption, a world in which economic forces create social divisions of such a kind that, in reaction to them, a level of autonomy hitherto undreamed may be attained. The communality of shared values gives way to the marketplace of 'free' individual choice. The overman's freedom, in this sense, teeters on the brink of becoming akin to the bogus choices afforded to consumers as a proclamation of their individual freedom within a modern mass market. Self-discovery, in this way, is rendered in terms of the possession of *one's own values* as a form of distinctive property.

> He [. . .] has discovered himself who says, 'This is *my* good and evil'; with that he has reduced to silence the mole and dwarf who say, 'Good for all, evil for all' [. . .] 'This is *my* way; where is yours?' – thus

> I answered those who asked me 'the way'. For *the* way – that does not exist.
>
> (*Zarathustra*, III, 'On the Spirit of Gravity', 2).

Humanity must be gone through in order to attain the overman. For Nietzsche, there is no other path: only a fool would believe that humanity might be 'skipped over' (ibid., 'On Old and New Tablets', 4). It is only by following the potential endowed to us in the form of our economic nature as primitive exchangers that it is possible to redeem humanity and make sense of its suffering at the hands of the self-imposition of culture. The parts must be made into a whole. All about us that is 'fragment and riddle and dreadful accident' needs to be assembled into something unified by way of enabling future humanity to realise its greatest potential (ibid., 3). In this way, the future lies in wait as something that may be *laboured upon* so that the past may receive its justification and redemption: 'To redeem what is past in man and to re-create all "it was" until the will says, "Thus I willed it! Thus shall I will it – this I called redemption and this alone I taught them to call redemption' (ibid.). Such redemption does not come cheap, as those who want things for free (the 'rabble') would like (ibid., 5). This very desire is their injustice, the wrong they perpetrate upon reality. *Even life*, Zarathustra says, should not be regarded as a matter of something for nothing. Life is only meaningful when it is understood as a matter of costs and returns on investments. That is why noble souls, who understand such things, 'do not want to have anything for nothing; least of all, life' (ibid.). Those who are of 'the mob', in contrast, desire 'to live for nothing [. . .]'. Life, in this way, becomes a giant exchange mechanism that is justified by those capable of paying up front. Even as the 'procreators and cultivators and sowers of the future' capable of redeeming humankind are in search of a new nobility, one immune from the taint of 'shopkeepers' gold' (ibid., 12), they are still bound by the same laws that bind it and have done since the time of the most primitive human communities where individuals first met and recognised one another by way of the creditor–debtor relationship. Zarathustra may seek a mode of exchange beyond the confines of the market and the realm of commodities, but the estimation and evaluation upon which this vision rests depends upon the economic modes of exchange and equivalence for its very formulation (cf. *Zarathustra*, III, 'On the Three Evils'). Central to this formulation is the question of futurity. It is to this I turn next.

5
Philosophical Temptations: Economy and Futurity

1. *The temporal articulation of Nietzsche's conception of philosophers of the future is significant in that by asserting the futurity of such thinkers he locates them within the framework of a specifically temporal understanding. They stand both in relation to the past as the fruition of the labour of human prehistory that made autonomy possible and against Nietzsche's own times as contradictions of its revulsion towards suffering and exploitation. As befits their economic articulation, philosophers of the future are akin to possessors of property. Their valued 'goods', however, are spiritual and intellectual.*

In Section 42 of *Beyond Good and Evil* Nietzsche envisages the coming of a new kind of philosopher. He might be right or wrong in venturing to do so, he tells us, but he in any case dares to give them a name. These new philosophers are 'attempters'. This characterisation implies many things. Principally, it presupposes the notion that the pursuit of some kind of *task* will characterise these future thinkers. One attempts something only in the light of some kind of purpose that is taken as a justification for the attempt being made in the first place. This desire for justification through purpose is, as Nietzsche is to put it later in *Twilight of the Idols*, something that frames the bounds of his 'happiness'. Such happiness is achieved by way of a formula: one proceeds via affirmation and negation to create a sense of direction culminating in a destination that signals the end of a journey.[1] Notable, likewise, is the manner in which these philosopher attempters are differentiated from other kinds of people. New philosophers are who they are in virtue of Nietzsche's situating them within a specific temporal register: these philosophers will first be 'philosophers of the future' (*Beyond Good and Evil*, 44). As such, their nature is delineated by way of an act of projection within an already presupposed temporal structure. Philosophers of the future are defined by their relation to what has gone before them, that is the realms of history and prehistory that (as we have seen) for Nietzsche made us the kind of beings we are. In this way, new philosophers stand upon the achievements of their forbears' prehistoric labour and its outcome in the form of the social realm. The economic conditions of this labour taken together are a necessary condition of the future philosopher's being possible, for such philosophers are only possible in consequence of the vast human labour upon itself that makes up the realm of prehistory. At the same time, the future kind of thinker stands out from these conditions as a new articulation of what it means to launch oneself on a flight of thought. Such a person will be daring, experimental, passionate, a risk-taker, an intellectual reveller and sufferer in equal measure. Above all, they will be capable of affirming their own existence.

Philosophers of the future stand on the achievements of the past. They also stand against their own times, against the present.[2] Nietzsche makes this point clearly enough: one ought not to confuse the new kind of philosophical attempters and tempters he envisages with the so-called 'free spirits' that can be seen at work within the social milieu of modernity. They differ in a specific way: they stand opposed to the dominant socio-political tendency of their times. New philosophers will not be like the 'scribbling slaves of the democratic taste and its "modern ideas" ' (ibid.). Free-thinking exponents of modernity of this stamp take suffering as objectionable and desire its eradication. Nietzsche and his imagined philosophical kin take the opposing view. Suffering, danger and the like, Nietzsche tells us, are what have always made humanity develop into something more admirable than it was hitherto. Simply put, we are beings that need to be challenged in order to develop – our advancement comes about only through struggle.[3] Humanity does not benefit from ease, nice as it might feel, but from trauma and trial – a point tellingly made in *On the Genealogy of Morality*.[4] The general rule applies to the past (a rule which is, for Nietzsche, a matter of empirical truth) that for the achievement of anything more than mere survival and everydayness to be possible the human 'life-will had to be enhanced into an unconditional power-will [. . .]'. In other words, culture and the highest cultural achievements that are possible in virtue of it spring from our being provoked into engaging with our environment with a view to mastering it. In less disconcerting terms, one might say that what makes us human is the fact that we are not mere playthings of nature. Although always susceptible to its overwhelming power, humanity has always stood facing nature armed with concepts and rituals with which it hopes to subjugate or at the very least appease it (the economic concepts of measuring, weighing, equivalence and the like being essential ones). Such concepts and the practices they are entwined with are outcomes and expressions of the suffering that provokes them. Suffering, it follows, does not represent an objection to anything – it is not an argument but a feeling and is, at best, a shaky basis upon which to construct moral theories. To the extent that Nietzsche affirms the essential value of suffering in human development he stands opposed to 'all modern ideology', which stresses the diminishment of suffering and easy living as an ultimate 'good'.[5]

> We think that hardness, forcefulness, slavery, danger in the alley and the heart, life in hiding, stoicism, the art of experiment and devilry of every kind, that everything evil, terrible, tyrannical in man, everything in him that is akin to beasts of prey and serpents, serves the enhancement of the species 'man' as much as its opposite does. (Ibid.)

One should recall at this juncture the manner in which the great economy of human preservation is outlined at the opening of *The Gay Science*. Here in *Beyond Good and Evil*, likewise, the great economy of preservation, the overall household budget of the drives making their various demands – a general economy which includes the violent and the so-called 'evil propensities' of humanity – is highlighted. The new philosophers take their point of departure from the embracing of this economy. As critics of the modern, over-sensitive attitude towards suffering such future thinkers will be tempters, akin to devils who seduce the faithful from the path of the universal truth that holds suffering and what engenders suffering to be objections to ways of living or existence itself.

Indeed, philosophers of the future are beings of trials and challenges right down to their very core. They positively seek out suffering in order to learn from it. In this way suffering becomes spiritual nourishment, something that stands in opposition to the comforts of modern life. No surprise, then, that the genuinely 'free spirit', as Nietzsche understands the term, rejects 'the lures of dependence that lie hidden in honors, or money, or offices, or enthusiasms of the senses'. New philosophers are ascetics, self-deniers who are cruel especially towards themselves, capable of exploring the most demanding intellectual territory. But they are also fetishists driven by the desire for possession and colonisation of the territories of others. He and his imagined fellows, says

Nietzsche, are 'conquerors even if we look like heirs and prodigals, arrangers and collectors from morning till late, misers of our riches and our crammed drawers, economical [*haushälterisch*] in learning and forgetting, inventive in schemas, occasionally proud of our tables and categories'. The future philosopher will be thrifty in their treatment of their own thought, the ideas that populate it being held as valued possessions. Their minds will be run according to a carefully regulated accounting of in-goings and out-goings. This will, in its own turn, seal their right to be considered as spiritually wealthy, as 'overflowing' with the goods and privileges of the spirit (*Beyond Good and Evil*, 219). Future philosophers are thrifty, but at the same time display spiritual excess; they are akin to property owners who gaze over an intellectual landscape as masters of what they survey. What is possessed and esteemed, as in the earlier works of the 1870s, is a spiritual wealth of such value that one needs to be miserly with regard to sharing it out. Just as a shaman initiates only a privileged few into the secret rights of a cult, so conqueror philosophers are keen to hoard their intellectual property.

2. *In their fearlessness and favouring of suffering and danger, philosophers of the future are also exploiters of the great economy of human preservation, which sanctions the most fearsome and most socially amenable attributes alike. In such philosophers, the great squandering of this economy (outlined in* The Gay Science, *1) is counterbalanced and justified. The social necessity of wastefulness finds its mirror image in the future philosopher's abstemious fastidiousness. This quality is bought at the price of the wastefulness and exploitation within the general economy that made it possible. This general economy is an ineluctable condition of human existence. Exploitation is regarded by Nietzsche as an organic function as evident in the social milieu as in the need for nourishment that is essential to any living being, which must exploit and appropriate its environment in order to survive. This, for Nietzsche, means that active exploitation takes precedence over mere survival, for it is the precondition of a being's survival that it engages with and appropriates its environment rather than merely responds to it. Normative structures are also subject to the same conditions. Norms are not 'natural', but must nevertheless deal with the requirements placed upon them by organic conditions. All social orders, in other words, have to deal with the need for exploitation in one way or another.*

The great economy is one of dreadful squandering. It is a domain in which much raw material and raw potential is wasted, where many unconscious 'experiments' go wrong without so much as a casual eye to bear witness to each individual disaster. The spiritual life of the new philosopher will, even as it embraces the truth of this general economy, act as counter-force and complement to such excess. That is why the future philosopher's inner life will be something akin to a well-run and strictly organised spiritual household, a regulated saving up of potential with a view to pursuing a chosen task in the face of the general squandering that goes on all about them. Such a scrupulous attitude gains its rationale precisely because of the general chaos of waste that is the necessary condition and consequence of our being here at all. It is the chaos that makes us what we are that is the justification of the philosopher of the future's self-appointed task. For the same reason, the notion that any form of social order could overcome this necessity needs to be quashed. As Nietzsche puts it, bluntly enough, the very idea of a social order that resists 'injury, violence, and exploitation' but is instead egalitarian, is itself a denial of the fundamental principle of (human) life, namely its natural tendency to expand rather than contract (ibid., 259). All expansion requires exploitation as a fundamental prerequisite. If there were no class of things or people suitable for exploitative appropriation there would be no development of any kind. One might express this as a general economic principle: social life is not static, it includes elements that either expand or contract, and every gain (expansion) by someone somewhere is possible only in virtue of there being an equal or greater than equal loss (contraction) on the part of someone or something somewhere else. This social requirement, as much a feature of the modern industrial mode of production which, as we have seen in Chapter 1, Nietzsche discusses in scathing terms in some of his earlier writings is now presented here in the most metaphysical and naturalistic of terms. To take the position of opposing exploitation means to take the (Christian) position of standing counter to the demands of 'life' itself as it must be lived:

> [L]ife itself is *essentially* appropriation, injury, overpowering of what is alien and weaker; suppression, hardness, imposition of one's own forms, incorporation and at least, at its mildest, exploitation – but why should one always use those words in which a slanderous intent has been imprinted for ages? Even the body in which individuals treat each other as equals [...] if it is a living and not a dying body, has to do to other bodies what the individuals within it refrain from doing to each other: it will have to be an incarnate will to power, it will strive to grow, spread, seize, become predominant –

> not from any morality or immorality, but because it is living and because life simply *is* will to power. But there is no point on which the ordinary consciousness of Europeans resists instruction as on this: everywhere people are now raving, even under scientific disguises, about conditions of society in which 'the exploitative aspect' will be removed – which sounds to me as if they promised to invent a way of life that would dispense with all organic functions. 'Exploitation' does not belong to a corrupt or imperfect and primitive society: it belongs to the *essence* of what lives, as a basic organic function; it is a consequence of the will to power, which is after all the will of life [. . .] the *primordial fact* of all history: people ought to be honest with themselves at least that far.
>
> (Ibid.)

For Nietzsche, all life involves the exploitation of resources. Any entity that lives must, by way of the most obvious example, take nourishment from its environment. In order to do so, it must in some manner or other appropriate aspects of that environment and incorporate them within itself (ingestion and digestion). Any entity needs, in this sense, not merely to negotiate but actually to master its environmental conditions (conditions that will include other organic entities) by making them conform to *its* nutritional requirements. Of course, such mastery may well be short-lived. What eats can always be eaten. However, in every case, exploitative interaction with the environment is what marks out all organic processes, from the most simple to the most complex. This kind of exploitation is, we might say, a 'natural' condition of our simply being here at all. Even the vegetarian (people about whom Nietzsche never seems to have anything kind to say) must exploit something else that lives in order to live.[6] What Nietzsche does, however, is force the argument a few steps further by conjoining the organic exploitation of environmental resources with social, political and colonial modes of exploitation. Societies, in this view, are exploitative because they are domains of culture constituted out of norms and their corresponding practices. These normative conditions are articulated in terms of the basic economy of organic conditions that must be embodied by any social order as its condition of possibility. You are a social animal. You need to eat and tend to a host of other organic functions in order to survive, and this means that you can and, if need be, *will* exploit others like you and that they will do likewise. Practices adopted in any social domain will make such exploitation not merely possible but even, in some cases, laudable (what sacrifices demanded in the pursuit of 'good' and 'holy' purposes, such as wars pursued in the cause of 'freedom', do not involve acts of exploitation somewhere?).

There is, for Nietzsche, no escape from this essential exploitative condition – even if some kind of egalitarianism is occasionally possible. Even if you are one amongst equals, then you and your peers will exploit those around you who fall within the category of those who are 'not one of us': 'we' will exploit 'them' – the social 'inferior', the 'foreigner', and so on. For Nietzsche the social body is, in terms of its functions and behaviour, no less organic than any other living body. An organism, by the same token, is for him always something organised along the hierarchical lines that typify rigid social divisions.[7] That is why Zarathustra, as we have seen,[8] envisages the self as a great reason that organises and masters the drives which are subordinate to it. The self is, in this sense, a political and economic structure in miniature whose principles of organisation are reflected in its biological nature and the human community alike. The body is a complex consisting of multiple functions: 'our body is but a social structure composed of many souls' (*Beyond Good and Evil*, 19). It operates like any well-built and happy political community in that 'all willing [. . .] is absolutely a question of commanding and obeying' (ibid.). As a notebook entry reflecting on the physiology of power from the mid-1880s puts it, the body is a structure ruled by a majoritarian aristocracy. It is a mutual struggle of biological tissue locked together in relations of domination. The 'division of labour' this implies is not peripheral; it is the body's necessary condition. Nietzsche's conclusion from this, 'concerning the evolution of mankind', is that 'perfecting consists in the production of the most powerful individuals, who will use the great mass of people as their tools (and indeed, the most intelligent and pliable tools)'.[9] In other words, an organic division of labour that characterises the body and the self finds its parallel in the social division of labour envisaged to serve the goals of culture and human enhancement. The economy of industrial labour, which represents the manipulation of the natural world with ever more powerful tools, finds its most powerful articulation in the economic manipulation of human populations.

3. *Nietzsche's commitment to a metaphysics of becoming provides him with further reasons for adopting the view that all bodies are economically mediated systems of colonisation and exploitation. This colonial aspect to the body is already found in Nietzsche's account of the primitive community dominated by custom and tradition. The supplicant trembles before and submits to the authority of tradition: they are one who simply*

> *obeys a command. Civilisation rests upon the exchange principle denoted by the creditor–debtor relationship* (Genealogy, *II*). *As such, civilisation implies exploitation since it involves relations of power and the uses persons make of others within such relations. The philosopher of the future embraces and refines these conceptions. Philosophy, in Nietzsche's view, is not a 'method' but a way of engaging with the environment with a view to mastering it. Such mastery is the most profound justification of human suffering. For, by asserting such mastery, the philosopher of the future transcends the normative conditions that made them possible. Economy is, in this way, transfigured. The economy of norms gives way to a new creative and spiritual economy. Nietzsche's criticisms of democracy can be situated within this context. Democratic ideals, for him, represent a reassertion of the normative coercion characteristic of the most primitive forms of social life.*

For Nietzsche, any talk about bodies is necessarily analogous with talk about social orders and vice versa. Organic bodies (including those such as us) are economically mediated systems organised for the gleaning and distribution of resources. Every living body is a colony of cells with colonial intentions, an aggressive social order in miniature. Organisms are hierarchies of elements organised to exploit what is available and, as a necessary conclusion of such exploitation, colonise it if possible by incorporating it. This colonial characteristic exists because nothing ever remains quite the same as long as life goes on. To speak metaphysically, which Nietzsche does no less than all philosophers sometimes do,[10] what exists is dependent upon the prime condition of *becoming*. Because things are always becoming they are either expanding or contracting in influence and power, and this means they are either exploiting and colonising or being exploited and colonised. Society, at least as Nietzsche would envisage it in its 'healthiest' state (i.e. one that corresponds to the functional demands made by any body), operates according to the same dictates. This conclusion probably forces us to consider Nietzsche as taking the position of what looks like a metaphysical apologist for social division in that he ontologises political subjugation through the naturalisation of class divisions. How far one wishes to pursue this issue with a view to resolving it would probably depend on how far one was concerned with the political ramifications of Nietzsche's thought and making use of them. Likewise, the extent to which one might *not* like to think about this would probably depend upon the degree to which one wanted to resist making Nietzsche 'political' at all – itself a political position. For present purposes, however, the point to note is that, for Nietzsche, society, in so far as it functions at all needs exploitation of some kind or another since no social orders exist that are devoid of hierarchy. All hierarchy presupposes organisation according to the principles of commanding and obeying, and one who obeys is always liable to be exploited simply in virtue of this role. One should recall here Nietzsche's account of the normative structure of the primitive community (discussed in Chapter 2). All observance of customs presupposes the commanding power of tradition, which in turn sanctions the roles of the commanding authority of the gods and the obedient supplicants who tremble before it. In this regard, all societies replicate the economic conditions that Nietzsche argues to be at work in the primitive prehistoric community in the second essay of the *Genealogy* and which themselves function in the context of the great economy of the affects outlined in *The Gay Science*. A world built on the practices and primitive notions of prehistoric traders is a world in which economic characteristics are, from the outset, amongst its essential features and all economy involves, to some degree or other, exploitation – even if it is perceived on occasion as being mutually beneficial.

In the same way as all that lives must desire to dominate its environment, or otherwise succumb to it, so any philosophy, too, if it is authentic, aspires to dominance. Hence Nietzsche's rejection of the conception of philosophy as nothing more than a scholarly discipline concerned with a narrow range of questions about what we can know, what morality is and the like. Such a concept of philosophy is for Nietzsche a poor excuse for the genuine article. Epistemology, especially, comes in for the deepest scorn: 'Philosophy reduced to "theory of knowledge", in fact no more than a timid epochism and doctrine of abstinence – a philosophy that never gets beyond the threshold and takes pains to *deny* itself the right to enter [. . .]'. Philosophy defined as epistemology is philosophy drawing its last breath, 'an end, an agony'. How, Nietzsche asks, could such a philosophy *rule* (*Beyond Good and Evil*, 204)? Against the conception of philosophy as mere *method* Nietzsche urges his readers to embrace a philosophy more worthy of the name. Such a conception doubtless follows Plato and the ancients in its ambitions,[11] for it is something that desires much more than merely the right to arbitrate on abstract questions or act as tidy-upper and rubbish-collector to the sciences. What really matters, in Nietzsche's view, is the ability to pose questions that concern justification in the broadest of senses, rather than in this narrow, academic one. Such broad justification has as its sphere the giving of reasons for the social divisions that are the prerequisite of the pursuit of large-scale cultural goals; it is the attempt to envisage human futurity as a plenitude of possibility. The modern desire for egalitarianism, made manifest by its faith in universally applicable norms or 'laws', stands most of all in the way of the pursuit of such possibility. The democratic character and resultant character-chaos that typifies modern subjectivity exemplifies the dominance of norms and the conformity they manufacture (ibid.).

It is as an uncompromising critic of the democratic spirit that Nietzsche is perhaps most profoundly at odds with the dominant tendency of his times.[12] One should resist going down any of the many tempting interpretative avenues that would allow one to respond to this disturbing aspect of Nietzsche's thought by effectively consigning it to the margins. Recuperating parts of Nietzsche's thinking that might seem suitable for democratic political purposes, dismissing his political attitudes as an aberration upon an otherwise glorious philosophical landscape, or simply denying that he had anything at all to say about politics, in their various ways do just this and are unsatisfactory. The whole point of what he says is, perhaps, to be found in the fact that we moderns are meant to be horrified and shocked. The problem with democratic culture, we are told, is that it is essentially regressive, for any increase in the political power of norms (popular power) is akin to a return to the most primitive social life of humanity, dominated by the power of convention and conformity. The view that democratisation represents any kind of advance on the past is hence, in his terms, a mere prejudice.[13]

4. *Philosophers of the future are experimenters. They thereby counter the dominance of convention that would impose limits on their experimentation. Their autonomy reflects the notion of the sovereign individual developed in the* Genealogy. *They transfigure and transform the significance of the prehistoric legacy of customs and traditions by standing as the reinterpretation and justification of the suffering they engendered. Genuine philosophers can be contrasted with 'philosophical workers'. The invocation of this contrast reveals that Nietzsche conceives of philosophy itself as being governed by an economic distribution of labour. The hard labour of critical knowledge becomes the preamble to creative thought, and gains its justification thereby. Philosophical creativity is commanding, it is legislative. In this, it replicates the authority of ancient tradition but in the form of an individuated and autonomous life. Above all the orientation towards futurity of genuine philosophers confirms their autonomy and authenticity. Our normative fashioning engenders self-understanding in terms of our future-oriented stance towards the world and our fate. The genuine philosopher is the highest and most self-conscious expression of*

> *this. The distinction between philosophical workers and genuine philosophers in turn replicates the modern industrial differentiation between labour power and capital. As with the questions of hierarchy and exploitation, so human futurity takes the form of an economically instigated temporal necessity.*

The stance Nietzsche takes against democratic 'prejudices' is an enactment of rebellion against the normativity he sees at work within the modern social milieu. The stance represents an *attempt* to think beyond the limits prescribed by what he takes to be the dominant moral discourse of his times. It is a piece of shocking experimentalism and, as such, an attempt at future philosophy. Philosophers of the future 'will be men of experiments' (*Beyond Good and Evil*, 210). As such, they cannot allow themselves the luxury of the democratic taste, for if their 'passion for knowledge' is to have full reign they must allow themselves to go beyond the restrictions to thought imposed by such considerations. Normative power demands a limit to experimentation, even of a person upon himself or herself. Just as the norm demands comfort so it frowns upon the discomfort that is necessary for such strict and rigorous spirits to be who they are.[14] As someone who stands beyond norms and traditions the philosopher of the future is an exemplar of the 'sovereign individual' who is envisaged as emerging from the economic fashioning of the self in the *Genealogy* (II, 2–3). This kind of human, the product of the discipline of an economy of primitive and violent compulsion stands as the justification of the enormous preparatory labour that humanity performed upon itself in the eras of prehistory. Unconsciously moulded, the outcome is an autonomous being capable of pledging their word independently of normative compulsion, a promiser whose pledge is no mere bond that binds them to the social body but an enactment of their own free individuality. In such beings, Nietzsche tells us, resides the justification of the most violent practices that were enacted upon the ancient human being in order to master him and teach him to master himself. The long prehistory of humanity signifies, in this sense, a preparatory labour, of which the autonomous individual is the goal. The prehistoric self-policing of humanity is thus a prelude as, in its own way, is Nietzsche's philosophy, for beings whose ability to promise has been transfigured into the most rigorously self-aware independence.

The prehistoric economic conditions consisting of creditor and debtor, the practices of discipline that brought about the mastering of the general economy of the affects that constitute our nature, find their outcome in the philosopher of the future as the most comprehensive form of autonomous being. Autonomy divides the philosophical worker from the real thing. Real philosophers are in many ways akin to philosophical workers and scholarly people in general. Like the latter, the real philosopher will need to have undergone the severity of an education that imparts discipline. No less than his or her 'servants', the real philosopher needs to ascend the ladder of knowledge. However, where such servants attain and then remain at one level of expertise, the real philosopher must pass beyond one competence in order to seek out and master others. Each level, however, is preparatory. The task of such a person is what matters: it demands nothing less than 'that he *create* values' (*Beyond Good and Evil*, 211). Nietzsche's choice as to who exemplifies such 'philosophical labourers' is perhaps surprising, given their deserved eminence: Kant and Hegel. The high-minded nature of such figures is reflected in their work, which consists in the fixing in place and expressing in formulae of a great stock of facts about highly esteemed values, be it in the realms of logic, politics or the arts. Such labourers prepare the ground for the real philosopher. They are like the workers on a building site who establish the foundations of a building, set in place its walls and roof, divide it up into rooms, compartmentalise it and thereby transform mere space into a space that can be lived in. Human life itself, however, is no mere compartmentalising activity. The tasks that can be pursued in existence do not find their destination in the vision of a well-established and neat living room. The labourer may establish the structure but his/her function is to fade conveniently into the background afterwards. They are, in this regard, people best suited to making things to be *used* by those who come after them. Philosophical labourers are like scholars, 'objective' people whose meaning is to be found in what end they serve but who cannot, as 'tools', ever be confused with being an end in itself (ibid., 207). Their task, it follows, is limited. It is up to these researchers to make every event and everything treasured up to now clear, easy to think over, intelligible, handy. Their task is ambitious, in that it consists in the compression even of time itself into something conceivable for those who can conceive of it thereby and put even this notion to their own uses. The researcher's is a tremendous and wonderful task. But 'genuine philosophers' are different. Their task is not one of servitude. They do not labour in service to others. Their lives are consumed in glorious selfishness (ibid., 211). Real philosophers are commanders and lawmakers: 'they say, "*thus* it *shall* be!"' In other words, their words are *decrees* wherein they seek to establish the 'Whereto?' and 'What-for?' of humankind. The work of all philosophical labourers lies at the genuine philosopher's disposal. With a 'creative hand' such beings pick up these preparatory achievements and then extend their grasp out towards the future, 'and all that is and has been becomes a means for them, an instrument, a hammer. Their "knowing" is *creating*, their creating is a legislation, their will to truth is – *will to power* [. . .] Are there such philosophers today? Have there been such philosophers? *Must* there not be such philosophers?'[15]

The presentation here of the domain in which philosophers of the future come about mirrors a world of economic production. The philosophical labourer does the work needed as a preliminary for the tasks of those capable of greatness. In other words, philosophy itself, as Nietzsche presents it, exemplifies the principle of the division of labour. The *genuine* philosopher is the property owner, the ruler whose right is expressed through legislative utterance and rule over his or her subjects (the workers who toil for his or her fulfilment). The genuine philosopher is a commander and as such he or she is possible only in virtue of the division of labour within a pre-existing social-philosophical order, a philosophical realm populated by masters and servants. In this way, the labour power of the critical philosopher acts as the economic base upon which the genuine philosopher's capital accumulation will be made. The will to power is then fitted into this: it is will to power which determines the world in terms of what is decreed by the genuine philosopher. It is the will to power that expresses itself through the desire for rule that the genuine philosopher would exhibit as a sign of their authenticity.

Genuine philosophers remain, however, locked in the future. Yet, at the same time, the text presents a demand that transforms them from the status of mere possibility into that of necessity: 'must' it not be the case that such philosophers will exist (ibid.)?[16] Doubtless, one could envisage the pathetic image of a lonely and largely ignored Nietzsche gaining some comfort from this – a man in solitude inventing fellow travellers on his philosophical path as a means of sweetening the bitterness of his isolation.[17] As he himself was prone to point out when castigating Christian conceptions of an afterlife in which the evil are punished and the good rewarded, the future is a comfort – and an often illusory one at that. The future is the promised land of hope where one's aspirations may yet come to fruition – even if one is not there to witness it, another kind of uncanny existence may still be possible after bodily extinction.[18] But the appeal to and celebration of futurity in the text is no mere coincidence of biography. It is essentially connected with Nietzsche's conception of the development of humankind from economic principles. Futurity is a defining component of the economy of human existence.

As is the case with questions of command, obedience, hierarchy and exploitation, we need to recall that here, too, according to the *Genealogy*, it is only because our primitive ancestors slowly tortured themselves into becoming creatures endowed with promising abilities that humankind emerged as a being that has one specific kind of orientation that no other animal has. Promising is what endowed us with the ability to have 'control over the future'. We are future-oriented animals. Futurity is underwritten into promising because a person who makes a promise is 'answerable for his own *future*!' (*On the Genealogy of Morality*, II, 1). Primitive economy, promising and futurity are facets of the human character that go hand in hand. The economic forces that drive the normativisation of the primitive communal individual give rise to a self-understanding that is thinkable only in terms of a sense of debt. Communal protection means that the individual stands as a debtor in relation to the communal body, which offers protection but demands normative obedience in return. Individuals, in turn, first meet and achieve mutual understanding in terms of the creditor–debtor relationship. The debtor makes a pledge. Failure to repay the debt brings with it a forfeit measurable in terms of the debtor's suffering and shame. The creditor has the right to demand as compensation from the bad debtor 'his body, or his wife, or his freedom, or his life (or, in certain religious circumstances, even his after-life, the salvation of his soul, even his peace in the grave [. . .])'(ibid., 5). In this way, the self emerges in the text of the *Genealogy* as something moulded by norms but at the same time moulded according to the demands of a temporal necessity. To be a normative being is, at the same time, to be a future-oriented one. To be human, in short, is to exist as a being endowed with a self-understanding that articulates itself in terms of a relationship with time. What has been the case, what is the case and what may or will be the case are the modes of self-understanding that characterise us. We stand, always, in some understood temporal relationship, be it in connection with our forbears, our present, or our future possibilities.

Philosophy, at its richest potential, takes the domain of human possibility understood as temporality and stretches its meanings to the limit. Every philosopher worthy of the name creates values (however sly they may be when it comes to disclosing it). It is as would-be creators that they are driven to the rejection of contemporary norms. This, for Nietzsche, follows as a matter of definition. Genuine philosophers are 'of necessity' opponents and protestors against their times (*Beyond Good and Evil*, 212) since they stand as embodied contradictions of the normative forces that make up all social order. As creative beings, philosophers of the future signify the transcendence of these normative structures, they are living evidence of the self-sublimation inherent within human life. Regularisation through the economy of norms serves humanity as a means of cultivating the independent individual, but such norms stand as unnecessary remnants and hindrances to the kind of being in whom such cultivation has attained its purpose.

5. *Norms are what make history. History is the conflict between different normative traditions which, when they meet, often comprehend each other as incompatible (foreign) and clash. Colonisation (violence) is thus, envisaged by Nietzsche as the opening of historical experience. Philosophers of the future are the fulfilment of the historical conflict between noble and slave that Nietzsche narrates in the* Genealogy. *Their new aesthetic challenges norms in its search for a transformation of humanity. This is the essence of their creativity. It is also the justification of the hardness that Nietzsche favours. Such beings need to be hard in order to take on the task of working on normative humanity with a view to its enhancement. This human material is pliable and undetermined. We are not like animals. Ours is not the snug fit between niche and nature. We are underdetermined beings and our openness in this respect is the basis of the futurity that the genuine philosopher seeks to exploit. It is also the reason why suffering is an inevitable part of the human lot. Unlike natural beings, we are devoid of a determinate nature and are consequently each of us a mass of contradictions. Nietzsche articulates this view in terms of an economy of investments and returns. Humanity attained its manifold nature through the painful investment in norms. These yielded a return in the form of futurity at the cost of suffering. Christianity and modernity, in so far as they have a hatred of suffering, fail to notice its necessity for human development. The aim to diminish suffering makes a farce of history in its exclusive desire for comfort and safety. Nietzsche's maxim that we ought to live dangerously is an invitation to follow the example of what he considers the genuine philosopher to aspire to.*

As Zarathustra makes clear when talking of values, norms are nothing less than the domain of what has counted as history hitherto. Only when our ancestors became creatures governed by custom and habit, only when they encountered each other and the world of nature alike as beings mediated by tradition, could human history even begin. History is also conflict, for conflicts must arise when traditions and hence *cultures* resting upon different articulations of the economic exchange principle become distinct from one another but remain sufficiently proximal so as to cross paths. From the outset the distinctness between cultural groups means that the sort of encounters this very differentiation initiates will be marked by necessary violence. The envisioning of a colonial pack of blonde beasts overrunning another community in the *Genealogy* is at the same time not merely a thesis concerning the origins of bad conscience, the state and law. With these invading and colonising beings comes genuinely historical experience. Historical experience is, in this sense, violence, pure and simple, since it is always the encounter between different cultures with heterogeneous traditions wherein one either appropriates and absorbs the other or succumbs to it. When in Section 7 of the 'Preface' to the *Genealogy* Nietzsche says that he is going to provide nothing less than 'the real history of morality', that historical analysis is in part the history of historicity itself. History, as the first essay of the *Genealogy* discloses it, is a narrative that unfolds only because of the initiation of physically and spiritually violent disputation between noble and slave. Such contest itself only came about in virtue of the communal fashioning of the individual through norms, and the subsequent violent establishment of the state, legality and society at the hands of the 'artists of violence' analysed in the second essay of the *Genealogy*. History, in its essence, is the working out of these violent conflicts, not least in terms of the creative bursts of imaginative inventiveness they engender. The slave's comforting consignment of the oppressive noble to a hellish afterlife is a daring act of narrative fancy born of impotence, but richly creative nonetheless. Without the impetus of pain and violence humankind would have been a far blander creature.[19]

The future philosopher stands as a kind of summation of this history and prehistory. The human prehistoric labour that manufactured us as promising animals created a kind of being that could think, project and overcome its own immediate desires through the self-policing of normative regularisation. But genuine philosophers always want more. They want 'to know of a *new* greatness of man, of a new untrodden way to his enhancement' (*Beyond Good and Evil*, 212). A building can be extended with new rooms in such a way that the extension does not represent a mere expansion in the space afforded for living. Rather, such an extension initiates a new aesthetic that retrospectively transforms the meaning of the whole. Likewise, humankind can be transformed and increased by experiment. Modernity is contrasted with the desire for such increase. Modern European taste and morality dilute 'the will'; ours is a period increasingly dominated by conformity. Resistance is the key:

> Today [. . .] nothing is as timely as weakness of the will. In the philosopher's ideal, therefore, precisely strength of the will, hardness, and the capacity for long-range decisions must belong to the concept of 'greatness' – with as much justification as the opposite doctrine [. . .] And the philosopher will betray something of his own ideal when he posits [. . .] 'Precisely this shall be called *greatness*: being capable of being as manifold as whole, as ample as full'.

Hardness, tremendous wealth in will, seclusion, differentiation, being manifold and yet entire: all these count as philosophical virtues for Nietzsche. They are so because of the prime demand that is placed upon the true philosopher: the *creativity* that characterises the attempter.

Hardness is most especially a virtue because of the nature of the material and conditions with which the creative philosopher spirit has to deal. We need here to recall a section of *Beyond Good and Evil* that was briefly considered in Chapter 3:

> There is among men as in every other animal species an excess of failures, of the sick, degenerating, infirm, who suffer necessarily; the successful cases are, among men too, always the exception – and in view of the fact that man is the *as yet undetermined animal*, the rare exception. But still worse: the higher the type of man that a man represents, the greater the improbability that he will turn out *well*. The accidental, the law of absurdity in the whole economy of mankind [*das Gesetz des Unsinns im gesammten Haushalte der Menschheit*], manifests itself most horribly in its destructive effect on the higher men whose complicated conditions of life can only be calculated with great subtlety and difficulty.
>
> (Ibid., 62)

Human enhancement is always gained at a cost. Like all living creatures, a logic of excess and squandering governs the production of every individual. Nature, one might say, proceeds wastefully. Under the sway of the foreground law of nonsensical ruination many individuals are born, but by far the largest number of them is (as presented here) akin to a myriad of unsuccessful experiments. This is the case even more so with humankind than with any natural being. To put it bluntly, we are, most of us, a mess, a mishmash. To have 'turned out well' a natural being such as a cat needs only to satisfy some rather rudimentary requirements. Leaving the physical requirements of development and fitness to one side, the cat's behaviour needs to fulfil only limited demands in order to satisfy the criteria that confirm its cat status (e.g. mercilessly hunting birds and small mammals, leaving scents in order to mark territory and engaging in behaviour appropriate for making yet more cats). A cat is a creature of instinct and, since it is built to be the way it is, cat-hood does not entail much difficulty for the average cat. People are different – even the average ones. A person cannot be said to be what they are on account of having fulfilled the kind of definitional criteria that make it possible with reasonable surety to say that a particular being is a cat. We have instincts and drives, but we do not live with them easily. We are layers of struggle, we are self-conscious, we are not at home with ourselves. The concept of personhood invokes a multiplicity of notions and thereby escapes simple definition. We are beings whose nature has not been fixed in place – at least, Nietzsche says, 'not yet'. Everybody thus embodies a potential openness when it comes to what kind of person he or she could turn out to be. What is average is in this sense available for recuperation as pure potential.

In a note from the mid-1880s Nietzsche comments that humanity up to now is understandable as 'an embryo of the man of the future'.[20] Human futurity, of which the genuine philosopher is an exemplar, is underwritten into the nature of the most average person. However average, we are all understandable as that specific kind of entity that is capable of escaping formal definition and this ability is linked inextricably with our futurity. Our nature is not yet fixed. In present humanity dwells the future, stored up and buried under layers of conformity. All the forces that mould us are aimed at *this* future possibility: our futurity is *constitutive* of our identity. And since these forces are, says Nietzsche, 'enormous', it turns out that the individual of the present who is most decisive for the future will necessarily *suffer* much for being so. The more futurity in a person the greater their ability to suffer. This, he adds, affords us 'the profoundest conception of suffering': the individual is a nexus in which the forces that fashion humanity pound into one another; and their collision evidences itself as inner turmoil. What the *Genealogy* characterises as 'internalisation' (II, 16) is no mere primitive characteristic of human nature that we have outgrown: it describes the living dynamic of what it means to be a person. The 'I' is a battleground, a field of conflict of the constitutive affects.[21] 'The isolation of the individual ought not to deceive us' for in truth 'something flows on *underneath* individuals'. Individual isolation, in other words, allows the expression of forces that govern human development. Loneliness makes you feel different, deviant. Loneliness goads the individual and thereby provokes them into seeking goals that lie beyond those stipulated by norms. Suffering is the inevitable consequence of standing apart from the norm. In doing so a person acts with the kind of independence and sovereignty characteristic of the genuine philosopher. In suffering they discover the openness of human existence. This very openness, understood as an unfulfilled potential, is the essence for Nietzsche of what it means to pursue the path of attaining authentic personhood.

Humanity as a self-created and an as yet unfixed being must, it follows, be a mass of contradictions. As self-proclaimed measurers of reality we at the same time initiated the means of placing ourselves beyond measure.[22] Our ascent into the realm of the 'unmeasurable' on the back of the concepts of number and weight (*The Wanderer and His Shadow*, 21) represents an ascent from a world that can apparently be calculated, weighed and estimated into one that pertains to a sublime enhancement of existence. The philosopher of the future is the appropriator and transformer of this achievement. As commanders and law-givers, philosophers of the future epitomise creativity, which is why their existence risks much. What they risk, however, is gleaned from the rest of humankind, it is only possible on the basis of the great accumulation that has preceded them. The rule of the 'foreground law' that dictates the great majority must turn out badly means that most of us fall short of what we could be and this cannot be countered. And, as with all investments, the greater the possible returns the greater the risk of calamity. Failure means suffering, regret, self-loathing, rancour. But we cannot and ought not to seek to cleanse the world of pain. One cannot remove suffering from the equation of the economy of life, as Christianity sought to do. One cannot divorce suffering and reality any more than one can remove exploitation from it. The attempt to do these things was Christianity's calamity: 'Men, not high and hard enough to have any right to form *man* as artists; men, not strong and far-sighted enough to let the foreground law of thousand-fold failure and ruin prevail [. . .] men, not noble enough to see the abysmally different order of rank, chasm of rank, between man and man – *such* men have so far held sway over the fate of Europe [. . .]' (*Beyond Good and Evil*, 62). Thus, the modern average, 'normal' person has been attained by lack of vision.

What this lack of vision amounts to, above all, is a lack of faith in humankind's future. The vision of the genuine philosopher is Nietzsche's contrasting statement of faith in human futurity. We have already noted that philosophers of this kind are attempters, experimenters and commanders. They are also teachers and their aim is 'To teach man the future of man as his *will*, as dependent on a human will [. . .]' (ibid., 203). Such beings would bring to an end 'that gruesome dominion of nonsense and accident that has so far been called "history" [. . .]'. They would endow purpose to the struggle of interests that make up history (its historicity). In doing so, such people would live *differently*: 'the genuine philosopher [. . .] lives "unphilosophically" and "unwisely" ' (ibid., 205) as attempter and tempter, 'he risks *himself* constantly'. Doubtless, this is why although the philosopher always stands for Nietzsche as the epitome of a 'higher species' of humanity[23] they have as a rule tended to turn out rather badly. This is for him certainly the case when compared with the artist, who may be a 'lower' kind of human being but is one that has nevertheless been more beautifully and 'richly developed'. But it is the real philosopher's lust for futurity that increases the risk of this just as it by the same token sets him or her apart from other 'higher' kinds of person. Futurity and legislative prowess together constitute the basic idea of the genuine philosopher: the highest human beings are understandable only as 'rulers of the earth and creators of the future'.[24]

6. *Human futurity is bound up with suffering. Our ancestors' passage from nature to culture was one in which the drives and passions were subjugated by convention. It is this subjugation that engendered specifically the human form of suffering, replete with accompanying tensions and conflicts within the community and the self. Human suffering thereby gained a unique significance. Its connection with norms meant that it came to be understood as something requiring justification, a meaning. This is because the outcome of communal life was the manufacture of people as beings who are part creature, part creator. This dichotomy epitomises, for Nietzsche, the essential contradiction of being human. We are an assemblage of conflicting qualities and this conflict is what drives us 'forward' into our own future. Human self-understanding is thus inexorably temporal. The price paid for futurity is that we suffer most from ourselves. The denial of suffering is, it follows, tantamount to the denial of our own humanity.*

Human futurity, however, is something that has to be purchased at great cost. This, as the narrative of prehistory offered in the second essay of the *Genealogy* makes clear, was always the case. Humanity left nature behind (or, at the very least, initiated a relationship with it that is unique) when it subjected itself to norms. In doing so it entered into a world dominated by economic principles that formed the basis whereby the individual was slowly and ruthlessly fashioned into the kind of regularised being able to understand and accept rules.

Humans thereby became able above all to police themselves when it came to mastering instinctive demands in order to satisfy the requirements of communal living. As a consequence of this, at every level our primitive ancestors suffered in new ways. In its exploration of this suffering, the second essay of the *Genealogy* effectively offers a history of the transformation of the meaning of pain. A natural being suffers and it does so for biological reasons. A creature is caught in an accident or a fight with another animal and injured. The injuries may be terrible and the suffering commensurate with them, but the meaning of such suffering remains limited and trivial in relation to the life of the species. An individual cat is significant because it is an instance of cat-kind, not an individual. As Heidegger remarks in *Being and Time*, animals cannot die like humans, they can only perish.[25] Likewise, the suffering of an animal lacks the spiritual resonance and meaningfulness of a person's. For an animal suffering is a biological function: it tells an individual when something is amiss. When something hurts it is best avoided, and if it cannot be avoided (if an injury is sustained) it is simply lived with or died from. People have to cope with this but they are also different. That they suffer is, for Nietzsche, an indubitable fact of life. That they suffer and seek to render their suffering meaningful is specific to them. One can categorise and dismiss various philosophies in the light of their attitude towards suffering – specifically, their retreat from it. Whether hedonism, whether pessimism, whether utilitarianism, whether eudaemonism: these paths of philosophical thought *all* 'measure the value of things' according to the standard of how much pleasure and pain they give rise to and can be judged accordingly (ibid., 225). They privilege secondary conditions and what is inessential, for they miss the point when it comes to the kind of beings we are. It is not possible to put an end to suffering, however much one might wish to:

> The discipline of suffering, of *great* suffering – do you not know that only *this* discipline has created all enhancements of man so far? [. . .] In man *creature* and *creator* are united; in man there is material, fragment, excess, clay, dirt, nonsense, chaos; but in man there is also creator, form-giver, hammer hardness [. . .] And that *your* pity is for the 'creature in man', for what must be formed, broken, forged, torn, burnt, made incandescent, and purified – that which *necessarily* must and *should* suffer? [. . .] [T]here are higher problems than all

> problems of pleasure, pain, and pity; and every philosophy that stops with them is a naiveté.
>
> (Ibid., 225)

One should not underestimate what is being claimed here, for it cuts to the heart of Nietzsche's conception of human nature as potentiality for autonomy and freedom. As in the second essay of the *Genealogy* it is tremendous suffering that is held to elevate humanity. Nietzsche bases his view on an empirical claim shot through with value judgements: humankind has always been raised beyond what it has been hitherto by trial, pain and displeasure. To be a person is to be a synthesis. In a person a merging and attempted reconciliation between what is creature and creator is contained in one and the same being. We are excremental and chaotic, as prone to the vicissitudes of chance as any natural being, and yet we are capable of extending ourselves beyond this condition. We can gaze upon the world as a divine being would, we have the form-giving abilities of the creator. Humanity can look forward, envisage the future and act with regard to it. As a synthesis of created and creator every person is also a site of conflict. For Nietzsche what is essential is grasping the significance of this conflict that makes up human identity. In bluntest terms: we suffer from ourselves, from the very fact of simply being here. To estimate values according to the criterion of minimising our suffering is not merely to misunderstand what it is to be human. Such an attitude precludes any genuine understanding of humanity altogether. Pain and pleasure are secondary because they are what humans have both imposed upon themselves and overcome as signs of being more than mere animals. Pain and pleasure signify embodiment, but such embodiment is only the 'stuff' to be worked on in the pursuit of something that exceeds our animal nature in the form of autonomy. Self-mastery is, at the same time, mastery of the perceptions, of the discomforts that make up life, but not with a view to their mere negation. A product of nature and yet profoundly unnatural, humanity is stretched across a divide between one kind of existence and another.[26] One can turn to the third essay of *On the Genealogy of Morality* in the light of this.

7. *The third essay of the* Genealogy *offers Nietzsche's most sustained account of the link between human suffering and futurity. This is the meaning of the ascetic ideal. Its power over humanity is testimony to our overwhelming need to explain and thereby justify our existence by endowing it with sense. It is this power that explains the role of asceti-*

> *cism in the history of philosophy. Philosophers have praised asceticism because it constitutes the best condition for their existence. Their self-denying propensity is a prerequisite of their thinking against the spirit of their times. Asceticism is a philosophical means. It allows the philosopher to deny their today and pursue their future. As such a means, asceticism was already available to philosophers and of sufficient power to be of use to them. They borrowed it from the religious cults of the priests. Ascetic priests exist at all times and in all places because they answer a human need for explaining suffering. As the being who suffers most of all from itself the human animal is replete with self-destructive potential. The ascetic priest counters this. In this way, the continuation of human existence is achieved.*

On the face of it, in the third essay of the *Genealogy* Nietzsche seems to be presenting the reader with an interpretation of the ascetic ideal. But the significance of asceticism, Nietzsche makes clear from the outset, lies not so much in what it is as in its power over humanity and what that power indicates. The meaning of asceticism is a matter that can only be resolved by way of an analysis of human nature, an analysis that will be conducted by Nietzsche in the light of the related notions of economy and suffering already outlined. '*That* the ascetic ideal has meant so much to man reveals a basic fact of the human will, its *horror vacui; it needs an aim* – and it prefers *nothingness* rather than *not* will' (*On the Genealogy of Morality*, III, 1). Asceticism is significant because it tells us something fundamental about our humanity. Because our nature is defined by an essential incompleteness we have a craving for purposes. The power of asceticism attests to this need. Nietzsche then reiterates and extrapolates this point in what follows. The starting point is the question of where to look for an instructive example when it comes to finding those who praise asceticism.

There are, of course, many avenues down which one could travel when it comes to analysing asceticism. Nietzsche dispenses with some of them quickly enough. When an artist like Wagner praises asceticism, for example, it is best to pass by in silence since artists are basically untrustworthy when it comes to such things (ibid., 4, 5).[27] More interesting is when a real philosopher such as Schopenhauer pays tribute to it (ibid., 5). Schopenhauer, like Kant, sought to conceive of aesthetic reflection as counteracting '*sexual* interestedness' (ibid., 6). As such, it represents for him an escape from the will, i.e. from the domain of the body. But is it not possible that Schopenhauer misunderstood himself, that he was no Kantian? Is it not the case that 'beauty pleased him, too, out of "interest", in fact, out of the strongest, most personal interest possible: that of the tortured person to escape from torture?'. Thus, the problem of the relationship between philosophy and the ascetic ideal raises its head as an issue that concerns what it means to confront or deal with *suffering*. At the same time, Nietzsche invites reflection of what has been said in the previous essay of the *Genealogy*, where the emergence of humankind as the promising animal was explored in terms of the fashioning of the self through an economy of violent procedures, i.e. torture. There is no reason, we are told, to feel too depressed when the word 'torture' is encountered. There is, Nietzsche says, sufficient to reckon against it, sufficient to pay off the debit side of the account and this must be considered in its favour (ibid., 7). Thus the significance of how philosophers deal with suffering is something that can be estimated in a manner akin to the way in which the cheques and balances of an account's calculations are worked through. Philosophers in general dislike sensuality – they are driven to asceticism. When they praise the ascetic ideal something speaks in them concerning the 'type' of being that each of them is. How is one to interpret the meaning of this? We are offered an answer:

> Every animal, including the *bête philosophe* [philosophical animal], instinctively strives for an optimum of favourable conditions in which fully to release his power and achieve his maximum power-sensation [. . .] (– it is *not* his path to 'happiness' that I am talking about, but the path to power, action, the mightiest deeds, and in most cases, actually, his path to misery).
>
> (Ibid., 7)

No less than any other kind of living being philosophers must obey an instinctive demand that is placed upon them. All that lives is driven to seek out the conditions most favourable to the expression of its drives. This is, in turn, translated into the feeling of power: the sensation of power is evidence of the drives asserting and expressing themselves. Philosophers, like other people, are driven by the desire to feel that they are able to give form and meaning to their world.[28] Their praise of asceticism is merely a precondition of the attainment of this. In praising asceticism they praise the turning away from the body. They praise the transformation of the body into an implement, an instrument that is thereby rendered amenable to the demands of their creative aspirations. Resistance to the body, to that in us which is a creature, is the first step on the path to freedom. Freedom, in its own turn, is a condition of the philosophical life. That is why the ascetic ideal means, in the philosopher's case, that he or she is simply cultivating those conditions necessary for the enhancement of the power-sensation that attests to the pursuit of spirituality. Affirmation of asceticism is 'an optimum condition of the highest and boldest intellectuality, – he [the philosopher] does *not* deny "existence" by doing so, but rather affirms *his* existence and *only* his existence [. . .]' (ibid.). Philosophers praise asceticism, it follows, out of *self-interest*. There is nothing saintly here. The 'three great catch-words' of asceticism, 'poverty, humility, chastity', signify characteristics present in the lives of 'all great productive, inventive spirits' (ibid., 8). This is not a matter of virtue, of morality, but of *necessity*. It is the case, for Nietzsche, that for the philosopher to achieve this optimal state his or her other drives must first be mastered. The philosopher's 'predominant intellectuality' acts 'in its capacity of a *predominant* instinct', imposing itself on all the other drives. We can note that intellectuality here is presented as an *instinct*: it is one (dominating) drive amongst others. Likewise, the selfhood of the philosopher is presented as a hierarchical structure consisting of commanding and obeying. In this regard, the innermost world of thought looks and behaves like a microcosm of social order: it is a domain of struggle between competing interests in which one must, of necessity, come out on top in order for the self to function as a self.

The philosopher's dominant intellectuality leads them to absent themselves from the normative world – thinkers always engage in the pursuit of 'deserts' apart from the realm of daily concerns and the marketplace – thus, 'Heraclitus withdrew into the courts and colonnades of the immense Temple of Artemis'. Such a retreat is, by definition, a retreat from the *present*: 'we philosophers need a rest from one thing above all: anything to do with "today"'. As with the invocation of philosophers of the future in *Beyond Good and Evil* here, likewise, philosophers are seen as essentially untimely.[29] However, their self-imposed exile is at the same time a kind of running ahead, since the philosopher is a kind of signpost towards the elevated kind of humanity that Nietzsche wishes for. Solitude, one needs to recall, is the precondition of difference and deviance. Solitude (which is no one place, but anywhere that is apart from the dominion of norms) is what goads the individual into thinking otherwise than according to the average. It is, in simpler terms, a creative space, which is why it defines the optimum condition of philosophical activity. To retreat into solitude is, at the same time, to remove oneself from discourse with others, to spurn the language of the everyday.[30] Asceticism stands amongst the necessary conditions that ensure the philosopher attains untimely status. In shunning the present, philosophers create their own world and with it their own *future*: the philosopher 'shuns his time and its "day". He inhabits it like a shadow: the more the sun sinks, the bigger he becomes.' What the philosopher constructs (a world of meaning) gains in autonomy and significance the further it is removed from the temporal conditions that mark its source. Philosophical origins are at the same time ascetic origins only in so far as asceticism was the 'leading-rein', the guiding and restraining hand that held up and protected philosophy when it first stepped and then tottered on the face of the earth (ibid., 9).

Imagine making a reckoning up of the 'drives and virtues of the philosopher', and setting them out in a row. The individual drives before us include the drive to doubt, negate, wait, analyse, research, look, risk, compare and balance out. The virtues are the will to neutrality and objectivity. These drives and virtues are anti-social. How can we doubt, says Nietzsche, that they all 'ran counter to the primary demands of morality and conscience for the longest periods of time?' That is why thinking *philosophically* means thinking *against* the norms and conventions of one's present.[31] At the same time, these drives are themselves indubitably social in origin. Doubting, waiting, analysing, researching and taking risks are all ways of acting that presuppose a social world in which such forms of behaviour and the practices associated with them exist before the philosopher can appropriate it. Likewise, comparing and balancing presuppose the estimating abilities of measuring and weighing that stand at the doorway of the social realm as its preconditions.[32] The philosopher thinks against norms and craves what is forbidden, but only does so in virtue of the work these norms have performed in rendering the human being into the kind of animal it is. In this way, the philosopher stands as the starkest embodiment of our contradictory nature. That is why philosophers are best advised to avoid understanding who they really are, why they need to guard against becoming self-aware. That is why philosophers had to borrow the appearance of the ascetic.[33]

What the philosopher borrowed from is as significant as the borrowing itself. Asceticism comes from the domain of the priest, 'the actual representative of *seriousness*' on earth (ibid., 11). The ascetic priest values life in a specific manner. The ascetic ideal of a timeless and pure reality is pitted against the world of becoming, change, appearance, the senses, and sensuality. Life is taken as 'a bridge to that other existence' that awaits the faithful in a blissful beyond. 'The ascetic treats life as a wrong path which he has walked along backwards, till he reaches the point where he starts.' The priest demands that others follow him and thereby 'imposes his valuation on existence'. What is interesting for Nietzsche, however, is the fact that this mode of valuation is not the exception but the rule. The ascetic priest is to be found everywhere throughout history. No time, society or class has even been devoid of priests. Why? 'It must be a necessity of the first rank that which makes this species continually grow and prosper when it is *hostile to life, – life itself must have an interest* in preserving such a self-contradictory type.' The self-contradiction is plain enough, at least on Nietzsche's account of it. Life, for the ascetic priest, is 'a self-contradiction' that must be mastered. The ascetic priest therefore expresses a deep desire to control the 'most profound conditions' of life itself rather than merely to control and master things in life. The ascetic priest is also a being of 'unparalleled *ressentiment*' and it is this *ressentiment* that wishes to master life. Imagine that such a 'will to contradiction and counter-nature can be made to *philosophize*: on what will it vent its inner arbitrariness?' It will 'look for *error* precisely where the actual instinct of life most unconditionally judges there to be truth'. Thus, the physical world will be dismissed as an illusion (e.g. 'Vendanta philosophy') (ibid., 12).[34] How, though, does one interpret the significance of the ascetic denial of life, of this form of 'life *against* life'? Nietzsche attempts an explanation: '*the ascetic ideal springs from the protective and healing instincts of a degenerating life* which uses every means to maintain itself and struggles for its existence' (ibid., 13).[35]

With this we encounter the central contention underlying the third essay of the *Genealogy* concerning what it is to be human. That humanity has been so dominated by the presence of the ascetic priest indicates that the effects that civilisation itself has had upon us. Civilisation (which is also none other than the 'taming of man', the regularisation and rendering of humanity in terms of the governance of norms) has created a humanity that suffers from an attitude of 'disgust at life'. In crude terms, humanity has developed the propensity for self-loathing. The ascetic priest is an expression of this hatred, but an expression of such a kind that the effect of the priest is to counter it. The ascetic priest represents 'the incarnate wish for being otherwise, being elsewhere [. . .] but the *power* of his wishing is the fetter which binds him here, precisely this is what makes him a tool, who now has to work to create more favourable circumstances for our being here and being man [. . .]' (ibid., 13). What seems initially to be a dreadful, contemptible and universal manifestation of human culture is now revealed in more complex terms. The 'apparent enemy of life, this *negative man* [. . .] actually belongs to the really great forces in life which *conserve and create the positive*'. To put the matter slightly differently: the ascetic priest is an articulation of the great economy of the preservation of the species. His existence is necessary because, however vile one might be inclined to find him, the priest embodies one of those 'evil' propensities that actively restores human trust and joy in life.[36] Humanity suffers from itself and the ascetic priest offers a way of making this suffering bearable by offering an explanation for it.

8. *A humanity that suffers from itself is a sick humanity. This is the outcome of the unconscious experimentation we have performed upon ourselves ever since our ancestors broke with the realm of nature and became normative beings. The philosopher of the future represents a refinement of this experimental nature. Philosophers of the future are envisaged by Nietzsche to be self-experimenters without equal. Like humanity as a whole they are seekers after meaning. Unlike the rest of humankind they seek to create rather than receive such meaning. In doing so, the philosopher of the future exemplifies the essential nature of humanity as that being endowed with futurity and self-understanding.*

That humanity is consequently sick is, for Nietzsche, beyond doubt: 'man [. . .] is *the* sick animal' (ibid.). The answer as to why this is the case leads us back to the notion of human futurity, of which the philosopher of the future is an exemplar. Philosophers, and especially philosophers of the future, are experimenters; above all, they are their own guinea pigs, their own laboratory animals. But in this they represent an extension of an already present and defining inclination in humankind. From the time of our ancestors' first communal attempt at self-regulation, from the first economically derived norms that were imposed as a means of fashioning the individual, what characterises human existence is, above all, *self-experimentation*. In the first, prehistoric instance this may have been unconscious. But, however unconscious, the attempt to come to terms with existence through struggling with it rather than letting conditions be dictated by circumstances, as the rest of the animal kingdom do, is a quintessentially human response to life. We want to be in control, we want to dominate our environment rather than let our environment dominate us. Domination, for us, means projecting meaning in a forward direction. In this regard, we always live within a domain bordered by the question of our own futurity, which means that our lives are haunted by the question of what simply being here at all means. Meaningfulness is a projection, an assertion of the relationship between human agency and the world. Every act of projection invokes the 'not yet', that which will be the case, a future state in which one considers one's own place as an active and responsible being. One *needs* this projection in order to be a person. Personhood is not something that can be boiled down to matters of fact or mere descriptions of states of things. Personhood is possibility, which is the interpretation of states of affairs rather than any particular state itself. In so far as one exists one needs to want this possibility, in whatever form, even if it is an illusory one. To this extent, humanity always lives in virtue of its desire for a *future*.

Philosophers of the future are an extrapolation of this essential aspect of human character. They exemplify a humanity that is in its fundamental nature 'the still-unconquered eternal-futurist'. To remain invincible with regard to being eternally future-oriented is to be human. But there is a price to pay for this. The thronging force that drives our forward-looking assertion of our identity prevents our finding peace. Our sense of who we are is a restless sense. How could it not be, given that who we are must always, in part, be thought of as somewhere else, not here but somewhere or other *ahead* of me. This relationship to one's sense of self amounts to a relationship with one's own being as that which suffers. The 'I' can contemplate itself but it is driven beyond itself even as it does so. Self-contemplation is never a mere *looking-in* upon the contents of a consciousness, as if they were akin to mere things stored away in a drawer and available for cataloguing. It is, rather, a comprehending of oneself within a movement of thought that is ceaselessly *looking-forward* and escaping from itself. Thoughts are not things, they are expressions of our dispositions and their relationship to our environment, temporal projections. We are beings who lean into the future and are, as a result, always in danger of toppling into a void. We suffer from our own futurity; our essence rebels in us against itself. The human being is such that 'his future digs inexorably into him like a spur into the flesh of every present: – how should such a courageous and wealthy animal not also be the most jeopardised, the longest and most profoundly sick of all sick animals?' (ibid.). Humanity is thus a manifest contradiction. We live and in living are affirmations of life, but even as we do this we turn *against* ourselves and life. We are like this simply because we do not fit into a niche, as all other animals do, but have taken the step of living in a manner that defies such modes of classification.[37] It is because it suffers from itself that humanity has become so adept as torturing itself. Torture, which began as the most physical of procedures aimed at reminding primitive humans that it was a good idea to obey communally beneficial regulations, has been transfigured and spiritualised.[38]

9. *The necessity of the ascetic priest can now be understood. It springs from the need of a sick humanity to be nursed. This has had a double effect. On the one hand, humankind has been saved from annihilation. On the other hand, it has 'ruined spiritual health'. However, the genuine meaning of the ascetic ideal does not reside in its consequences (the damage it has done) but in the need it satisfies. Humankind needs meaning, which for Nietzsche means that it needs to believe in a unifying and universal purpose that justifies existence. Nietzsche's analyses of suffering, futurity and the need for meaning are extrapolations of the great economy first discussed in* The Gay Science. *The first section of this work can, it follows, be read as a kind of commentary on the later text of the* Genealogy.

The state of 'sickliness' that Nietzsche has been discussing typifies humanity; it is the norm. This being the case, we should value all the more the unusual '*strokes of luck*' that create humans of 'spiritual and physical powerfulness' (*Genealogy*, III, 14). Such beings need to be protected from the danger that the norm presents to them – above all the danger of being nauseated by man and of feeling sympathy for those who suffer most from themselves. You can find evidence of the struggle between the 'sick and healthy' all over the place. For Nietzsche, it is manifest in the writings of contemporary philosopher and political economist, Eugen Dühring, 'that apostle of revenge from Berlin [. . .] today's biggest loudmouth of morality, even amongst his kind, the anti-Semites'. Such people are characterised by a self-hatred that expresses itself as the desire to hold *others* to account for the fact that they suffer from themselves. They embody the maxim 'It's a disgrace to be happy! *There is too much misery!*'. Sick beings need nursing. We can now understand 'the necessity of doctors and nurses *who are sick themselves*: and now we have and hold with both hands the meaning of the ascetic priest' (ibid., 15). The priest ministers with regard to rancour, and is therefore 'the *direction-changer* of *ressentiment*'. The direction of *ressentiment* is altered by the sufferer being offered a reason for his or her distress, above all 'a *guilty* culprit'. Pain is alleviated by release of the most satisfying of compensatory emotions: blame, 'Someone or other must be to blame that I feel ill [. . .]'. This urge to explain pain creates a metaphysical explanation that disguises the real 'physiological' reasons for suffering. The priest's explanation does not stop at mere blame, it names the culprit: someone is indeed to blame for your suffering: it is *you*. The direction of bad feeling engendered by suffering is, in this way, focussed inward, playing on the internalising tendency inherent in human psychological life. The concepts of guilt, sin, and damnation serve to turn the resentment of the sufferer back on its source. In this way, the sufferer becomes trained to survey, discipline and overcome his or her own feelings. The ascetic priest is in this way an expression of 'the healing instinct of life' (ibid., 16).

The ascetic priest is the great user of emotion: above all, guilt. In the second essay Nietzsche argues that guilt and bad conscience (defined succinctly here as 'cruelty turned back on itself' (ibid., 20)) emerged when the inhabitants of primitive communal creditor–debtor social orders were imprisoned within the confines of society as a consequence of invasion and colonisation. The priest, he now tells us, took this sense of guilt and reinterpreted it in terms of 'sin'. The 'sick man' became 'the sinner'. In this way suffering was radically misunderstood. This interpretation of suffering gave rise to all forms of self-torture (physical and mental): 'the scourge, the hair shirt, the starving body, contrition'. What did this achieve? Oddly enough, things began to look better: 'the old depression, heaviness and fatigue were thoroughly *overcome* by this system of procedures, life became *very* interesting again: awake, eternally awake, sleepless, glowing, burned out, exhausted and yet not tired, – this is how man, the "sinner", looked when initiated into *these* mysteries'. In this way the ascetic priest stimulated an interest in life and hence overcame exhaustion by creating conditions under which yet *more* pain came to be desired. More emotion, more suffering: all received their justification from the concept of the 'sinner' deserving of endless punishment. The power of the ascetic ideal thereby reveals itself in all its glory. Certainly, much self-contempt and much self-torture resulted from the dominance of the ascetic priest, with the result that humankind was perhaps irreparably damaged by it (ibid., 21).[39] A self-scourging humanity is a lacerated and disfigured humanity, both physically and mentally. That is why, for Nietzsche, asceticism in its priestly guise has 'ruined spiritual health' (*Genealogy*, III, 22). At the same time, it saved humanity from itself, from the fact that it suffers from its existence. In this regard, the genuine significance of the acetic ideal does not turn so much on what it has done as what it has forestalled and what its appeal indicates. Its true meaning consists in 'what it *means*, what it indicates, what lies hidden behind, beneath and within it and what it expresses in a provisional, indistinct way, laden with question marks' (ibid., 23).

For Nietzsche, such issues are issues of *power*. If we are to answer the question of the meaning of the ascetic ideal adequately we need to do so by way of an appreciation of the power that this ideal has exerted over humanity for millennia: 'What does the *power* of that ideal mean, the *monstrosity* of its power?' Nietzsche's answer is straightforward enough and is linked to his conception of the futurity that is the essential component of human existence. What is at stake here in so far as it concerns power is at the same time a question of *purposes*. The ascetic ideal 'has a *goal*'. But this is not just any old goal. The ascetic ideal does not offer a goal like the purposes that crop up as part of the everyday fabric of life. One can have limited goals, purposes that stretch from the trivial to the life changing in their implications. One person can also have many different goals and these need not harmonise with one another to form a coherent whole: 'I must clean my teeth'; 'Today I will read that book'; 'Next year I will get that promotion, even if it means loosing against my boss at golf'; 'I want to be a pop star'; 'I want to be prime-minister'; 'I want to live a moral life'; 'I want to be happy'. The ascetic ideal does not offer humanity goals of this sort. Rather, its goal is of such generality that all others are capable of being fitted into it, interpreted in terms of it, and will appear trivial in contrast with its over-arching significance. The ascetic ideal presents humanity with a sense of purpose that claims universality: all 'the interests of human existence appear petty and narrow when measured against it [...]'. It is supreme in so far as it ventures to offer an interpretation of all times, races, humanity in general; an interpretation that seeks to subordinate all of them to a *single purpose*. The ascetic ideal 'rejects, denies, affirms, confirms only with reference to *its* interpretation' of the world. It believes it has 'unconditional *superiority of rank* over any other power [...]' (ibid.). The ascetic ideal makes manifest an unconstrained desire for domination; and it is this *desire* that endows life with meaning. This is asceticism's gift to the human race, for without it 'the *animal* man, had no meaning' (*Genealogy*, III, 28). The ascetic ideal therefore endowed humanity with a much-needed sense of purpose.

The meaning of the ascetic ideal can now be grasped: '*This* is what the ascetic ideal meant: something was *missing*, there was an immense *lacuna* around man, – he himself could think of no justification or explanation or affirmation, he *suffered* from the problem of what he meant.' The key problem that the ascetic ideal addresses is not suffering itself but *what this suffering signifies*. *Suffering* is what makes us human, but not in relation to the fact that we simply suffer, as all sentient life can and usually must do, but because we are driven to search for a meaning, an answer to the question 'Why do I suffer?' There is, for a person, no such thing as mere pain. For us, all pain demands reasons, its role in the narrative that constitutes someone's understanding of their life cannot be underestimated. Nietzsche's contempt for utilitarians and any others with the attitude that takes suffering and any of its manifestations to be an objection and mere obstacle is hence not some quixotic matter of individual temperament. It springs, rather, from his contention that a life, so long as it is truly human (which means, so long as it has left behind and beneath it the realm of mere animality), cannot be rich in meaning if avoiding suffering in all its possible forms becomes the prime consideration. 'Man', Nietzsche tells us, is 'the bravest animal and the most prone to suffer [. . .]' (ibid.). We do not, he claims, really seek to avoid suffering or deny it. Rather, we are even prone to search for it, so long as we are given 'a *meaning* for it, a *purpose* of suffering'.

What has plagued humanity was, it follows, not suffering itself but the very meaninglessness of its suffering. The great achievement of the ascetic ideal was that it managed to provide a reason, a justification, for our pain – a pain that is not merely physical discomfort but one of spiritual turmoil. 'Within it, suffering was given an interpretation [. . .]'. The problem was that this interpretation actually made humanity *suffer even more*: ever prone to internalisation, it internalised suffering through its use of the concept of guilt and its reinterpretation of this concept in terms of sin. 'But in spite of all that – man was *saved*, he had a *meaning*, from now on he was no longer like a leaf in the breeze, the plaything of the absurd, of "non-sense"; from now on he could *will* something [. . .] the *will itself was saved*' (ibid.). The will was saved, but only at the cost of being given a specific 'direction by the ascetic ideal'. A humanity fashioned by this ideal came to hate the senses, the body and the animal aspect of human existence, likewise recoiling from beauty.[40] It also found itself driven to escape from appearance, becoming, growth, development, and death. To put it more simply, humankind came to desire *nothingness*. This is the essence of the *will to nothingness* that Nietzsche castigates Christianity and asceticism generally for endorsing. All the things that life is are, from this perspective, lesser things, pale shadows of a reality whose essence can only be intimated in thought and entered after death. The short section that began the third essay of the *Genealogy* now stands revealed in all its meaning: 'And, to conclude by saying what I said at the beginning: man still prefers to *will nothingness*, than *not* will . . . '.

Human existence, on the above conception, is not merely bounded by the notions of suffering, meaning and futurity found in the text of the *Genealogy* itself. At the same time, Nietzsche's analysis represents an extrapolation of the great economy first presented in *The Gay Science*. The craving for meaning is an essential component of this economy, for endowing life with sense is, we need to recall, precisely what constitutes the 'economy of the preservation of the species' (*The Gay Science*, 1). As Nietzsche says in that work, all religious and ethical teachings, even poetical works that dwell upon the tragedy of human existence, promote human continuance by satisfying our need to give some kind of sense to our lives. In the classical or Shakespearean tragedy the fate of the individual becomes a universal paradigm for human suffering transfigured into art and thereby richly endowed with meaning. The sense of narrative order communicated by the tragedy no less than the promise of future eternal bliss for observing divine commandments provokes us consider life worthwhile: it tempts us to affirm life. The essential promise made here is that life itself is not mere surface and farce; that one's existence has been given a meaning that is reassuringly out of one's own bungling hands.

The *Genealogy* operates as a commentary on the earlier postulation of the economy of human preservation offered by *The Gay Science*. The *Genealogy* fills out the earlier text's contention that all humankind needs to have 'faith in *reason in life*' in order to cope with the idea of existing at all. It does so by exploring an example of such a faith (asceticism) and the consequences it has when it comes to moulding human existence. Along with the analysis of human prehistory in the *Genealogy*'s second essay, the analysis of asceticism also offers perhaps the most daring example of Nietzsche's enactment of the kind of experimentalism he extols. It is an experimentalism of costs and benefits. The benefits of asceticism are weighed up against the price that had to be paid for them. The economy of human preservation in *The Gay Science* becomes in the *Genealogy* by turns the violent instigator of the realm of communal and social life and the means whereby the individual was constituted in relation to the other as measurer, creditor and debtor. Normativity and economy in this way become one and the same thing. Norms are codes signifying measures, estimations of actions and relations between people and their world. They gain significance because of their role within the grand story Nietzsche seeks to tell of the unconsciously pursued development of human autonomy and independence in the shape of the 'sovereign individual' or overman. In this way, the economy that grounds human preservation is transformed into the motivating force that powers human development and social evolution by endowing it with futurity and simultaneously offering a kind of goal (in the form of individual autonomy) that satisfies the demands placed upon us by our futurity.[41]

10. *Nietzsche wishes to overcome primitive economy. He turns to the notion of self-sublimation as a means of doing this. But even as he does so, economy returns to haunt it.*

As the notions of the sovereign individual and the philosophers of the future should make clear, Nietzsche does not want to remain trapped within the economy that is constitutive of our species. The point about enabling conditions is that it is always possible to go beyond them – or ought to be. The passage from creature to creator is, at one and the same time, a move away from the economic conditions that mark out human emergence and its maintenance. Thus, the sovereign individual is envisaged as transforming the conditions that gave rise to human futurity in its ability to spurn the economic logic of exchange underlying the compensatory notions that constitute justice (*Genealogy*, II, 10). The power of sovereignty here becomes equivalent to the overcoming of justice in the form of 'mercy'. Justice is pure economy, a manifestation of the notions and practices that gave rise to the individual out of the creditor–debtor relationship. Justice presupposes exchange, measure, 'weight', equality: it holds that, when faced with a wrong, some form of compensation equivalent to the deed can be offered up by the culprit, that the full power of contractual and legal obligation can be brought down upon them and recompense exacted.[42] For Nietzsche, individual sovereignty at its most worthy would turn its back on all feelings of revenge; the economy of exchange would be broken. Understood this way, justice would conclude 'like every good thing on earth, by *sublimating itself*' (ibid.).

Yet, even as sovereign autonomy is seen as overcoming economical-normative constraints, these notions return to haunt it. Our futurity no less than our ancestors' futurity is a direct consequence of the primitive exchange principle. We are built as the kind of beings that *must* think in terms of our future, and we carry about with us every moment of every day the ancient legacy our ancestors endowed to us in this regard (*Daybreak*, 18). The need for a reason for being here at all that is explored in the concluding essay of the *Genealogy* (the related questions of the 'Where-to?' and 'What-for?' of humanity) points forward as much as it points back. The basic character of humankind as the creature that can be formed, moulded, re-formed, lacerated, as the being that is cultivated and cultivator, exploiter of others and exploited by its own kind, does not change. Everything about humankind, Nietzsche argues at the beginning of *Human, All Too Human*, has 'become'. But the *what* that becomes us, our basic constituent propensities, the original 'eternal' text of *homo natura* (*Beyond Good and Evil*, 230), the assemblage of affects that make us what we are,[43] remain constant once set in place. That is why prehistory, the era of untold communal violence that prefigures the 'centuries *before* the history of mankind' is not only 'the genuine and decisive historical period which determined man's character' (*Genealogy*, II, 14, 9). It is also that which 'exists at all times or could possibly re-occur' (ibid., 9). The influence of the prehistoric economy of communal norms is, in other words, universal. Economy does not merely engender futurity and then pass away. It abides as a constitutive condition of human existence. In this sense, our communal past always precedes us. The economic origins of our prehistoric understanding and its historical articulations are not remnants trapped in a distant past, but form the basis for all projection, striving and hope for our own kind.

Conclusion

We have followed Nietzsche upon a path that begins with his criticism of economic culture and ends with the employment of economy as a tool for articulating his vision of human potential. Economy bestows upon humankind the gift of being able to become more than it is. As such, it articulates the condition of futurity that is fulfilled in the figures of sovereign individual, in the allegorical figure of the overman and in the philosophers of the future. In their transcendence of norms these images of human potential represent possible answers to the question posed by Nietzsche in *Human, All Too Human* as to 'whether mankind could *transform itself from a moral to a knowing mankind*' (*Human, All Too Human*, 107).[1] As Nietzsche is all too well aware, a knowing humanity is also always already an economically organised one. Modern Europe, a mass society, a sphere of burgeoning mass culture, increasingly decentralised, flowing, shifting and redistributing itself as a result of the impetus given to it by ever more efficient industrialised production, can lead to an accumulation of the very forces that he sets his hopes by. This hope marks the opening of a dichotomy between Nietzsche's earlier texts, separating the *Untimely Meditations*, the *Human, All Too Human* volumes and the *Daybreak* from the writings that begin with *The Gay Science* and culminate in the *Genealogy* and *Twilight of the Idols*. All are conjoined by a common concern. This is that, in the words of *Twilight*, 'what matters most [. . .] always remains culture' (*Twilight of the Idols*, 'What the Germans Lack', 3). The concern may remain consistent and the context, too, is consistently that of 'the age of labour' (*Twilight*, 'Skirmishes of an Untimely Man', 30), but the path to its attainment alters. The economic model becomes increasingly Nietzsche's chosen paradigm for articulating the emergence of civilisation and the meaning of culture alike.

In Nietzsche's mature works, the language of value becomes increasingly dominated by the logic of exchange. It becomes increasingly the case that for him the nature of culture, society, humanity and human potential are matters that can be considered through a language of costs and benefits. 'The value of a thing sometimes does not lie in that which one attains by it, but in what one pays for it – what it costs us' (*Twilight*, 'Skirmishes', 38) becomes an ever more generally applicable maxim. Even though initially expressed here in *Twilight of the Idols* in relatively tentative terms as a principle that applies from time to time, the notion that the exchange incurred for a thing determines its value is almost immediately restated in categorical terms. Freedom is not the right of the tired old soldier who desires to be left alone in peace. Freedom is a possession by right of conquest, it belongs to the 'warrior'; and as such one must be prepared to sacrifice oneself and others to its cause. Freedom, it follows, is 'measured' by the individual and by entire cultures and peoples alike in terms of the degree of 'resistance which must be overcome'. That is why the aristocratic commonwealths epitomised by Rome and Venice were like great 'hothouses'. They were places of cultivation where the drives of their subjects were forged and beaten like resilient but pliable metal to make beings who desired conquest, a desire that was itself an expression of the will to freedom. The ancient commonwealth becomes like a workshop in which the violent labour of humanity upon itself first begun in the primitive community can be conducted and refined with a view to attaining some kind of perfection. Freedom comes only when one has invested sufficiently in the means to its attainment.

Modernity is problematic because it lacks the means (i.e. the will) to the attainment of such freedom: 'The whole of the West no longer possesses the instincts out of which institutions grow, out of which a future grows [...]' (ibid., 39). Yet, although modernity may be contemptible the development of Nietzsche's thought bears witness to an increasing temptation to see it as ripe for appropriation by those endowed with the means. The genuine philosopher as the mature Nietzsche understands such a being, a 'man of the most comprehensive responsibility who has conscience for the over-all development of man' (*Beyond Good and Evil*, 61) is such a person. This is a spiritually endowed person. But it is a person who no longer stands like Epictetus as a solitary in the marketplace. Instead, the philosopher of the future stands amidst contemporary life waiting in preparation to enter the swirling morass of modernity with a view to plundering it like a warrior. The genuine 'philosopher will make use of religions for his project of cultivation and education, just as he will make use of whatever political and economical states are at hand'. Future legislative philosophy does not shirk from entering into the world of political and economic strife.

It is not, however, simply a matter of the experimental thinker's willingness to seize hold of whatever happens to be handy in their desire to fulfil their drive to create. The going to ground and cultural sterility that the young Nietzsche sees in his times remain, but the very negativity is now regarded as what makes the material suitable for appropriation and transformation. What characterises Nietzsche's mature conception of philosophical futurity is also, it turns out, made most manifest by the world of modern economic production. As attempters and experimenters, philosophers of the future at the same time exemplify one aspect of modernity of which Nietzsche evidently approves wholeheartedly: 'our whole modern existence is nothing but *hubris* and godlessness, in so far as it is strength and awareness of strength rather than weakness' (*Genealogy*, III, 9). This self-awareness of strength finds its foremost expression in industrial technology and the manner in which we engage in 'nature-rape', treating our natural environment as an instrument and resource. We tear our world to pieces with machines. We knead and batter it into convenient shapes and force it to conform to our demands with the assistance of the technician's and engineer's unconcerned resourcefulness. The industrial-scale mastering of nature characteristic of modernity is, in other words, another expression of the primitive drive to futurity that springs from our promising nature. Through industrial practice, nature is colonised and subordinated no less than the originally unpredictable early human seized by the passions and desires of the moment was, through being forcibly rendered an obedient servant to tradition, colonised by norms. The violation of nature with a view to its being rendered fit for human purposes is, of course, an act of pure instrumentalism, its unthinking, unreflective nature as conventional as the most uncritical conformity. The drive to fashion humanity according to the creative demands of the future philosopher's legislative desire that Nietzsche advocates thereby finds an uncomfortable parallel in modernity's desire to wrestle with its environment and transform it into mere material.

The question arises of the extent to which the profound opposition to his times that Nietzsche extols slips away with this conciliatory gesture towards modern hubris. The philosopher of the future opposes the norm. Yet, in the celebration of the hubris of modernity's treatment of nature, this norm returns to colonise the thought that conjures the future philosopher and their means of escape through legislative mastery. In a society where mass production methods increasingly dominate, such methods come to serve as the most unthinkingly observed conventions, they constitute the morality of custom of the day. As soon as it is celebrated in terms that invoke the modern machine and the industrial procedures that accompany it, the future philosopher's self-experimentation becomes susceptible to being rendered little more than a poeticised extension of the formalised methodologies that characterise the technical-industrial process. And it is celebrated: 'we experiment on ourselves in a way which we would never allow on animals, we merrily vivisect our souls out of curiosity [. . .]'. The experimenter turns on his or her own subjectivity as if it were no more than thing-like, a piece of nature that can be dug up, dug into, tested, manipulated and used up by a masochistic curiosity. With this celebratory gesture, the purportedly autonomous self that Nietzsche celebrates becomes enmeshed in a world dominated by the know-how of technicians and engineers. The 'vast experimental workshop'[2] of nature that the genuine philosopher must inhabit no less than the normative individual is, at the same time, an experimental order of industrial production that signifies a social world bounded by forces greater than those of mere creative imagining.

Technical facility lies beyond the philosopher's sphere of influence precisely because he or she cannot stand outside of it. To live in the modern world is to dwell in a realm that is ever more technically replete. It is a world where the concepts of labour and creativity are ever more intertwined with the narrow specialism of the expert and so also become increasingly dependent upon it. Technical knowledge eclipses poetic and creative knowledge. The fact that one may today even pause when tempted to conjoin the word 'knowledge' with 'poetry' and 'creativity' is symptomatic. The ability to make instruments that satisfy desires, and which takes the worth of those desires as a given, ultimately subordinates the critical ability to think about and create values to its own demands and so absorbs it. Nietzsche, no less than us, stands in the midst of this dilemma. We may recall Zarathustra urging his followers to build a dwelling for the overman and to make ready 'earth, animal, and plant for him' in order that he may give justification to our futurity and redeem our past sufferings (*Thus Spoke Zarathustra*, I, 'Prologue', 4). Such urging is simultaneously open to being read as a demand to pursue the human project of labour on an industrial scale. The project takes its justification from a vision of the future that is attainable through the technical transforming of the earth.[3] Nietzsche would rather this seizing hold of reality than any form of acceptance: 'Do we desire for mankind and end in fire and light or one in the sand?' (*Daybreak*, 429). The attitude this expresses places itself unthinkingly in the hands of those whose aptitude it wrongly thought to be a mere resource for its own goals. The earth becomes encircled by a vision of technical facility that exceeds the control of the self-appointed evaluator and esteemer. Enclosed within a belt of instrumentalism, the globe becomes a sphere where the increasing subordination of natural resources to the short-term but universal goal of profiting from the satisfaction of human desires is attained at the cost of ever-greater wastage.

The problem with such instrumentalism is that its consequences are strictly speaking *unthinkable*. That an instrument can break is, of course, easy enough to comprehend. But that the world itself, the ever more manipulated environment which is the condition of all instrumentalism, might be used up and disappear even as we grasp it, *that the future might vanish because of our striving for it*, is too shocking to envisage in concrete terms. It is consigned to our poetic imaginings, the fearful yet distant projection of a dim possibility. Yet, Nietzsche's use of the notion of 'earth' invokes something that must at the same time provoke this thought in us in more concrete terms. The earth precedes the primitive economy of exploitation still evident in modern industrialism even if it does not necessarily stand apart from the organic economy that Nietzsche is frequently tempted to envisage as being constitutive of 'life itself'. Zarathustra, we should recall, urges us to keep faith with the earth not merely in order to render it suitable for use but also that it may one day become a domain of healing (*Thus Spoke Zarathustra*, I, 'Of the Gift-Giving Virtue', 3). Likewise, the human being of genuine futurity is, for Nietzsche, someone who 'gives the earth purpose and man his hope again' (*Genealogy*, II, 24). The question we may ask, perhaps the one that today we *must* ask above all others, concerns the extent to which the global exploitation of the earth is justifiable. Nietzsche's work stands as one of the most imaginative conceptual landscapes in relation to which such questions can be raised. In this, his enactment of the violent, exploitative aspects of economy in the language of philosophy makes it possible to reflect upon in thought what is all too often left to mere unthinking practice. By turning economy into philosophy, Nietzsche renders it questionable.

Raising the question of economy also means raising the question as to whether the relationship between self and other is exhausted by the kind of accounts that Nietzsche offers in texts such as *Human, All Too Human, Daybreak* and the *Genealogy*. Although taking a stand against metaphysical philosophy, Nietzsche does not take a stand against transcendence. The vision of human futurity is a vision of transcendence: through it humanity transcends its own present to yield an as yet unrealised potential. Yet, Nietzsche does not pause to consider the possibility that the kind of transcendence he craves is not something located in the realm of his fondest imaginings but in the everyday world of the street and others like him. His consideration of others is usually starkly contrasted between the impersonal (the 'herd', the machine-like slavery of modern life, etc.) and the realm of personal friendship. The neighbour is always inferior to the friend. The other, understood as 'you', denotes for Nietzsche the most ancient and normative of social relations. The 'I', in contrast, is new, rich in individual potential, a prefiguring of the overman's uniqueness: 'I teach you not the neighbor but the friend [... which is...] an anticipation of the overman [...] Let the future and the farthest be for you the cause of your today: in your friend you shall love the overman as your cause' (*Zarathustra*, I, 'On Love of the Neighbor'). Friendship in this way becomes an analogue of the transcendence of humanity sought in the overman. The overman's transcendence, in turn, lies in his enjoyment and revelling in the sense of mastery that his peculiar kind of affirmation makes possible. What Nietzsche's approach recoils before is the possibility that the other itself (the 'you') is what inspires in us such desire for transcendence. In terms expressed by Emmanuel Levinas, such desire as the Other inspires in the 'I' overruns the latter's inwardly focussed sense of enjoyment and pleasure in mastery.[4] In simplest terms, even before subjects meet as creditor and debtor they must already be able to recognise their common humanity, and they do not do so not by an inner dwelling on the contents of their own minds or by reacting to their own internalised instinctual demands. Rather, humanity emerges as an encountering of the Other as a being that cannot be mastered or thought of as an object. The external nature of the Other is never a matter of a mere being-outside. The Other is not an entity that can be grasped in the manner akin to which knives, forks, spoons and other objects around us can be. True, one can seek to 'get hold' of another's physical body, one can wrestle them to the ground, silence them and use them as a means to an end. Yet, their existence is necessarily already understood, Levinas argues, as a mode of transcendence that overruns all notions of exteriority that the existence of mere objects may be grounded in. As soon as someone opens their mouth and speaks they are more than a mere object. They are a *somebody*, a being 'like me' who cannot be considered merely in terms of their use-value, as a debtor whose existence is merely a means of my attaining subjective satisfaction. I never merely 'see' or 'grasp' the Other as a thing. I respond to its expression *as language*. When someone else speaks, they enact a transcendence that comes from a height, not from somewhere merely 'outside' me but *beyond* me. This transcendence remains at the same time within the world that the 'I' dwells in and lives off.

This relationship between the 'I' and the Other as Levinas articulates it necessarily presupposes 'a certain form of economic life'.[5] Spheres of economic life concern the world around us. A world is only held in common, recognised as something that is dwelled in *together* because it is broken up into possessions, places in which 'I' live, and you live, and the like. To this extent, Levinas's and Nietzsche's thought conjoin: 'No human or interhuman relationship can be enacted outside of economy; no face can be approached with empty hands and a closed home'.[6] For Levinas, as much as for Nietzsche, every person dwells in a world characterised by economy. Language, what affirms the generality of this possession, the fact that a world that is initially comprehended as 'mine' in the manner in which a child sees everything as an extension of its own awareness, was already placed 'in common' as the precondition of that comprehending.[7] In this way, the world is endowed with meaning through economy. However, economy exists in whatever form one might care to envisage it only because others are there, too. In this way, economy ceases to be open to the kind of speculative and mythologising projection that Nietzsche ultimately proffers with his vision of futurity as mastery.

That said, the realm of economy remains as much a matter of our present as Nietzsche's. When the world at large faces the ramifications of a global economy that fashions subjectivity as inexorably as it does motor cars and computers, engagement with the richness of his thought in precisely this register attains greater relevance than ever before. The attitude that renders the earth and those on it no more than mere tools for use, akin to things thoughtlessly regarded as just other kinds of handy entity at one's disposal and, consequently, disposable according to the demands of the moment, is conjoined irrevocably with the question of economy. To see in Nietzsche's dual celebration of mastery and earth an inconsistency that needs addressing is to place his thought in question in such a way that its excesses place *us* in question. The normative world of commerce that Nietzsche fights against, employs and in his late writings even succumbs to is more embracing in the concrete expression of its power today than in his time. To raise the question of economy is, even more today than in Nietzsche's time, to raise the question of futurity. This much, at the very least, we must learn from him, for most truly it has been said 'the weights of all things must be determined anew' (*The Gay Science*, 269).

Primary Texts

Friedrich Nietzsche, *Untimely Meditations*, trans. R.J. Hollingdale (Cambridge: Cambridge University Press, 1983).

——. *Human, All Too Human*, vols I and II (which includes *Assorted Opinions and Maxims* and *The Wanderer and His Shadow*), trans. R.J. Hollingdale (Cambridge: Cambridge University Press, 1986).
——. *Daybreak: Thoughts on the Prejudices of Morality*, trans. R.J. Hollingdale (Cambridge: Cambridge University Press, 1982).
——. *The Gay Science*, trans. Walter Kaufmann (New York: Vintage Books, 1974).
——. *Thus Spoke Zarathustra*, trans. Walter Kaufmann, in *The Viking Portable Nietzsche* (New York: Penguin, 1976).
——. *Beyond Good and Evil*, trans. Walter Kaufmann, in *Basic Writings of Nietzsche* (New York: Modern Library, 1968).
——. *On the Genealogy of Morality*, ed. Keith Ansell Pearson, trans. Carol Diethe (Cambridge: Cambridge University Press, 1994).
——. *Twilight of the Idols*, trans. Walter Kaufmann, in *The Viking Portable Nietzsche* (New York: Penguin, 1976).
——. *The Antichrist*, trans. Walter Kaufmann, in *The Viking Portable Nietzsche* (New York: Penguin, 1976).
——. *Ecce Homo*, trans. Walter Kaufmann, in *Basic Writings of Nietzsche* (New York: Modern Library, 1968).
——. *The Will to Power*, trans. Walter Kaufmann and R.J. Hollingdale (New York: Vintage Books, 1968).
——. 'On Truth and Lies in a Nonmoral Sense', trans. Daniel Breazeale, in *The Nietzsche Reader*, eds Keith Ansell Pearson and Duncan Large (Oxford: Blackwell, 2006).
——. *Sämtliche Werke: Kritische Studienausgabe*, eds Giorgio Colli and Mazzino Montinari, 15 vols (Berlin: Walter de Gruyter, 1980).
——. *Briefwechsel: Kritische Gesamtausgabe*, eds Giorgio Colli, Mazzino Motinari, Norbert Miller and Annemarie Pieper, 20+ vols (Berlin: Walter de Gruyter, 1975).

Notes

Preface

1. See Jacques Derrida, *Spurs: Nietzsche's Styles*, bilingual edition, trans. Barbara Harlow (Chicago & London: University of Chicago Press, 1979).
2. See Walter Kaufmann, *Nietzsche: Philosopher, Psychologist, Antichrist* (Princeton: Princeton University Press, 1974), p. 412. For a more recent exponent of this kind of view see Brian Leiter, *Nietzsche on Morality* (London: Routledge, 2002). Those who see Nietzsche's thought as expressly political in its implications include Daniel W. Conway, *Nietzsche and the Political* (London: Routledge, 1997), and Mark Warren, *Nietzsche and Political Thought* (Cambridge, Mass.: MIT Press, 1988). An interesting overview of this area of Nietzsche research is provided by Herman Siemens in 'Nietzsche's Political Philosophy: A Review of Recent Literature', *Nietzsche-Studien*, 30 (2000).
3. In connection with this, I am quite content here to avoid addressing the issue of Nietzsche's so-called 'postmodernist status'. I would suggest that it is best to follow the example of Jean-François Lyotard and abandon using the word. See Lyotard, 'Rewriting Modernity', in *The Inhuman: Reflections on Time*, trans. Geoff Bennington and Rachel Bowlby (Cambridge: Polity Press, 1991). The later Lyotard used other terms to characterise the experimental attitude he advocated, for example 'rewriting' modernity, implying that there is no escape from the modern: 'Postmodernity is not a new age, but the rewriting of some of the features claimed by modernity, and first of all modernity's claim to ground its legitimacy on the project of liberating humanity as a whole through science and technology' (*The Inhuman*, p. 34). In other words, the phrase 'rewriting modernity' denotes a political project that questions the Enlightenment belief in the possibility of liberation by way of technological and scientific forms of knowledge. Such self-critical refection on technology may well, however, take us back into a new variant of the Enlightenment project that Lyotard spurned. As David Harvey has argued, what is needed is 'a renewal of historical materialism and of the Enlightenment project. Through the first we can begin to understand postmodernity as an historical-geographical condition.' See David Harvey, *The Condition of Postmodernity* (Oxford: Blackwell, 1990), p. 359.
4. Ronald Hayman, *Nietzsche: Nietzsche's Voices* (London: Phoenix, 1999), p. 16.
5. What constitutes much of Nietzsche's greatness as a thinker is this seductive ability to appeal to manifold sensibilities. Laurence Lampert's interpretation, which argues for an environmentalist philosophy inspired by Nietzsche is a recent case in point. See Laurence Lampert, *Nietzsche and Modern Times: A Study of Bacon, Descartes and Nietzsche* (New Haven & London: Yale University Press, 1993). Likewise, the plethora of interpretations that appeared in the 1980s that sought to detect in Nietzsche a postmodern sensibility testify amply enough to this appeal.

6. See Rudolph Steiner, *Friedrich Nietzsche, Ein Kämpfer gegen seine Zeit* (*Friedrich Nietzsche: A Fighter Against His Times*) (1895) (Dornach: Philosophisch-Anthroposophischer Verlag am Goetheanum, 1926). English translation: *Friedrich Nietzsche, Fighter for Freedom*, trans. Margaret Ingram deRis (New Jersey: Rudolf Steiner Publications, 1960). For Steiner, the fact that Nietzsche's thought runs counter to the spirit of its times is exemplified by the latter's conception of the 'overman' as the antithesis of the modern norm of what constitutes personhood (Section 41). At the same time, Nietzsche has been taken as signifying and expressing something quintessentially modern. For Thomas Mann, for example, 'We have from him [...] the experience of modernity'. Thomas Mann, quoted in Rüdiger Safranski, *Nietzsche: A Philosophical Biography*, trans. Shelly Frisch (London: Granta, 2002), p. 324. Likewise, consider the comments made by the author of one of Nietzsche's obituaries: his thought embodies 'a creed which has been called hideous, ferocious, abominable, insane, but which is nevertheless a direct, we might almost say a legitimate, product of the age' (Anon., *The Academy and Literature*, 59, 1st September 1900, pp. 175–6).
7. See, for example, *The Gay Science*, 356, 372, 375, 379; *Beyond Good and Evil*, 215, 224, 247; *Twilight of the Idols*, 'Skirmishes of an Untimely Man', 37. As will become apparent from Chapters 1 and 2, I am inclined to disagree with Alexander Nehamas's contention that 'Far from being a symbol and hero of Modernity, for good or ill, Nietzsche, despite his talk of "us moderns", has deep doubts about the very existence of such a period.' Alexander Nehamas, 'Nietzsche, Modernity, Aestheticism', in *The Cambridge Companion to Nietzsche*, eds Bernd Magnus and Kathleen M. Higgins (Cambridge: Cambridge University Press, 1996, p. 242). Nehamas is surely right in contending that Nietzsche has a complex attitude with regard to modernity; modernity is for Nietzsche an amalgam of features (including the unrelentingly new and transient, the ancient and the primitive – a point I make in Chapter 2) but this does not seem to me to license the contention that Nietzsche never thinks in periodising terms about modernity. He does, and with a view to characterising it as such: the death of God, for example, is 'the greatest modern event' – it has social and historical implications that imply the possibility of transformations in self-understanding (see, *The Gay Science*, 344).
8. It is this sense of discomfort at our own powerlessness that possibly underlies the feeling of unstoppable decline that attests to modern consciousness. Such decline, of course, is part of Nietzsche's conception of the modern: 'Modernity represents some sort of epochal, unique "twilight", or "decline", or "degeneration", or "exhaustion", to use his frequent descriptions.' Robert B. Pippin, 'Nietzsche's Alleged Farewell: The Premodern, Modern, and Postmodern Nietzsche', in *The Cambridge Companion to Nietzsche*, op. cit., p. 256.
9. David Harvey, *The Condition of Postmodernity* (Oxford: Blackwell, 1990), p. 10.
10. In this connection, I must confess to finding the term 'postmodernism' of little value when it comes to any attempt to grasp our own times, and so avoid it.
11. See Daniel W. Conway, *Nietzsche's Dangerous Game: Philosophy in the Twilight of the Idols* (Cambridge: Cambridge University Press, 1997); and Derek Hillard, 'History as Dual Process: Nietzsche on Exchange and Power', *Nietzsche-Studien* 31 (2002).

12. See Graham Parkes, *Composing the Soul: Reaches of Nietzsche's Psychology* (Chicago: University of Chicago Press, 1994). Parkes's aim is to offer an interpretation of Nietzsche that uses 'perspectives [. . .] of depth-psychology and certain forms of East-Asian thought' (p. 1). He provides a sustained discussion of Nietzsche's conception of the economy of the soul, showing the manner in which notions of husbandry and cultivation permeate Nietzsche's works (pp. 171ff).
13. See *Friedrich Nietzsche (1844–1900): Economy and Society*, eds Jürgen G. Backhaus and Wolfgang Drechsler (New York: Springer Verlag, 2006).
14. In this regard, my argument follows Jean-Joseph Goux's contention that 'one cannot help but notice a parallel between the emergence of a stock market paradigm of values (in neoclassical economics) and the anti-Platonist explosion that shook postmodern philosophy. Walras and Nietzsche, let us not forget, were contemporaries.' Jean-Joseph Goux, 'Ideality, Symbolicity, and Reality in Postmodern Capitalism', in *Postmodernism, Economics and Knowledge*, eds Stephen Cullenberg, Jack Amariglio and David F. Ruccio (London: Routledge, 2001), p. 180.
15. Graham Parkes notes the possible influence here. See *Composing the Soul*, op. cit., p. 45.
16. See Walter Bagehot, *Physics and Politics, or Thoughts on the Application of the Principles of 'Natural Selection' and 'Inheritance' to Political Society* (Westport: Greenwood Press, 1973). On 28 December 1879, Nietzsche wrote a postcard to his bookseller, Ernst Schmeitzner, enquiring about the availability of a translation of Herbert Spencer's *Data of Ethics*. He also wanted to know about everything by Bagehot available in German (*Briefwechsel: Kritische Gesamtausgabe*, II_5, p. 474; Schmeitzner's reply, listing available texts, is in *Briefwechsel*, II, 2, p. 11). Five years prior to this Nietzsche had already quoted Bagehot's *Physics and Politics* with approval in the third of the *Untimely Meditations* (Section 8). He also discussed him in a letter to Paul Rée (*Briefwechsel*, II_5, p. 266).
17. The creditor–debtor relationship is the one in which subjects first encountered one another as subjects, according to *On the Genealogy of Morality* (II, 8).
18. Bagehot's *Lombard Street: A Description of the Money Market* is one of the books listed by Schmeitzner in his reply to Nietzsche's enquiry about Bagehot (see the Endnote 7). This text makes plentiful reference to Adam Smith, the founder of modern political economy. See Walter Bagehot, *Lombard Street: A Description of the Money Market* (London: Scribner, Armstrong, 1873). Gregory Moore and Thomas H. Brobjer cite Bagehot as an example of the manner in which 'scientific knowledge and methodologies spilled over into wider cultural debates'. See *Nietzsche and Science*, eds Gregory Moore and Thomas H. Brobjer (Aldreshot: Ashgate, 2004), p. 4.
19. See, for example, Gregory Moore, *Nietzsche Biology and Metaphor* (Cambridge: Cambridge University Press, 2002), Chapter 1; Walter Kaufmann, *Nietzsche: Philosopher, Psychologist, Antichrist* (Princeton: Princeton University Press, 1974), Chapter 5; Keith Ansell Pearson, 'Nietzsche Contra Darwin', *Nietzsche: Critical Assessments*, Vol. IV, eds Daniel Conway and Peter Groff (London: Routledge, 1998); John Richardson, *Nietzsche's New Darwinism* (Oxford: Oxford University Press, 2004). Kaufmann argues that Nietzsche

can be read as a Lamarckian (*Nietzsche*, pp. 132, 293–4), a view countered by Ansell Pearson, who argues he is in fact much closer to Darwin than one might think ('Nietzsche contra Darwin', p. 8).

20. Darwin 'borrowed those ideas Malthus had applied to humans and generalized them to cover the plant and animal kingdoms', E. Ray Canterbury, *A Brief History of Economics* (Singapore: World Scientific, 2001), p. 77.
21. Charles Darwin, *The Origin of Species*, ed. J.W. Burrow (Harmondsworth: Penguin, 1976). The phrase 'economy of nature' occurs on several occasions: pp. 116, 127, 131, 147, 194, 320, 325, 332, 398, 399, 403, 411, 444.
22. Darwin even writes of 'natural selection' as if it were some kind of agency 'continually trying to economise in every part of the organisation' of a being (*The Origin of Species*, p. 186 – a point reiterated on p. 432). He is also concerned to show the manner in which the 'natural' or 'general economy' of a 'country' or 'land' influences this (pp. 149–50, 158, 166, 207). Nature is thereby rendered amenable to being grasped in terms of credit and debit – Darwin cites Goethe's 'Fragment on Nature' in this connection: 'in order to spend on one side nature is forced to economise on the other side' (p. 185). He also writes of 'the whole economy of any one organic being' (p. 224), ponders the economic use of resources (wax) by bees (p. 253) and discusses the manner in which such use becomes a 'newly acquired economic instinct' (p. 256). Doubtless, the deployment of the notion of economy here could be traced back, at least in part, to the influence of economist Thomas Malthus's *Essay on the Principle of Population* (1797). Darwin read this work in 1838, 'borrowed those ideas Malthus had applied to humans and generalized them to cover the plant and animal kingdoms' in the form of the famous 'struggle for life' (E. Ray Canterbury, *A Brief History of Economics*, op.cit., p. 77).

Economy and Society in Nietzsche's 'Middle Period' Works: *Human, All Too Human, Assorted Opinions and Maxims, The Wanderer and His Shadow, Daybreak*

1. This point is made by Paul de Man in *Allegories of Reading: Figural Language in Rousseau, Nietzsche, Rilke, and Proust* (New Haven: Yale University Press, 1979), p. 86.
2. 'On Truth and Lies in a Nonmoral Sense', trans. Daniel Breazeale, in *The Nietzsche Reader*, eds Keith Ansell Pearson and Duncan Large (Oxford: Blackwell, 2006), p. 117.
3. *Ökonomie*. Nietzsche also makes use of the word *Wirthschaft*, a term that encompasses such things as economic and business affairs (the realm of commerce and industry) and good housekeeping (frugality).
4. That is, *Wissenschaft*: the word encompasses scholarly and systematic enquiry in general rather than merely the physical sciences.
5. How one stands against one's time is always a problematic question, however. To take issue with something does not prevent that something colonising you even as you oppose it. As Eberhard Lämmert has commented, 'To a greater degree than ever before, Nietzsche raised the noncontemporaneity

of the entrepreneurial author to a principle of thought and outward existence.' Eberhard Lämmert, 'Nietzsche's Apotheosis of Lonliness', trans. Shari Holmer-Lewis, in *Nietzsche, Literature and Values*, eds Volker Dürr, Reinhold Grimm and Kathy Harms (Wisconsin: The University of Wisconsin Press, 1988), p. 57. As entrepreneur of the spirit, Nietzsche at the same time risks recuperation within the mercantile culture he seeks to stand aloof from.

6. Socialism, for Nietzsche, epitomises this threat, which is why he regards it as regressive in its essential impulse: 'Socialism is the fanciful younger brother of the almost expired despotism whose heir it wants to be; its endeavours are thus in the profoundest sense reactionary. For it desires an abundance of state power such as only despotism has ever had; indeed it outbids all the despotisms of the past inasmuch as it expressly aspires to the annihilation of the individual [. . .]' (*Human, All Too Human*, 473).
7. Such conformity is what typifies the modern. See Robert B. Pippin, 'Nietzsche's Alleged Farewell: The Premodern, Modern, and Postmodern Nietzsche', in *The Cambridge Companion to Nietzsche*, eds Bernd Magnus and Kathleen M. Higgins (Cambridge: Cambridge University Press, 1996), p. 270.
8. This, as David Harvey notes, expresses 'the collapse of space' characteristic of modernity. *The Condition of Postmodernity* (Oxford: Blackwell, 1990), p. 273.
9. This comparison is indebted to an analogous point made by Theodor Adorno in 'The Essay as Form', trans. Bob Hullot-Kentor and Fredric Will, *New German Critique*, spring–summer, 1984, pp. 151–71, cf. p. 161.
10. Who, or what, one wonders, would regulate the trade in money and transport if private individuals were denied the right to do so? Nietzsche's antagonism towards the state would suggest that this would hardly be his first alternative choice. Yet, it is hard to see where his argument might lead if not to the extolling of some kind of public or community ownership of these spheres, or at the very least state regulation and limitation of their financial potential.

Humankind, the Measurer of All Things: Modernity and Primitive Economy in *Human, All Too Human, Daybreak* and *The Gay Science*

1. The announcement of this event, one may note, is made in terms of the theme of sacrifice explored in this chapter and in terms of issues of credit and debit. After announcing the death of God the madman asks, 'What festivals of atonement, what sacred games shall we have to invent [to justify this deed]?'. The death of God, as an act of violence akin to a murderous sacrifice performed with knives, will require atonement: it will have to be *paid for*.
2. Nietzsche, *Werke*, V_1, 6[129].
3. By way of comment on this, one can cite Duncan Large: 'Nietzsche's and Zarathustra's today is a falling-off, an epigonal age unworthy of producing greatness and indeed incapable of doing so (*Z* iv, 5/2) for the modern period lacks decisiveness and resolution [. . .]'. Duncan Large, *Nietzsche and Proust: A Comparative Study* (Oxford: Clarendon Press, 2001), p. 217.
4. This portrayal seems to contradict *Daybreak*, 203 (discussed in Chapter 1 in this book), which paints the scholar as equally prey to the pressures

of capital. That said, one could argue that whereas the latter concerns the demonstration of social status due to the pressure of modern norms (excessive consumption as a symbol of high social rank), this section of *The Gay Science* is concerned with the use of knowledge as a means to such success. In this regard, the genuine scholar is characterised by a refusal to exchange their scholarship within a money economy dominated by the demand for readily consumable (i.e. superficial) titbits of 'wisdom'.

5. See Adam Smith, 'The Theory of Moral Sentiments', in *The Essential Adam Smith*, ed. Robert B. Heilbroner (Oxford: Oxford University Press, 1986), p. 123.
6. The 'family failing' of philosophers is that they take man as he is as a constant, they think of him as 'a sure measure of things' (*Human, All Too Human*, 2).
7. One can take as an example a constantly endangered community. Here, says Nietzsche, the most demanding morality will of necessity have come to dominate. The extent of the demands of tradition is exhibited in such communities by the presence of one key pleasure: cruelty. In this, their judgement reflects the conditions of their life. A life that is hard is given meaning when it is seen as one that is approved of by the gods. Consequently, joy in cruelty becomes a virtue, for it reflects the conditions that the gods have imposed upon the community. 'Thus [in such communities] the concept of the "most moral man" of the community came to include the virtue of the most frequent suffering, of privation, of the hard life of cruel chastisement – *not*, to repeat it again and again, as a means of discipline, of self-control, of satisfying the desire for individual happiness – but as a virtue which will put the community on good odour with the evil gods and which steams up to them like a perpetual propitiatory sacrifice on the altar' (*Daybreak*, 18).
8. '[W]hoever wanted to elevate himself above it had to become a lawgiver and medicine man and a kind of demi-god: that is to say, he had to *make customs* – a dreadful mortally dangerous thing!' (ibid., 9).
9. The struggle against the morality of custom, for Nietzsche, is what epitomises the task of philosophy. In this sense, at least, philosophy aspires to stand if not strictly 'outside' then as an embodied contradiction of the prevailing conventions of all times and places. See, for example, ibid., 496: 'Plato has given us a splendid description of how the philosophical thinker must within every existing society count as a paragon of all wickedness: for as a critic of all customs, he is the antithesis of the moral man, and if he does not succeed in becoming the lawgiver he remains in the memory of men as "the evil principle".'
10. From the Latin *mensura*, from *metiri mens-*.
11. 'For he [Protagoras] says, as you know, that "Man is the measure of all things: of the things that which are, that they are, and of the things which are not, that they are not" ', Plato, *Theaetetus*, trans. M.J. Levett, revised Myles Burnyeat (Indianapolis: Hackett, 1992), 152a.
12. Nietzsche's account of the development of religion is a case in point. Early humanity attempted to tame nature by seeking to make it amenable to the same regulative conditions that constituted the foundations of social order. Primitive consciousness posed the question, is it possible to find a 'means of regulating these powers [of nature] through a tradition and law in just the

way you are regulated by them? – The believer in magic and miracles [thereby] reflects on how to *impose a law on nature* [. . .]' (*Human, All Too Human*, 111). Nature, initially seen as lacking the conformity to rule of the community and individuals, is tamed by ritual and ultimately grasped in terms of rules. Religion is what results: an organised cult designed to propitiate nature and thereby render it as law-like as the tradition-dominated social realm itself. Religion, in other words, is part and parcel of the human sensibility that responds to the power of custom and tradition. Because of this, even from the outset humanity has never been the mere plaything of natural forces, but has approached the world with a view to comprehending and thereby influencing it: 'Even at very low stages of culture man does not stand towards nature as its impotent slave, he is *not* necessarily its will-less servant [. . .]' (ibid.).

13. Nietzsche's examples include punishing wrongdoers by stoning, breaking on the wheel, immolation, dismemberment, boiling alive, flaying (a real favourite, according to him) and even smearing the miscreant with sweet honey and leaving them in the heat of the sun to be devoured by insects.
14. See Peter Sedgwick, 'Violence, Economy and Temporality'. Plotting the Political Terrain of *On the Genealogy of Morality*', *Nietzsche-Studien*, 34, 2005.
15. One could note that this account has something in common with Hegel's analysis of self-consciousness in the *Phenomenology of Spirit*. See G.W.F. Hegel, *Phenomenology of Spirit*, trans. A.V. Miller (Oxford: Oxford University Press, 1977), para. 175.
16. For a perceptive account of the exchange principle as it is manifest in the *Genealogy* see Derek Hillard, 'History as Dual Process: Nietzsche on Exchange and Power', *Nietzsche-Studien*, 31, 2002.

The Great Economy

1. Which is why people may sometimes participate in fostering the very conditions that subjugate them.
2. This is the reinterpretation of the now formalised civil law relationship between debtor and creditor into one that concerns the relationship between the community and its ancestors. This reinterpretation of the creditor–debtor relationship conceives of the living in the community as existing in a state of indebtedness to the ancestors who founded it. The more successful the community, the greater the feeling of indebtedness. The outcome of this most monstrous sense of indebtedness is that the ancestor is ultimately transfigured into a god. Thus, religion and religious worship are likewise expressions of our fundamental economic characteristics. For Nietzsche, the fusing of primitive organised religion with the sense of guilt characteristic of the bad conscience is what underpins the birth of monotheism and ultimately Christianity. See the discussion of this in the *Genealogy*, II, 19ff.
3. This view is developed in the third essay of *On the Genealogy of Morality*. See the discussion in Chapter 5.
4. Such passing would, following Foucault, announce 'the disappearance of "man" as the standard bearer of an all-too-serious anthropocentrism [. . .]'. Alan D. Schrift, 'Nietzsche's French Legacy', in *The Cambridge Companion to*

Nietzsche, eds Bernd Magnus and Kathleen Higgins (Cambridge: Cambridge University Press, 1996), p. 328.
5. Discussed in Chapter 2.
6. *Werke*, VIII_3, 4[185]; *The Will to Power*, 291.
7. Cf. the brief discussion of this at the end of the Chapter 2.
8. Utilitarianism is numbered by Nietzsche amongst the 'false' '*Modern Ideas*', cf. *Werke*, VIII_3, 6[82].
9. Graham Parkes's account sees this as forming the foundation for Nietzsche's psychology. See *Composing the Soul: Reaches of Nietzsche's Psychology* (Chicago: University of Chicago Press, 1994), p. 7.
10. *Ecce Homo*, 'The Birth of Tragedy', 2: 'Nothing in existence may be subtracted, nothing is dispensable [. . .]'.
11. Nietzsche cleaves to this view, as witnessed by *On the Genealogy of Morality*, III, 7. Philosophers, Nietzsche declares, detest marriage as a hindrance to their spiritual freedom. Their asceticism, in other words, increases spiritual independence; but at the same time it ensures that such great thinkers do not leave something lesser in their wake.
12. For illuminating discussion of this see Graham Parkes, *Composing the Soul*, op. cit., pp. 171ff. Parkes concentrates on elucidating 'what Nietzsche calls "the great economy" of the soul', showing the manner in which economic imagery of husbandry and cultivation permeates his discussion of the psyche.
13. Nietzsche refers to the entire 'economy of my soul [*Die gesammte Ökonomie meiner Seele*]' (*The Gay Science*, 338).
14. To ask the questions that need to be asked about truth and value, what is needed is a 'will to the economy of the great style [*Wille zur Ökonomie grossen Stils*]' (*Antichrist*, Preface).
15. For a discussion of this see Chapter 4.
16. The question of why the ascetic priest exists at all is discussed in Chapter 5.
17. See Jean-François Lyotard, *The Differend: Phrases in Dispute*, trans. Georges van den Abeele (Manchester: Manchester University Press, 1988), Sections 25ff.
18. Lyotard characterises Parmenidean ontology, from which Plato draws his own, in the following way: 'what it phrases, Being, is also what is phrased through its mouth; the referent is also the addressor. "Being and thinking are the same thing" ' (*The Differend*, Section 20). In other words, any ontological sentence must obey the rules of formation that characterises ontological talk in general. In order to have ontological status, a sentence would need to present us with a universe that exhibits the properties of absoluteness and necessity. This kind of universe would be, on its own terms at least, one which affirms itself, that is the reality it offers must simply be acceded to – if this is reality as such it is not open to question. The sentence's assertion of its own necessity means that it would have to be a self-referential sentence. However, even if one accepts the ontological claim thereby formulated, what is presented by the sentence cannot be commented on without an inevitable curtailment of its ontological status. The ontological veracity of the initial sentence will vanish since, in order to note that an ontological sentence has been asserted, another sentence is needed which is not ontological, for example an ostensive sentence that tells us 'Here is an ontological sentence.' What happens, however, is that the ontological primacy of the first sentence is thereby shown to be dependent on the second and hence sundered.

19. Protagoras makes use of this strategy. The 'pious' argument might run: the gods can do no wrong. In turn, one who truly believes in the gods as prescribed by law can do no wrong, nor utter 'lawless discourse' (Plato, *The Laws*, 885b). A person who does not believe in the gods holds this view because either (a) they do not believe the gods can respond to human actions (they are not the addressees of our prayers), or (b) they accept the gods are addressees of our actions, but just do not care what happens to us anyway, or (c) they hold the gods to be unreliable and fickle and hence not worthy of trust. All these are impious sentences which can be rendered (using the second person) as 'you do not exist; you do not speak; you say what I make you say' (*The Differend*, Section 21). In this way, according to Lyotard, Being is prevented from attaining the status of a given. What reality is can now be worked through by way of procedures of argument and recourse to the criterion of falsification. What was considered as a given and an absolute (the gods and their veracity) has now been placed in question by an inversion. The gods, who are by definition (i.e. in virtue of their identity) 'the strongest ones' (kreittonès) are rendered the weaker. The impious utterance is, it follows, rendered possible in virtue of our ability to address ourselves to the world in a variety of ways. The gods are no longer *spoken to* (addressees) but *spoken about* (referents) and thereby undermined.
20. *Werke*, VIII_3, 14[182]. See *The Will to Power*, 864.
21. This notion, too, I argue, is itself infiltrated in significant ways by the economic notion of measurement.
22. Ibid.
23. *The Will to Power*, 889; *Werke*, VIII_2, 10[10].
24. *The Will to Power*, 927; *Werke*, VIII_2, 10[134].
25. Ibid.
26. *On the Genealogy of Morality*, II, 2–3. The sovereign individual is the outcome of a long period of breeding through violent compulsion. The long prehistory of humanity signifies, in this sense, merely eras of preparatory labour, of humanity working unconsciously upon itself in order to create this autonomous being. The training and cultivation of humanity is thus a prelude, it is the rendering of a creature initially driven by instinct and desire into a being whose promising ability can be transfigured into self-aware autonomy.
27. *The Will to Power*, 888; *Werke*, VIII_2, 10[11].
28. *On the Genealogy of Morality*, III, 4. The comment here concerns the relationship between artist and artwork.
29. The question of how far up to now every stronger kind of human, he tells us, has stood upon the level of the lowly cannot be ignored. *The Will to Power*, 890; *Werke*, VIII_2, 9[17].
30. *The Will to Power*, 786; *Werke*, VIII_2, 10[57]. This allocation, Nietzsche adds, would be the task of a 'Tractatus politicus'.
31. Ibid.
32. *The Will to Power*, 931; *Werke*, VIII_2, 10[133].
33. *On the Genealogy of Morality*, II, 2.
34. *The Will to Power*, 969; *Werke*, VIII_2, 9[45].
35. *Werke*, VIII_2, 9[137]; *The Will to Power*, 896.
36. *The Will to Power*, 933; *Werke*, VIII_2, 9[139], VIII_3, 16[6]: Advanced education is regarded here as 'a system of means, in order to direct good taste against

the exceptions, favourable to the average'. Such an attitude, Nietzsche adds, is harsh 'but viewed economically completely sensible'.

37. *Werke*, VIII_3, 24[2].
38. An allusion to the greatest ironic of them all, Socrates. Nietzsche's development of this thesis in *Twilight of the Idols* ('The Problem of Socrates') makes clear the extent to which he perceives history of near cyclical terms.
39. *Werke*, VIII_3, 15[23]; *The Will to Power*, 93.
40. Ibid.
41. *Werke*, VIII_3, 16[6].
42. See *Werke*, VIII_3, 15[30]: 'We are not the result of [. . .] one will, of one wish: with us *no* attempt is being made to reach an "ideal of perfection" or an "ideal of happiness" or an "ideal of virtue" [. . .] it is a great refreshment, in it lies the innocence of all existence.'
43. A tendency epitomised by 'The Last Man' in *Thus Spoke Zarathustra* ('Zarathustra's Prologue', 5). As Robert B. Pippin notes, this rather smug tendency epitomises for Nietzsche the self-misunderstanding of modernity: in it, the average sees itself as the goal of culture, but this itself is a sign of nihilism and lack of culture. See 'Nietzsche's Alleged Farewell: The Premodern, Modern, and Postmodern Nietzsche', in *The Cambridge Companion to Nietzsche*, op. cit., pp. 255ff.
44. *The Will to Power*, 881; *Werke*, VIII_2, 10[111].
45. Ibid.
46. *The Will to Power*, 90; Werke, VIII_3, 15[8].
47. See also *The Will to Power*, 339; *Werke*, VIII_3, 11[226]: Humanity is 'an inextricable multiplicity of ascending and descending life-processes [. . .] refuse and decaying matter are found everywhere [. . .]'. Thus, human existence is characterised by the kind of excess that typifies modern consumer-culture: the production of *waste*; rubbish.
48. *The Will to Power*, 888; *Werke*, VIII_2, 10[11].
49. By way of another example, Nietzsche can write of 'higher men' as people who 'for the sake of their superior claims and tasks also freely accept a life more full of peril (expressed economically [*ökonomisch ausgedrückt*]: a rise in the cost of the undertaking [*der Unternehmer-Kosten*: the enterprise costs] in proportion to the decline in the probability of its success) [. . .]' (*The Will* to Power, 252; *Werke*, VIII_2, 11[55]).
50. *The Will to Power*, 866; *Werke*, VIII_2, 10[17].
51. Nietzsche's phrase is the 'common economic management of the earth [*Wirtschafts-Gesammtvertwaltung der Erde*]' (ibid.).
52. Ibid.
53. *The Will to Power*, 462; *Werke*, VIII_2, 10[28].
54. *The Will to Power*, 731; *Werke*, VIII_2, 10[15].

Zarathustra and the Economy of the Overman

1. Laurence Lampert, *Nietzsche's Teaching: An Interpretation of Thus Spoke Zarathustra* (Yale & London: Yale University Press, 1986), p. 5.
2. See, by way of contrast, Maudmarie Clark, *Nietzsche on Truth and Philosophy* (Cambridge: Cambridge University Press, 1990), who regards *Zarathustra*

as 'a work of fiction. It articulates Zarathustra's cosmological vision, which may or may not also be Nietzsche's (p. 210). Given Nietzsche's own high estimation of the value of this text such a view is perhaps questionable.

3. Ibid., pp. 13, 83, 155.
4. Ibid., p. 287.
5. Early-twentieth-century readers like the critic Havelock Ellis saw Nietzsche as 'poetic', 'prophetic', a 'seer' and 'spiritual force'. Ellis is quoted in an anonymous review, as claiming that Nietzsche is 'one of the greatest spiritual forces to have appeared since Goethe' (see *The Academy and Literature*, vol. 52, 8 July 1899, pp. 31–2). This was not an isolated view. For others, too, Nietzsche was 'an artist among philosophers rather than a pure philosopher' (Anon., review of *The Dawn of Day*, trans. Johanna Volz (London: T. Fisher Unwin), *The Athenaeum*, No. 3932, 7 March 1903, pp. 298–300). He was a figure whose works embody a 'teaching' (F.W. Hacquoil, letter to *The Academy and Literature*, vol. 59, pp. 197–8). For a detailed discussion of this aspect of Nietzsche's reception history see Peter Sedgwick, 'Nietzsche as Literature/Nietzsche as German Literature', *Journal of Nietzsche Studies*, 13, Spring 1997, pp. 53–71 and also 'The Nietzsche Legend: A Genealogy of Myth and Enlightenment', *Ecce Opus: Nietzsche-Revisionen im 20. Jahrhundert*, eds Rüdiger Görner and Duncan Large (Gottingen: Vandenhoek & Ruprecht, 2003).
6. An image of the philosopher to be repeated in the 'Preface' to the *Genealogy*.
7. See Immanuel Kant, *Critique of Practical Reason, and Other Writings in Moral Philosophy*, trans. Lewis White Beck (New York: Garland, 1976).
8. See Chapter 2.
9. Graham Parkes analyses the 'arboricultural imagery' used here in *Composing the Soul: Reaches of Nietzsche's Psychology* (Chicago: University of Chicago Press, 1994), cf. p. 175.
10. I borrow the phrase from Heidegger; see 'The Question Concerning Technology', in *Martin Heidegger: Basic Writings*, ed. David Farrell Krell (London: Routledge, 1996).
11. Some of Zarathustra's examples include the following: one attacks one's own pride; one mocks one's wisdom; one shuns one's fondest causes precisely at the point of their victory; one invites and endures temptation; one spurns comfort in illness, seeking instead conditions that intensify suffering.
12. Zarathustra says he knows this all too well, for he has held such beliefs himself.
13. Occasionally, Nietzsche speculates about the adequacy of even the notion of the body. However, the point for him is that 'in all ages there has been more faith in the body, as our most personal possession, our most certain being [. . .] It has never occurred to anyone to regard his stomach as a strange or, say, a divine stomach: but to conceive his ideas as "inspired", his evaluations as "implanted by God" [. . .] – for this tendency and taste in men there are witnesses from all ages of mankind [. . .] For the present, belief in the body is always stronger than belief in the spirit; and whoever desires to undermine it, also undermines at the same time most thoroughly belief in the authority of the spirit!' (*The Will to Power*, trans. Walter Kaufmann and R.J. Hollingdale (New York: Vintage, 1968) p. 659).

14. These are the conditions I have already discussed in the previous two chapters, detailed in *Daybreak* and the *On the Genealogy of Morality*.
15. That is, mental stuff and physical stuff. Descartes's rendering them distinct in this way, of course, is what initiates his abiding problem of answering the question of how mind and body are linked.
16. That is, those 'evil' instincts that form an essential component of the great economy of our species' preservation (*The Gay Science*, 1; see Chapter 3).
17. 'The *Übermensch*, according to Zarathustra, is continually experimental, willing to risk all for the sake of the enhancement of humanity.' Bernd Magnus and Kathleen M. Higgins, 'Nietzsche's works and their themes', in *The Cambridge Companion to Nietzsche*, eds Bernd Magnus and Kathleen M. Higgins (Cambridge: Cambridge University Press, 1996), p. 40. The question of experimentalism and enhancement is pursued further in Chapter 5.
18. The Will to Power, 866; *Werke*, VIII_2, 10[17].

Philosophical Temptations: Economy and Futurity

1. *Twilight of the Idols*, 'Maxims and Arrows', 44: 'The formula of my happiness: a Yes, a No, a straight line, a *goal*.' This conception of philosophy as goal-seeking does not preclude there being many journeys and a multitude of possible tasks.
2. This, of course, typifies the philosopher generally. It is 'a feature of the philosopher's lot to be in contradiction to the norms of his day'. Duncan Large, *Nietzsche and Proust: A Comparative Study* (Oxford: Clarendon Press, 2001), p. 219.
3. 'Nietzsche's conception of health is not of a pain free state – on the contrary, he sees pain as a necessary constituent of great health.' Giles Fraser, *Redeeming Nietzsche: On the Piety of Unbelief* (London: Routledge, 2002), p. 90. Fraser's central contention, powerfully argued, is that Nietzsche's philosophy ultimately fails to confront the reality of suffering, 'that after Auschwitz Nietzsche's soteriology looks like the imaginings of a more comfortable and innocent age' (p. 123).
4. To recall, the second essay of the *Genealogy* envisages human society as emerging out of conditions that consist of a violently imposed normativity governed by the exchange principle of creditor and debtor. In turn, colonial and political violence subsequently refashions the bad conscience and spiritualises humankind. Thus, the human soul and spirituality is born of violence and trauma.
5. Hence, his contempt for utilitarianism.
6. This does not, of course, preclude our being exploited in return even by flora. The plant that is much eaten by humans is, in return, cultivated and spread across the globe (as is the case with wheat). Doubtless, one could possibly say the same about various kinds of animal – if one is not feeling too sentimental.
7. Nietzsche's fondness of naturalising and organic metaphors is no accident or unconscious affectation. To take just a few examples: the feelings of '*ressentiment*' and 'bad conscience' are 'plants' (*Genealogy*, II, 11, 14) as are works of art (*Genealogy*, III, 4); the genuine philosopher is akin to a piece of fruit growing on a tree (*Beyond Good and Evil*, 205).

8. See Chapter 4.
9. *The Will to Power*, 660; *Werke*, VIII_1, 2[76].
10. Most notably, he does so when he envisages the distinction between 'metaphysical' and 'historical' philosophy in *Human, All Too Human*. Historical philosophy is anti-metaphysical to the extent that it spurns the search for origins in a timeless realm of eternal truths. However, this attack on the timeless truths of metaphysics does not stop Nietzsche from promulgating a metaphysical claim of his own: 'everything has become: there are *no eternal facts* just as there are no absolute truths' (*Human, All Too Human*, 1).
11. *Beyond Good and Evil*, 204: 'Let us confess how utterly our world lacks the whole type of a Heraclitus, Plato, Empedocles, and whatever other names these royal hermits of the spirit had [. . .]'. One should note, also, that in Nietzsche's view the 'strength' of Plato is the greatest that any philosopher up to now has been able to turn to in order to fulfil his or her goals (*Beyond Good and Evil*, 191).
12. *Beyond Good and Evil*, Nietzsche tells us, 'is in all essentials a *critique of modernity*, not excluding the modern sciences, modern arts, and even modern politics, along with pointers toward a contrary type that is as little modern as possible – a noble, Yes-saying type' (*Ecce Homo*, '*Beyond Good and Evil*: Prelude to a Philosophy of the Future', 2).
13. By stressing the claim that democratic attitudes are *prejudicial* Nietzsche at the same time demands of those readers who would follow him a concession: a shift in understanding (which would certainly have to be concession if they are democratically inclined readers, as presumably he must suspect). This shift introduces a feeling of suspicion that undermines the assumption of the positive nature of democratic values by questioning both the *giveness* and the usefulness of these values themselves. Modern prejudices are democratic prejudices, and these can be deceptive. Consider, for example, *On the Genealogy of Morality*, II, 11, which argues that modern scholarship, in so far as it has a tendency to favour the role of 'hatred, envy, resentment, suspicion, *rancune* and revenge' in its accounts of justice and the like is itself an expression of *ressentiment*. *Ressentiment* perspectives decree all things to be equal in virtue of the sense of inferiority they express. Science reveals its prejudiced nature when it uses the concept of equality (the notion of universal 'laws') or when it favours reactivity over positive assertion when it comes to social or biological considerations. But, as far as Nietzsche is concerned there are emotions 'of much greater biological value than those of reaction [. . .]: namely the actual *active* emotions such as lust for power and possessions and the like'. Nietzsche pursues the point in Section 12 in connection with his postulation of a power thesis. Modern, democratic prejudices, he tells us there, have an in-built resistance to the view that a coercive, exploitative 'will to power' is enacted in all events. Nietzsche's promulgation of what he calls a 'major point of historical method' is thus mounted in direct resistance to the dominance of the 'democratic idiosyncrasy of being against everything that dominates and wants to dominate'. This idiosyncrasy effectively ignores the 'basic concept' of physiology and biology, 'that of actual *activity*' and stresses, instead, its opposite, reactivity. According to Nietzsche, when one 'forces "adaptation" into the foreground, which is a second rate activity, just a reactivity', one in effect denies 'the essence of life, its *will to power*', that

is the 'spontaneous, aggressive, expansive, re-interpreting, re-directing and formative powers'.

14. 'What is foremost at issue for Nietzsche is the question of value [. . .] and finding a solution to the "problem of value" defines "the future task of the philosophers" (GM, I, 17, note)'. Alan D. Schrift, *Nietzsche and the Question of Interpretation: Between Hermeneutics and Deconstruction* (London: Routledge, 1990), p. 61. Schrift has argued that philosophers like Derrida and Foucault stand as thinkers who address themselves to this task; they occupy a 'place in the history of philosophy as two of the "philosophers of the future" to whom Nietzsche's writings were addressed'. See Alan D. Schrift, 'Foucalt and Derrida on Nietzsche and the End(s) of "Man" ', in *Exceedingly Nietzsche*, eds David Farrell Krell and David Wood (London: Routledge, 1988), p. 146.
15. As Richard Schacht has argued, this creativity is, for Nietzsche, something inherent in reality: 'Nietzsche holds [. . .] that the world is to be conceived as something which has made itself [. . .] that the course taken by the world as it thus proceeds to fashion itself is *creative* (and thereby also destructive) rather than merely mechanical or nomalogical or "logical" .' Richard Schacht, *Nietzsche* (London: Routledge & Keegan Paul, 1983), p. 211. The notion of Nietzsche's conception of creative destruction has become important in recent economic theory. See Hugo Reinert and Erik S. Reinert, 'Creative Destruction in Economics: Nietzsche, Sombart, Schumpeter', in *Friedrich Nietzsche (1844–1900): Economy and Society*, eds Jürgen G. Backhaus and Wolfgang Drechsler (New York: Springer Verlag, 2006).
16. Wolfgang Müller-Lauter interprets this must as a sign of Nietzsche's inability to achieve a philosophical resolution of the harmonisation of power and wisdom: 'The conflict between wisdom and power remains unsolved in the highest man. Nietzsche must, however, cling to the possibility of a solution [. . .] Because the philosophical proof of this possibility does not succeed, it can be kept open only as an *object of faith*. In the end nothing remains but stubborn hope [. . .]'. Wolfgang Müller-Lauter, *Nietzsche: His Philosophy of Contradictions and the Contradictions of His Philosophy*, trans. David J. Parent (Urbana and Chicago: University of Illinois Press, 1999), p. 83.
17. A view that typifies the 'Nietzsche legend'. See R.J. Hollingdale, 'The hero as outsider', in *The Cambridge Companion to Nietzsche*, eds Bernd Magnus and Kathleen M. Higgins (Cambridge: Cambridge University Press, 1996), pp. 84ff.
18. 'Some are born posthumously' (*Ecce Homo*, 'Why I Write Such Good Books', 1).
19. 'The history of mankind would be far too stupid a thing if it had not the intellect of the powerless injected into it [. . .]' (*On the Genealogy of Morality*, I, 7).
20. *The Will to Power*, 686; *Werke*, VII_2, 26[231].
21. This conception is developed in the Genealogy. By way of one example, take the analysis of noble and slave morality in the first essay, Section 16. This section makes the (dubious) historical claim that the battle between noble morality and slave morality has been fought on earth 'for thousands of years'. This battle remains undecided. Nietzsche expresses the hope that this struggle has 'in the meantime become ever deeper and more intellectual'. A mutual and reciprocal influence on the part of the two types of morality is

envisaged. The feature that Nietzsche obviously values in his invocation of spiritual deepening is one derived from slave/priestly morality, that is intellectuality (cf. *Genealogy*, I, 6, 7). In other words, he is not advocating the case for a return to a 'pure' form of noble morality (which is, after all, non-intellectual and essentially 'unconscious' in its mode of expression) but the fusion of elements of this with the spiritual elements generated by *ressentiment* thought. The last point is then pressed home: 'there is, today, perhaps no more distinguishing feature of the "higher nature", the intellectual nature, than to be divided in this sense and really and truly a battle ground for these opposites'. As with so many instances of Nietzsche's thinking the opposition between noble and slave has been collapsed. Nietzsche is advocating the reinterpretation of slave morality, not its mere abandonment but its sublimation and transfiguration into something affirmative that thereby cancels out its reactive (rancorous) features. He is, in other words, advocating a new conception of morality, one 'beyond good and evil' that is at the same time intellectual and spiritual. The self, in its own turn, is the sphere of conflict, the 'battle field' upon which the struggle between values is fought out.

22. This is why we must forever remain furthest from, and hence unknown to ourselves (*Genealogy*, 'Preface', 1).
23. *Werke*, VII_2, 26[138].
24. *Werke*, VII_2, 26[258].
25. See Martin Heidegger, *Being and Time*, trans. John Macquarrie and Edward Robinson (Oxford: Basil Blackwell, 1962), p. 291.
26. 'Man is a rope tied between beast and overman – a rope over an abyss [. . .]' (*Thus Spoke Zarathustra*, I, Prologue, 4).
27. Purity is, Nietzsche notes elsewhere, merely part of 'the economy of an artist' (*Werke*, VIII_3, 14[117]).
28. Hence Richard Schacht's contention that Nietzsche's philosophy, especially in its mature phase, is 'a *sense-making* activity'. See Richard Schacht, 'Nietzsche's Kind of Philosophy', in *The Cambridge Companion to Nietzsche*, op. cit., p. 176. The importance of meaning (especially our *need* for it) is, as I have argued here, fundamental to Nietzsche's conception of human nature. It arises from the economically instituted normative conditions that constituted human identity.
29. This is why both the *Genealogy* and *Beyond Good and Evil* mount attacks on modernity that take the question of futurity to be central to their critical approach. According to Bernd Magnus and Kathleen M. Higgins, the central concern of *Beyond Good and Evil* is the role that philosophy itself must play in such a future. See 'Nietzsche's Works and Their Themes', in *The Cambridge Companion to Nietzsche*, op. cit., p. 45.
30. '[W]hoever thinks in *words* thinks as a speaker and not a thinker (which indicates that, basically, he does not think in facts, factually, but in relation to facts, so that he is actually thinking about himself and his listeners)' (*Genealogy*, II, 8).
31. This is why the origins of the philosophers are to be numbered amongst 'the most dangerous of all origins [. . .]' (*Werke*, VII_2, 26[160]).
32. One only needs to recall that Nietzsche claims 'the contractual relationship between *creditor* and *debtor*' (*Genealogy*, II, 4) to be the 'most primitive

personal relationship there is' (ibid., 8). The first encounter between persons is, in line with this, envisaged as taking place upon the already established basis of calculation. It was as creditor and debtor that 'person met person for the first time, and *measured himself* person against person' (ibid.). Measurement, in other words, is the precondition of all subjective self-awareness, and presupposes others like us. The measurer who sees himself does so only in virtue of envisaging the gaze of another like them.

33. Turn to the times of prehistory and it is possible to engage in conjecture as to what happened when philosophy first developed under the yoke of the tyranny of the morality of custom (*Genealogy*, III, 10). In this period, the 'earliest race of contemplative men', thinking against the conventions of their own times, would have been obliged to live as beings who were 'despised when they were not feared'. They needed, above all, to be feared, just as the priest needs to be feared in order to survive: 'The earliest philosophers knew how to give their life and appearance a meaning, support and setting which would encourage people to learn to *fear* them: on closer inspection, from an even more fundamental need, namely in order to fear and respect themselves'. This appearance is the appearance of the ascetic. Because their value judgements were actually turned *against* themselves philosophers had to fight off every kind of self-awareness concerning their real identity. Philosophers, in other words, were not just beings divided against their times but against and within themselves. The *philosophical drive* thereby sought to preserve itself through disguise. Philosophy, in emerging from primitive social conditions that were hostile to it, needed subterfuge, misunderstanding and self-delusion.
34. This is not wholly bad, since philosophy has learnt from this. The desire 'to see differently to that degree, is no small training and preparation of the intellect for its future "objectivity" – the latter understood not as "contemplation without interest" [. . .] but as *having in our power* our "pros" and "cons": so as to be able to engage and disengage them so that we can use the *difference* in perspectives and affective interpretations for knowledge'. What is thereby gained from the discipline of wanting to see differently is the insight that there is no such thing as a 'pure, will-less, painless, timeless, subject of knowledge [. . .]'. In other words, we can come to realise that all knowledge is embodied and dependent upon perspective. This, for Nietzsche, forms the basis of his conception of perspectivism.
35. This, of course, has parallels with Nietzsche's discussion of Socrates in *Twilight of the Idols* (cf. 'The Problem of Socrates'). Socratic thought is degenerate, a reaction against its own decadence and an attempt to overcome degeneration through the invocation of reason.
36. 'Priests make *everything* more dangerous [. . .] with some justification one could add that man first became an *interesting animal* on the foundation of this *essentially dangerous* form of human existence, the priest, and that the human soul became *deep* in the higher sense and turned *evil* for the first time [. . .]' (ibid., I, 6). Priests are, it follows, to be numbered amongst the most evil enemies (ibid., 7). Thus the two features (profundity and evil) that constitute the basis for human superiority over animals are owed to the priest.

37. An insight that, by the way, begs the question with regard to the language of types that Nietzsche is sometimes tempted to resort to.
38. The spiritualisation of torture allows humanity to carry on living, just as Schopenhauer's 'enemies' tempted him back towards the very existence he renounced in his philosophy. We hurt ourselves in order to provoke our desire to live: 'even when he [man] *wounds* himself, this master of destruction, self-destruction, – afterwards it is the wound itself which forces him *to live* . . . ' (*Genealogy*, III, 13).
39. It is, says Nietzsche, 'the *real catastrophe* in the history of the health of European man' (ibid., 21).
40. This is doubtless why 'the self-preserving strategy seems to have played itself out' and requires both critical interpretation and replacement. Robert B. Pippin, 'Nietzsche's alleged farewell: The premodern, modern, and postmodern Nietzsche', in *The Cambridge Companion to Nietzsche*, op. cit., p. 263.
41. In the phrase 'man still prefers to *will nothingness*, than *not* will . . . ' David B. Allison sees an affirmation of a philosophy of 'intensity of will' and of 'ordinary human life and its value'. See David B. Allison, *Reading the New Nietzsche* (Lanham: Rowman & Littlefield Publishers, Inc.: 2001), p. 245. This is certainly the case in so far as humankind, for Nietzsche, is oriented in its everydayness toward its future. It is, however, the value of our future potentiality, our ability to go beyond the ordinary, that is celebrated here.
42. See *Genealogy*, II, 8. Here Nietzsche argues that notions of duty, right, debt, and compensation derived from the creditor–debtor relationship were subsequently given a social and legal dimension. In this way, specifically *legal* entitlements (notions of rights, of formal means of gaining compensation for suffering a wrong, etc.) are seen as having their origin in conventions (formalised and made statute in the first instance by the foundation of state and law under the power of colonial rule). See also *Werke*, VIII_1, 5[82].
43. The fact that we must think in some ways and cannot think in others, for example. See *The Will to Power*, 516; *Werke*, VIII_2, 9[97]. We are beings who deal with our environment by way of concepts. Our use of these is governed by limitations. Thus, we are incapable of simultaneously affirming and answering in the negative about something. This, Nietzsche argues, is a subjective experiential matter, and in that respect expresses no objective 'necessity', *but only an incapacity* on our part. The inability to think in certain ways is linked to the conditions that gave rise to human development. In this sense, it is impossible to escape the influence of these conditions even though, at the same time, our nature is not exhausted by these limitations. Human freedom, for example, is only possible in virtue of limits, but such limits do not of themselves determine the sphere of human freedom as anything more than a space of possible acts – they have no predictive power.

Conclusion

1. 'Nietzsche's history of philosophy shows that great health, recovery from resentment and bad conscience, is not the end of conscience; it is not a move backward into the premoral or submoral but a move forward into the postmoral.' Laurence Lampert, *Nietzsche and Modern Times: A Study of Bacon,*

Descartes and Nietzsche (New Haven & London: Yale University Press, 1993), p. 438.

2. *The Will to Power*, 90; *Werke*, VIII_3, 15[8].
3. In this regard, I would, at least at present, find it hard to reconcile this aspect of Nietzsche's thought with Laurence Lampert's forcefully argued contention that it is possible to conceive of his thought as forming the basis of an environmentalist philosophy. See *Nietzsche and Modern Times*, p. 432.
4. Emmanuel Levinas, *Totality and Infinity*, trans. Alphonso Lingis (Pittsburgh: Duquesne University Press, 1998), pp. 171 ff.
5. Ibid., pp. 172.
6. Ibid.
7. Ibid., p. 174.

Index